The Carolina Rice Kitchen

Fanning Rice, Santee River, South Carolina
Courtesy of The Rice Museum, Georgetown, South Carolina

The Carolina Rice Kitchen:
The African Connection

by Karen Hess

Featuring in Facsimile the
Carolina Rice Cook Book

Compiled by Mrs. Samuel G. Stoney
Charleston, South Carolina [1901]

With Additional Collected Receipts
Making a Total of Some
Three Hundred Historical Receipts for Rice

UNIVERSITY OF SOUTH CAROLINA PRESS

Other Books by Karen Hess:

The Taste of America, 1977, 1989,
coauthor with John L. Hess.

English Bread and Yeast Cookery
by Elizabeth David,
editor of American edition, 1980.

Martha Washington's Booke of Cookery, 1981.

The Virginia House-Wife
by Mary Randolph (1824),
editor of facsimile edition, 1984.

Copyright © 1992 University of South Carolina

Published in Columbia, South Carolina, by the
University of South Carolina Press

Manufactured in the United States of America

Library of Congress Cataloging-in-Publication Data
Hess, Karen
    The Carolina rice kitchen : the African connection / by Karen Hess
; featuring in facsimile the Carolina rice cook book compiled by
Mrs. Samuel G. Stoney, Charleston, South Carolina (1901) ; with
additional collected receipts making a total of some three hundred
historical receipts for rice.
    p.   cm.
    Includes bibliographical references and index.
    ISBN 0-87249-666-X (hardcover : acid-free paper)
    1. Cookery (Rice)—History. 2. Rice—South Carolina—History.
3. Cookery—South Carolina—History. 4. Afro-American cookery—
History. 5. South Carolina—Social life and customs. I. Stoney,
Samuel G., Mrs. Carolina rice cook book. 1992. II. Title.
TX809.R5H46   1992
641.3'318'09757—dc20   91-46341

To the memory of the African women,

torn from their ancestral homelands

and forced to live out their days as

chattel slaves, as were their daughters

and granddaughters after them.

Save for an occasional slave name,

such as Maum Sarah,

their names are forgotten,

but it was they who created

the celebrated rice kitchen of

the South Carolina Low Country.

Contents

Acknowledgments and Explanations

FIRST I MUST THANK the University of South Carolina Press for having entrusted this work to me. Little did any of us realize at the beginning just how compelling the subject was and how much time it was going to take. It was a singular gesture of confidence, which I appreciate, as I appreciate the patience shown as the work dragged on and on. I want to thank everyone there who has had any responsibility whatsoever for editing and producing this book. Warren Slesinger, in particular, was endlessly helpful in providing me with materials that otherwise would have been unavailable to me. And while I'm about it, I should thank the Press for having put back into print the work of Sarah Rutledge, the grand lady of Charleston who, back in 1847, recorded the cookery of the Low Country, not only that of her aristocratic milieu but that of the more humble inhabitants as well, including old slave dishes, in short the cookery practiced by the African-American women cooks, whether in the Big House or in their own cabins.

As always, I express my gratitude to Elizabeth David, who showed us all that it is possible—despite much evidence to the contrary—to write about cookery with erudition and elegance, but above all, with honesty. We can only strive to emulate her as best we can. (I might note here that she is one of the few English cooks, past or present, who understand the cooking of rice.)

I want to thank John Martin Taylor of *Hoppin' John's,* culinary historian and bookseller of Charleston, who has been so generous with time and materials. Over the years he has sent this Yankee a steady stream of books and articles, even part of his precious store of Carolina Gold rice, including the panicle used by Betti Franceschi for her drawing. Whatever understanding of the uniqueness of the cookery of South Carolina Low Country I was able to bring to this task is largely due to him. He also took time to read the manuscript, not once but twice, and I have followed his suggestions as best I was able. Much of this reading he did while digging out from the devastating hurricane of 1989 and desperately trying to finish his own work, *Hoppin' John's Lowcountry Cooking.* A smaller mind might have felt that I was encroaching on his territory. Bless him. He also put me in touch with Harriet McDougal, granddaughter of our Mrs. Stoney, to whom I am also grateful for having taken time from a busy schedule to talk about her grandmother as well as about Faber, the Stoney family cook cited in these pages. John Taylor also put me in touch with John Bennett, a grandnephew of Mrs. Stoney, who graciously chatted about "Aunt Lou," that is, Mrs. Stoney, whose full name was Louisa Cheves Smythe before she married "Uncle Boss" Stoney.

I am beholden to a number of colleagues in culinary history, first of whom is Dr. Rudolf Grewe, a man of learning who has been of immeasurable help to me in locating various manuscripts and other works, often sending me photocopies of them as well as answering endless questions with admirable patience. (I am not certain that he will always entirely agree with some of my conclusions, but he is a gentleman.) He, too, has been busy finishing a book, a bilingual edition, Arabic with a facing English translation, of an early Arab culinary manuscript from Spain.

I also want to thank Dr. Jessica B. Harris, who read my manuscript and provided invaluable advice, caught errors, and answered questions on various aspects of West African dishes, the *chiebou niebe* of Senegal, for instance.

Jan Longone, bookseller of Ann Arbor, Michigan, went beyond all normal obligations to a client when I asked her help in chasing down the elusive Mrs. Parker to whom Mrs. Stoney had attributed so many receipts. Jan had never seen but a single copy of Mrs. Parker's cookbook, her own—which she was not about to sell—but she sent me photocopies of every page on which rice appeared. And I thank her.

I also want to thank Marilyn Einhorn, bookseller of Manhattan, who volunteered to lend me a rare copy of *Fifty Years in A Maryland Kitchen,* another of Mrs. Stoney's sources. (I ended up buying it, to be sure.)

In remembering other colleagues who have been helpful, I start with Anne Mendelson, whose eagle eye caught things that she knew would be of interest to me, often sending me photocopies. I remember Philip and Mary Hyman of Paris, who volunteered to send me photocopies of Escoffier's rare work on rice and did; also Amelia Wallace Vernon, who generously sent me excerpts from her as-yet-unpublished work on subsistence rice-farming in South Carolina, of which I made good use. My thanks also to Nancy Harmon Jenkins, Sheila Johnson, Laura Shapiro, John Thorne, Jules Rabin, Pranay Gupte, Joan Nathan, Rosa Rasiel, Andréas Freund, Julie Sahni, and Nahum Waxman, bookseller of Manhattan, all of whom I imposed on in some measure. If memory has failed and I inadvertently omitted someone, I beg forgiveness.

It is not customary to acknowledge the help of an author's published work other than properly attributing it, but I want to express my deep appreciation of the work of Daniel C. Littlefield, whose *Rice and Slaves* was the key work in my research. So much of what I learned in other ways fell into place on studying that work.

I have a special debt of gratitude to Veronica Walker, who answered my questions about her grandmother's rice kitchen in Georgia with patience and charm. And, of course, I am full of admiration for the indomitable Pearlie Walker, her grandmother.

I also want to thank Tommy Hill and his sister-in-law Nell Hill for their willingness to talk to me about their ways with rice.

I am deeply grateful to The South Caroliniana Library for its generosity in supplying me with materials that would otherwise have effectively been unavailable to me as well as for the copy of Mrs. Stoney's *Carolina Rice Cook Book* used for the facsimile.

I here express my appreciation to the distinguished artist Betti Franceschi, who did the drawings of the Charleston rice spoon and the panicle of Carolina Gold and to Martha Hess, who photographed the drawings. Also, I thank Dale Rosengarten for her assistance in choosing the photograph used for the frontispiece, as well as Jim Fitch of the Rice Museum of Georgetown, South Carolina, who dug it up and granted permission to use it.

And I thank the staff of the Schomburg Center for Research in Black Culture for their helpfulness. The staff of the Oriental Division of the New York Public Library was also helpful, particularly the Arabists.

I thank Mary Lou O'Keefe at the Hermann-Grima Historic House in New Orleans for her friendly assistance in obtaining for me photocopies of all-but-unfindable rare books, of which I have made good use.

At the Rice Council for Market Research in Houston, Texas, Kristen O'Brien and Julie Gibson were most helpful, as was Lisa Pasquale in giving me sources, elsewhere credited.

Thanks are also due to Giro Press, PO Box 203, Croton-on-Hudson, N.Y. 10520, for permission to use "*Riso del Sabato*" from *The Classic Cuisine of the Italian Jews* by Edda Servi Machlin; to the University of South Carolina Press for "Roast Squab with Rice Pilau" and "French Pilau" from *Two Hundred Years of Charleston Cooking*, as well as "Journey Cake," two receipts for "Rice Bread," and "To Make A Cassorol" from *The Receipt Book of Harriott Pinckney Horry*, Richard J. Hooker, editor; to South Carolina Extension Homemakers Council for "Hoppin John" from *South Carolina Book*; to the University Press of Virginia for "Rice [*Chello*]" from *Persian Cooking* by Nesta Ramazani;

to Mireille Johnston for *"Riz au Safran"* from *The Cuisine of the Sun*; to the Junior League of Charleston, Inc., for lines from "Foreword" from *Charleston Receipts*; to Dinah Ameley Ayensu for *"Yoo-ke-Omo"* from *The Art of West African Cooking*; to Maguelonne Toussaint-Samat for *"Vary Apang oro"* from *La Cuisine Rustique: Afrique Noire [et] Madagascar*; and to Raymond Armisen and André Martin for *"Ris ai fava"* from *Les Recettes de la Table Niçoise*. All are used by permission. Scattered phrasings in my section on Johnny Cakes previously appeared in a paper delivered at a symposium held at Schlesinger Library of Radcliffe College; also, certain passages from the present work were first presented in a paper delivered at a symposium held at the Hermann-Grima Historic House in New Orleans.

A number of explanations may be helpful to the reader. I have introduced a great deal of material into my text in a parenthetical manner, matter which might better have gone into the notes, perhaps, in that it often involves digressions, sometimes discussions of historical method, that I feel are illuminating in some way. I have learned, however, that few people read the notes. For that reason I also mention sources and dates as much as I can within the text as I go along.

Concerning certain questions of usage: In South Carolina the consecrated term is *receipt,* a perfectly valid word in English but not one in much use elsewhere in the United States. I attribute this charming anomaly to the presence of the Huguenots, who would have used the French term *recette*. I feel that it is almost a question of good manners to use the South Carolina term when writing about South Carolina cookery. On a somewhat related subject, I feel that it is likewise a matter of courtesy and respect to use the forms of address to which historical women writers would have been accustomed, so that it is *Miss Rutledge* and *Mrs. Randolph,* for example.

When referring to page numbers in the *Carolina Rice Cook Book,* here reproduced in facsimile, I indicate them thus: (F 10), for example. My system of differentiating among the many receipts for rice croquettes—there are six, of which only two are attributed—is to add a number, thus: "Rice Croquettes [1]," for example, followed by the page number in parentheses, all a bit awkward, perhaps, but the best I could do. The same system is used for receipts in certain other categories.

All citations from French works are translated by myself, even those that have been published in English. A reader—neither of those named as such—criticized my translation of *à peine crevé* as "scarcely cooked" in regard to the cooking of a pilau, claiming that since *crevé* means "burst," *à peine crevé* means "to cook till it just begins to burst and no longer," showing a remarkably poor grasp of French and of French culinary jargon in particular. The source was Provençal and was making the point precisely that the rice must *seem* not quite cooked to the average French cook. For confirmation of my reading, I direct the reader to Durand's receipt *"Riz en pilau"* (pp. 52–53), where the rice is to be *peu cuit,* that is, "undercooked," or "scarcely cooked." I make a point of this because it has to do with understanding the nature of a pilau.

This brings up the always vexing problems of the proper transcription of words from certain languages, Arabic being notoriously difficult in this regard, often with several equally valid transcriptions to choose from. I have used the transcription as given in any particular instance, making no attempt at uniformity, all the more since I have no knowledge of Arabic. But even in French there are problems, especially with diacritical marks, many of which have changed historically. In my edition of 1753, for example, the title page gives a pristine *La Cuisiniére Bourgeoise,* the correct form being *Cuisinière.* I normally follow archaic, capricious, or even wrong, spellings to the letter, reserving the irritating and insulting *[sic]* for use *in extremis,* but this instance presented a different problem. I did not want first-year French students to think that I did not know how to use accents, so I followed the lead of Georges Vicaire, the eminent French bibliographer, who simply ignored the question of the wrong accent. Likewise, in some works from New Orleans, for example, even in English titles, it is *Créole,* in others, *Creole.* Here, I have followed copy, but if a helpful copy reader were to "correct" it one way or the other or if the printer were to make a typographical error, I do not guarantee that I would catch it. I do not always catch my own errors.

I do not regard this work as definitive. There are a number of areas of investigation where I simply had neither the means nor the time to do primary research. I was fortunate in finding certain secondary sources of exceptional quality, such as the works by Daniel C. Littlefield, Peter Wood, and Louis Stouff, for example. But such quality is rare, and as regards culinary research, where quality is even more rare, a Stouff, admirable as he is, was not necessarily seeking what I would, had I access to those documents. That is only one very small aspect of the many areas of research that my project has entailed. In addition, there is a terrible paucity of records. Who, for example, among the early slaves brought from Africa to South Carolina was in a position to write down her receipt for the rice-and-bean dish that came to be known as hoppin' John? Not even the French Huguenot women thought to record receipts for pilau from Provence—those who came from Provence—as I propose they must have done. (They did, however, give hints, as with "To Make a French Pilau.") As a culinary historian, my primary sources are receipts, sometimes having to reconstruct them, working backwards from such evidence as we have, a task perhaps not all that different from the problems faced by linguists in reconstructing Frankish, for example. I make use of all possible ancillary disciplines, always against a general historical background. But finally, it is the study of the evolution of cookery in the many parts of the world that have any bearing on a particular subject—always insofar as I can find primary material or reconstruct it with some confidence—that forms the basis for my conclusions. Take the Baghdad manuscript from 1226, for example, which I cite so often. Clearly, a Persian manuscript from the same period would have been closer to the source of pilau, the earlier the manuscript, the better. Yet we learn more about the dispersion of pilau from the Arab document than we might have from a Persian one. We must work with what we have. All of this I have made use of in reconstructing the journey of the pilau from Persia to South Carolina, on the one hand by way of Jews fleeing Persia for Provence and the Huguenots fleeing France (some of whom were from Provence) for South Carolina, and on the other hand by way of Baghdad and the known Arab penetration of Africa, including the rice lands of West Africa from which the slaves of South Carolina were brought, this last concerning specifically the bean pilau known as hoppin' John. I believe that my hypotheses hold up from every point of view, culinary, historical, and linguistic, but there is an element of conjecture, hence possibility of error.

But I would like to think that my work will encourage further research, particularly in the area of African and African-American contributions to American cookery, a much neglected subject—so neglected that an academic historian was able to write in a book published by the scholarly Oxford University Press the following: "Even before independence, waves of immigrants from Europe and Africa washed onto America's shores, but left few traces of their cuisines on the American table."[1] If this were so, why have I spent years unearthing and analyzing evidence of African and French influences—not to mention those of the Persians and Arabs—in the cookery of Low Country Carolina?

And finally, as always, returning to acknowledgments, I thank John for having put up with it all. I could never have become a writer without his active support; inevitably, household matters are neglected, sometimes shamefully. Really, one writer to a household is quite sufficient. His expert criticisms on my writing are always to the point, and I deeply appreciate them. He is always right.

I want to thank all the members of my family, who had to eat a lot of rice—and bear with my enthusiasm on the subject—but in a special way my daughter Martha, who brought me information about rice and sowers of rice, as well as magnificent photographs of rice fields and women transplanting rice and practicing primitive methods of irrigation and milling—not to mention the pot of rice and black-eye peas, for all the world a hoppin' John seasoned with lemon grass, being sold on the streets of Saigon—from Vietnam, India, Bali, Cambodia, Thailand, etc., in short many of the primeval rice lands.

The Carolina Rice Kitchen

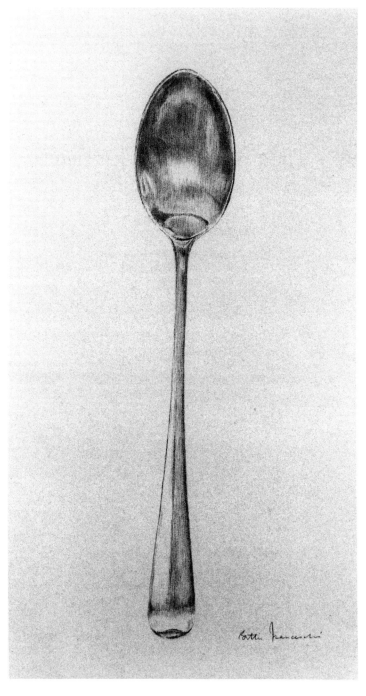

The Charleston Rice Spoon, as depicted by Betti Franceschi.

CHAPTER 1

The Rice Kitchen of the South Carolina Low Country

To Boil Rice

Take a pint of rice well picked and Clean'd. Set on a saucepann with one Gallon of water and a handful of salt, when the water boils put in the rice, about a quarter of an hour will boil it enough according to the quickness of the fire or by tasting it; but be sure to avoid stirring the rice after 'tis in the saucepann for one turn with a spoon will spoil all. When 'tis tender turn the rice into a sieve; when the water is quite draind off return it to the same pann and let it stand near the fire for an hour or more to be kept hott and if the process is well observed it will be white, dry, and every grain Separate.

—Mrs. Blakeway, as recorded in *Rect. Book. No: 2. Eliza Pinckney, 1756*

On every proper Charleston dinner table [there is] a spoon that is peculiar to the town. Of massive silver, about fifteen inches long and broad in proportions, it is laid on the cloth with something of the reverential distinction that surrounds the mace in the House of Commons at Westminster....If you take away the rice spoon from the Charleston dinner table, the meal that follows is not really a meal.

—Samuel Gaillard Stoney, in *Charleston: Azaleas and Old Bricks,* 1937.

And speaking of rice. I was sixteen years old before I knew that everyone didn't eat rice everyday. Us being geechees, we had rice everyday. When you said what you were eating for dinner, you always assumed that rice was there. That was one of my jobs too. To cook the rice. A source of pride to me was that I cooked rice like a grown person. I could cook it till every grain stood by itself.

—Vertamae Smart-Grosvenor, in *Vibration Cooking, or The Travel Notes of A Geechee Girl,* 1986.

The *Chilau* [of Persia], which is a triumph of cookery, comes in the form of a white pyramid of steamed rice, every grain of

which is dry outside, but inside is full of juice, and is served with
a large number of entrees.
—Lord Curzon, in *A New Account of East India and
Persia, Being Nine Years' Travels, 1672–1681,*
by John Fryer.[1]

THIS WORK IS A HYMN OF PRAISE for Carolina rice, the fabled Carolina Gold of yesteryear, the chosen rice of the emperors of
China, or so 'tis said, a rice so esteemed that its very name early became a
generic term in much of the world for the finest long-grain rice obtain-
able. Indeed, it was sought as seed rice in many lands where the culture of
rice was ancient. And considering that the cultivation of rice dates back
millennia, while Carolina rice at the height of its importance as an industry (around 1860) dated back substantially less than two centuries, this is
truly remarkable.

This hymn of praise has elegiac overtones. Since the effective demise
of commercial production in the 1920s, Carolina Gold is no more. (That
is, there has been a joyful resurrection on one plantation on the Carolina
side of the Savannah River, with the first crop in 1988 of certified Carolina Gold in more than a half a century. But this is a labor of love, based
on the passion of one Richard Schulze and in no way commercially com-
petitive.)

This is also a hymn of praise for the rice kitchen that evolved around
the use of Carolina Gold. The ancient way of cooking rice developed in
the primeval rice lands of India and Africa became the Carolina way; directions assuring that the rice "will be white, dry, and every grain Separate" appear in various forms in myriad South Carolina receipts, almost
as a litany. The princely pilau, described by "a seventeenth-century En-
glishman" as "Rice boiled so artificially [artfully] that every grain lies
singly without being added together, with Spices intermixt and a boil'd
Fowl in the Middle," is as at home in Carolina Low Country as in old Persia.[2] We shall explore how this came to be, along with related questions,
as best we can in the following pages.

What we do know is that the early history of the rice kitchen in
South Carolina is inextricably bound up with slavery; it was the black
hands of African slaves who cultivated the rice and cooked it. This is primordial. Other influences were present, to be sure, but we cannot begin
to understand the history of the Carolina rice kitchen except in the light
of this association. So this is also a hymn of praise for the African men
and women torn from their homelands so long ago who made it all
possible.

Let us first define what we mean by a rice kitchen. In its most traditional forms, it is characterized by something approaching the worship of rice. Where rice was the only staple, it was reasonably enough equated with life itself and was often deified. Every aspect of its cultivation was accompanied by propitiatory rites, some of which may have been based on sound agricultural practice in any given area. Even the cooking of rice had to be done so as not to offend the gods; poorly cooked rice was a desecration. Rice was so identified with fertility that even in many lands where rice has never grown, a bridal couple would be showered with rice in a fertility rite, a custom that persists to this day.

In more modern terms, one may say that a rice kitchen means that rice appears on the table every day and is treated with due respect as one of our oldest and most prized grains. Early man in Java, one of the points of origin of rice, may have had little choice; but the peoples of some of our most ancient and dazzling civilizations, the Chinese, Indians, and Persians, for example, *chose* to be eaters of rice and have long held it in veneration. (That is, it either replaced other grains, as in southern China, or coexisted in a position of honor with wheat, as in Persia and northern India.)

The rice kitchen of Carolina is largely derivative; it could hardly have been otherwise, since it came on the world rice scene very late. But it became for all of that a genuine rice kitchen with some highly distinctive notes, which is all the more astonishing considering that rice had not previously been the staple of the European plantation owners, nor was it the only staple; in spite of the strong presence of wheat and maize, rice was revered and eaten at virtually every meal, not only as the great standing dish but also in dishes that were part of every course: soups, main dishes, side dishes, desserts, and breads, as well as invalid foods. All this is admirably documented in the 237 receipts included in the little work compiled by Mrs. Samuel G. Stoney in 1901. The unfailing presence of rice on a Low Country table determined to a great extent the character of *every* dish on that table so that, in a sense, Mrs. Stoney's is an incomplete work in that it presents only receipts in which rice is an ingredient or the obligatory accompaniment. (For example, *atzjar*, a mixed pickle, was nearly as typical of the early South Carolina rice kitchen as the pilau. [Variously spelled, the word comes from Persian *achar;* in India, the word was taken over to refer to any sort of pickle.] Harriott Pinckney Horry recorded a receipt *"Ats Jaar"* in her cookery manuscript dated 1770. It is significant that forms of the Persian/Indian name *achar* seem to have been nearly peculiar to the Low Country insofar as English or American cookery is concerned; that is, with one exception, I do not find it in other English-language cookbooks of the period, although similar concoctions are

fairly common under various other names. [The exception is a receipt for
Atx Jar Pickle, surely borrowed from Carolina sources, given by Mrs. Ho-
ward in *Fifty Years in A Maryland Kitchen* (1873).] As early as 1755, for
example, Hannah Glasse had given a similar receipt in *The Art of
Cookery*—virtually identical in later editions—under the name *India
Pickle.* Considering Mrs. Horry's use of the name *Ats Jaar,* I do not be-
lieve that Mrs. Glasse's work was the source of Mrs. Horry's receipt.]
Sarah Rutledge essentially repeated this early South Carolina receipt in
The Carolina Housewife [1847], variously calling it *atzjar* and *atsjar.*)[3]

What is also surprising is the extent to which this rice kitchen survived the end of commercial rice production in South Carolina, particularly among African-Americans. To be sure, it has suffered under the
onslaught of industrialization, much as American cookery generally has
suffered, although again perhaps not so severely among African-
Americans. In this regard, Nancy Harmon Jenkins's *New York Times* interview with Anna Pinckney, an African-American caterer of Charleston,
is very much to the point. After explaining that as a child she ate rice and
corn her parents had raised and drank clabbered, or slightly soured, milk
from the family cow, she added scornfully, "not milk that somebody
brought to the door," and went on: "Let me tell you something. When we
were children, being black and being poor, we thought we ate that way
because we were poor, but we were eating the best of food, nothing but
natural food. I never ate anything from a can." And her partner, Lucille
Grant, remembers that as a child, "We had all fresh vegetables, everything out of the garden. And we had seafood. My daddy was a fisherman, too; he used to catch shrimps, oysters, clams, crabs. Nowadays we
appreciate what we had." Her father also planted rice, and she says: "We
ate rice at every meal. That is a real lowcountry dish."[4]

There are still scattered traces of these customs, even outside South
Carolina. Pearlie Walker, African-American, seventy-four years old and
the mother of twenty-four children including five sets of twins, still cooks
pretty much as her grandmothers did. As her granddaughter Veronica
Walker said when asked about it, "Nothing's changed. Nothing's
changed." They had rice at every meal, and her grandmother cooked it
"the same old way." When asked what she served it with, Veronica
sounded surprised and puzzled. "Why, *everything,*" she replied. When
pressed, she added, musingly but with increasing enthusiasm: "Greens.
Collard greens. Mustard greens. Or neck bones. Or black-eyed peas. Or
baby lima beans." Sometimes her grandmother would bake a steak and
lay it on a bed of rice, then cover it with more rice and bake it some more.
Of course, the steak was all seasoned and had a nice gravy. Of course. In
short, pretty much Low Country cooking, even though Mrs. Walker lives

in Albany, Georgia, which is well inland. Veronica claims that nothing tastes as good as her grandmother's cooking. When asked if she were learning what her grandmother had to teach her, she replied, "I'm trying." There is yet hope.[5]

Things have changed, of course, and continue to change. Nor do I want to be seen as painting a rosy picture of the old days. But from a culinary point of view, there was an honesty, a regard for and understanding of produce, along with an admirable simplicity of concept eschewing the unnecessarily complicated, that characterized the Carolina rice kitchen of yesteryear that we would do well to emulate. And while the cuisine in the Big House on the plantation and the aristocratic homes of Charleston was as sumptuous as any in England or Virginia, for example, it had more in common with that of the slaves than was the case in Virginia. Wherever African-Americans did the cooking, there were subtle African influences even when they followed the receipts read aloud by their English mistresses as conscientiously as they were able. As I have written elsewhere, such cooks had known other products, other fragrances, and because of a phenomenon known to the Chinese as *wok presence,* they insensibly changed the English palate into the Virginia palate, which came to expect headier sauces.[6] It was this African presence that accounted for the near mythic reputation of Southern cookery. To be sure, slavery enabled plantation owners to live the baronial life, to enjoy the bounties and elegance of a highly labor-intensive cuisine, but there was more to it than mere numbers in kitchen and garden. Actual African dishes occasionally appeared on the master's table—this in addition to the African thumbprint on receipts from elsewhere. And the master liked what was put on his table. The resulting Southern cuisines varied with myriad factors, such as climate, place of origin of both European and African immigrants, and social structure. In South Carolina the determining factor was the role of rice itself, the peculiarly characterizing staple of both slave and master. That is, in the South Carolina rice kitchen it was the African cook, not the mistress, who was the teacher.

Further on I shall return to the pilaus and other goodies, and discuss the influence of the Carolina kitchen on the mainstream of Southern cookery as well. I shall identify, insofar as I am able, the contributors of the receipts compiled by Mrs. Stoney and include a few South Carolina rice receipts from other sources in addition to rice receipts from elsewhere that seem to cast light on the history of a dish or are significant in some way. But methods of cooking rice evolve around the peculiar qualities of the local product, always reflecting the cultural and social structure of the community; even massive borrowings change to accommodate these characteristics. So before going on to the Carolina Gold and finally to the actual receipts, let us take a quick look at the society in which the Carolina rice kitchen evolved.

A BIT OF HISTORY

South Carolina was unique among the Thirteen Colonies in that it was less English in its beginning than were the others. Even the English who settled at Albemarle Point on the Ashley River in 1670 were less English than those who had come to Virginia early in the century, for example, in that most of them came to Carolina, bringing their slaves, from Barbados and the Bahamas, both of which had been settled by the English early in the century, so that they had already become appreciably Creole in their attitudes. (In 1670 the Bahamas were granted by the Crown to the Lord Proprietors of Carolina, who did not give up their claim until 1787.) This connection was so strong that according to the historian Peter H. Wood, "Wills and travel documents referred to 'Carolina in yᵉ West Indies' upon occasion" well into the eighteenth century.[7] And then, nobility was actually bestowed by the Crown upon the Lord Proprietors (which later lapsed), the very idea of which would have been anathema to settlers in other Colonies, at least in principle. In point of fact, a quasi aristocracy existed in varying degree in all the Colonies by virtue of inherited wealth and station as well as land grants. Still, by and large, more egalitarian ideals were professed in other Colonies than in South Carolina.

In addition, perhaps as high as 45 percent of early European settlers were French Huguenots; they may have been very nearly as numerous as the English, since there were scattered numbers of other Europeans as well. (This "other" category was to increase appreciably, but not until after the Revolution.) French seems to have been spoken along the Santee River not only by the French but also by their slaves as late as 1774. The Huguenot Church in Charleston still uses the French liturgy on special occasions, and the singing of French hymns by the choir is being revived. Some of the proudest names in South Carolina are Huguenot: Ravenel, Lucas, Porcher (pronounced *pohr-SHAE*), Huger (pronounced *YOO-JEE*, clearly a corruption of the French) Horry (pronounced *OH-REE*), Gaillard (pronounced *gil-YAHD*), and Doar, among others. Judging by the membership rolls of the Huguenot Society of South Carolina in 1954, the names of distant French Huguenot forebears were a matter of pride and were retained as often as possible.[8] The names above are variously cited in this work.

But the most important distinguishing feature of South Carolina society, by far, was the fact that very early, before 1710, African slaves began to outnumber white inhabitants; by midcentury there were roughly twice as many Africans as whites, and the trend continued. In Lower All Saints Parish, on the Waccamaw River, the ratio reached the point of nine Africans to each white. During the long hot months when all who were able fled the miasmal swamps for higher ground, the only white face on a plantation may have been that of the overseer. Even so, the drivers, who were slaves, were effectively foremen and would have been more directly involved with the laborers. While rare, there were instances of overseers having been African slaves.

The result was a Creole society where the work was done by large numbers of black slaves, the fruits of which were enjoyed by a very few white owners and their families. This situation had far-reaching effects, most of which are beyond the scope of this work. That is, this work does not attempt to document the inhumanity of slavery, nor its corrupting effect on the fabric of white society, nor the whites' ever-growing fear of the black majority verging at times on paranoia. But an unintended benefit for the slaves was that they were largely housed among themselves in one-family dwellings, living in virtual villages, so that they were able to develop some sense of community and maintain certain aspects of their African culture, including culinary traditions, to a far greater extent than was possible, or even permitted, in other Colonies. This is not to say that these Africans were a homogeneous group. In spite of having come almost entirely from West Africa, they were nevertheless of many tribes and as many languages and dialects. The development of Gullah was in response to their need for a secondary language, one sufficiently flexible to serve in communicating not only with each other but also with their white masters and overseers insofar as was necessary. This *lingua franca,* employing a largely English vocabulary essentially organized in various African grammatical systems (to oversimplify a bit), was a phenomenon of the Low Country. It is thought to have originated in the Sea Islands, a result of African demographic superiority and relative isolation from the white proprietors there. Elsewhere in the Colonies slaves usually learned the language of their masters as best they could, according to opportunity. In Virginia, for example, "Africans were expected to become Negroes as soon as possible," according to historian Michael Mullin, writing on a related aspect, their African "national character."[9] And so it was that slaves in South Carolina Low Country remained more African than elsewhere in the Colonies; the very existence of Gullah bears testimony to that fact. Gullah as it has survived must be a pale shadow of the rich language it once was; since it was then solely oral, we shall never know just how much it has changed. Attempts to transcribe Gullah phonetically, even when done in good faith, give a patronizing impression that interferes with an appreciation of its richness and beauty.

While work on rice plantations was far more arduous and dangerous than other plantation work, there were certain compensations. For one thing, work was organized on the task system, as opposed to the gang system in use elsewhere, meaning that once a specific task was accomplished—be it clearing, planting, hoeing, controlling inundations, repairing dykes and ditches, harvesting, or pounding—slaves were allowed to work for themselves and their families until time for the next task. Many observers have remaked on this fact; apparently the system was reasonably codified and was honored. That is, harvesting or urgent repairs for example, might require working straight through, but workers on such projects expected compensatory days off. Slaves' skills in fishing or hunting or snaring of game were legendary, enabling them to eke out their rations and add variety to their diet, even supposing that much of what they caught was sold. (Firearms were generally forbidden, and the sale of goods by slaves was in theory regulated, but enforcement seems to have been spotty. On occasion, such activities were assigned as tasks.)

Perhaps even more important is the fact that slaves were given the use of a plot of land, generally running about an acre per family, where they were encouraged to grow rice and to garden for themselves, so that they were able to grow their own vegetables, a circumstance of which they seem to have made good use.[10] Above all they grew greens, but presumably they also raised such African favorites as okra, sorghum, black-eye peas, eggplant, and benne seed, for example. They also usually kept poultry and perhaps a hog. The testimony of Anna Pinckney, Lucille Grant, and Pearlie Walker opens a window on this past; their parents must have been following patterns that had endured generations.

Finally, there were the forces of geography and climate. The remarkable river systems and the subtropical weather provided optimal conditions for the cultivation of rice. (It should be noted that some of the finest long-grain rices grow on relatively cool, terraced hillsides, as in Kashmir, for example, but in general, tropical or near-tropical conditions similar to those in the lands of origin favor the growing of long-grain rice.) Also, large-scale production was facilitated because the cultivators were able to harness not only the water itself but also the motive power of the tidal rivers to accomplish the necessary repeated floodings and drainings of the rice fields. The great rice rivers, north to south, are as follows: Waccamaw, Pee Dee, Black, Sampit, Santee, Cooper, Ashley, Edisto, Ashepoo, Combahee, and Savannah. Similar conditions continued down the Georgia coast, and indeed the cultivation of rice spilled over into that Colony, but a good half-century later. And the political history of Georgia was very different. For one thing, many plantation owners there remained loyal to the Crown during the Revolution; as a result, their lands were confiscated, many of which were taken over by families of South Carolina proprietors. Also, the period following the 1780s, lasting into the nineteenth century, was a period of expansion, and such prominent Carolina family names as Blake, Clinch, Elliott, Hazzard, Heyward, Huger, Kollock, Manigault, Pinckney, and Wightman established themselves as proprietors of rice lands in Georgia, while not relinquishing Carolina holdings.[11] So there were traces of South Carolina cookery that showed up in Georgia, as can be seen by the fact that many of the names above show up as contributors of receipts, either in the Stoney collection or in other works which I have cited. And, of course, the cookery presented by Mrs. Hill in *Mrs. Hill's New Cook Book* (1872), from which Mrs. Stoney chose nineteen receipts, reflects those ties. It should be noted that when the culture of rice took hold in Georgia following the lifting of the prohibition of slavery in 1750, similar forces produced similar customs in regard to the task system and the use of Gullah, with all that implied. Eventually, of course, the commercial culture of rice spread yet further down into Florida and especially Louisiana, as well as into many other areas of our country, but all that occurred well into the nineteenth century and is not part of our subject, at least not directly.

THE PLANTERS OF RICE

It is only from the more closed society of later times, which placed a high premium upon fostering ignorance and dependence within the servile labor force, that white Americans have derived the false notion that black slaves were initially accepted, and even sought, as being totally "unskilled." The actual conditions of the colonial frontier meant that workers who were merely obedient and submissive would have been a useless luxury.
—Peter H. Wood, in *Black Majority: Negroes in Colonial South Carolina,* 1974.

As one views this vast hydraulic work [the rice plantation], he is amazed to learn that all of this was accomplished in face of seemingly insuperable difficulties by every-day planters who had as tools only the axe, the spade, and the hoe, in the hands of intractable negro men and women, but lately brought from the jungles of Africa.
—David Doar, in *Rice and Rice Planting in the South Carolina Low Country,* 1936.

It is a region [the Southern Rivers, land of the Bagas] containing some of the richest soil in West Africa, admirably suited to rice culture but so difficult to work that, in the words of

one scholar, one would think that it might be abandoned to "the
fish, the crocodiles, the crabs, the mosquitoes and the birds" were
it not inhabited by some of the most industrious agriculturalists in
Africa.
—Daniel C. Littlefield, in *Rice and Slaves: Ethnicity and
the Slave Trade in Colonial South Carolina,* 1981.[12]

The cultivation of any grain requires generations of continuing experience regarding optimal choice and development of a strain for a specific
soil and climate, optimal planting and harvesting times, learning to cope
with the vagaries of nature as well as with specific pests and diseases, and
learning to prepare and store the grain for eventual consumption. In addition, the cultivation of wetland rice entails judging the appropriate
times of inundation and draining of the rice fields, a matter of crucial importance. In turn, these operations require various skills of high sophistication. David Doar, of Santee, the last planter of his line, cites an
unidentified plantation owner thus: "A rice plantation is a huge hydraulic
machine, maintained by constant fighting against the rivers; the manager
and the labor must be ready at a moment's notice for the most exhaustive
efforts. The whole apparatus of levels, floodgates, trunks, canals, banks,
and ditches is of the most extensive kind, requiring skill and unity of purpose to keep in order."
       By the time commercial cultivation of rice in South Carolina was
coming to an end, many plantation owners had convinced themselves
that the only African contribution to rice culture had been the unskilled
labor of "intractable negro men and women, but lately brought from the
jungles of Africa," as Doar expressed it. Based on nothing more than his
admiration of paintings showing Chinese methods of cultivating rice, for
example, Duncan Clinch Heyward, in *Seed from Madagascar* (1937) suggested that Carolina methods had come from China; he did not address
the question of who among the early settlers of South Carolina would
have been familiar with Chinese methods nor, for that matter, the fact
that the two systems were quite dissimilar.[13]
       The truth is that early English and French proprietors knew nothing
of rice culture. How would they have learned? John Gerarde wrote in
1597 concerning the rice that he had grown in his garden that "the floure
did not shew itself with me, by reason of the injurie of our unseasonable
yeare of 1596." He listed the places where it grew, all hot countries, and
noted that "it prospereth best in fenny and waterish places." True
enough, but this seems to very nearly exhaust what the English knew
about the cultivation of rice until the Virginia experience, when in 1647
Governor Sir William Berkeley "caused half a bushel of Rice. . . to be so-

wen, and it prospered gallantly," so gallantly that the Virginians decided to continue because, in their words, "we perceive the ground and Climate is very proper for it as our *Negroes* affirme, which in their Country is most of their food." It is reasonable to infer that it was their African slaves who cultivated the rice. (We have no records concerning the source of the rice or cultivation methods; there is some reason to believe that it was upland, or "dry," rice, that is, rice raised more or less as are other grains. Virginia exported rice to the West Indies and New England as late as 1697, so the project must have been fairly successful. Littlefield notes that the success of tobacco ended the cultivation of rice in Virginia, but I propose that increasing competition from the undoubtedly superior rice of South Carolina may have been an equally important factor. Also, there was a growing importance of Virginia wheat, which was much esteemed and fetched high prices.)

Nor were the French any more knowledgeable. I know of two desultory attempts in the seventeenth and early eighteenth centuries to grow rice in France; not until this century was a modicum of success achieved in the Camargue, the saline marshes on the Mediterranean.

This leaves the Africans. There were of course countless peoples elsewhere who knew how to grow rice but, as Littlefield so succinctly puts it, "Africans were on the scene." Given that it was they who cleared and prepared the rice fields, constructed the canals, dikes, and lock systems, planted and hoed the rice, ran the flooding and draining operations, and harvested and pounded the rice, it should hardly be necessary to elaborate the point. And indeed, the early proprietors were quick to recognize the particular skills of African slaves in the cultivation of rice. Littlefield suggests that "Englishmen, from the beginning, could have made a conscious effort to import slaves from those regions known to produce rice."[14] That is, to put it more bluntly, the proprietors, recognizing that they were bumbling about, turned to experienced cultivators of rice for help. Unfortunately, figures on slave imports are not available for those crucial early years, but those for later periods make such an interpretation altogether reasonable, even compelling. We shall return to this aspect, but to better understand African contributions to the success of rice culture in South Carolina, it is useful to know a little something about rice and its origins.

RICE AND ITS ORIGINS

Rice is our most important grain, in that it constitutes the basic diet of over half the world's population. As to name, the most common Middle English form was *rys,* from Old French *ris* (Modern *riz*), Latin *oryza,*

Greek *oruza,* perhaps derived from (unattested but reconstructed) East Iranian *vrīz-,* which is akin to Sanskrit *vrīhi.* According to the botanists, rice (*Oryza sativa* and related grasses, *not* including our own "wild rice," which is not botanically a rice) originated in India, Indonesia (including certain associated areas), and Africa. Most of us are rather more likely to associate rice with China than with Africa, but the fact is that rice came to China relatively late, historically speaking. Over time, thousands of cultivars of *O. sativa* have been developed, which fall into two groups: *O. sativa indica,* or long-grain rice, and *O. sativa japonica,* or short-grain rice. Long-grain rices generally prefer hotter climates, take longer to mature, and are less starchy and sticky when cooked than are short-grain varieties. (Nothing is ever quite that simple; there are medium-grain rices, but they tend to share the characteristics of short-grain varieties.) I might note here that eaters of rice are finicky about the choice and quality of rice. Those who prefer short-grain rice complain that long-grain rice is "less absorbent," while those of long-grain persuasion find short-grain rice "sticky" and "mushy." In addition, there are scores of other characteristics, such as aroma and flavor, that are equally important to aficionados, at least once the question of texture has been settled.

Rice has been cultivated in Africa since around 1500 B.C. according to evidence cited by Littlefield. The centers were in the Central Niger Delta and Senegambia; the rice cultivated was *Oryza glaberrima,* thought to have been domesticated from *O. Breviligulata,* the "red" rice of West Africa. Another indigenous rice, *O. Barhil,* was cultivated between the River Senegal and the White Nile, reaching as far south as Angola and Tanzania, again according to Littlefield. One must suppose that those wild rices had been gathered for millennia; domestication bespeaks long acquaintance. By the sixteenth century, perhaps earlier, the cultivation of *O. glaberrima* had spread along a large stretch of the Atlantic coast. Details concerning the introduction of *O. sativa* into Africa are unclear; Arab travelers made "numerous references to the presence and use of rice in the Sudan," beginning in the eighth century, according to Littlefield, but it is not certain that it was *O. sativa.* Some historians place its introduction to the sixteenth century with the Portuguese. Whatever the date of introduction, "it took root in those areas where the cultivation of rice was already known," as Littlefield notes.[15]

Curiously, in all the discussion about when and how Asian strains of rice were introduced into Africa, no mention is made of the introduction of *O. sativa indica* from the Malay Archipelago to Madagascar by the Malagasy in their migration around 500 A.D. Madagascar is, after all, part of Africa; Malagasy is a Malayan language but is peppered with Bantu words in such a way as to suggest long association. In addition, the

Arabs came to Madagascar around 1000 A.D.; they were not only prodigious eaters of rice—*O. sativa,* that is—who planted it wherever it would grow all around the Mediterranean, including North Africa, but also prodigious traders who had long crisscrossed Africa, and continued to do so. That is, the Arabs knew rice when they saw it, or to put it another way, *O. sativa* followed Islam. (In Gambia, for example, Arabic was spoken among the Fula in addition to their own language. The Hausa were predominantly Muslim, and so remain. And a number of Arabic-speaking Africans were among those brought to South Carolina as slaves. As we shall see, Gambia was rice country. According to the historian Charles Joyner, some African-born slaves in the Low Country "retained their belief in Islam as late as the mid-nineteenth century," in sufficient number, it would seem, to warrant the recorded substitution of beef for pork rations for such slaves.) In time, *O. sativa* largely displaced indigenous rices in Africa, primarily because of its higher yield.[16]

According to Wood, the principal rice region of West Africa was along the Windward Coast (Sierra Leone), stretching westward from the Gold Coast; in slaving times a portion of that area was specifically known as the Rice Coast. Among other documents, Wood cites a notice from the [Charleston] *Evening Gazette* of July 11, 1785, announcing the arrival of "a choice cargo of windward and gold coast negroes, who have been accustomed to the planting of rice." That is, plantation owners were perfectly aware of the superiority, from their point of view, of African slaves from rice country. Littlefield writes that "as early as 1700 ships from Carolina were reported in the Gambia River." And this continued. In a letter dated 1756, Henry Laurens, a Charleston merchant, wrote: "The slaves from the River Gambia are preferr'd to all others with us save the Gold Coast." The previous year he had written: "Gold Coast or Gambias are best[;] next To Them The Windward Coast are prefer'd to Angolas." As Littlefield says, "Thus went the hierarchy of regional preferences."[17]

Such records as are available show that Angolans were more numerous in South Carolina than the "preferred" ones from Gambia or the Gold Coast. This was most likely a matter of availability and expediency. It was not necessary that every slave know how to cultivate rice; it sufficed that a good proportion know. Littlefield estimates that 43 percent of the Africans brought during the eighteenth century, for example, came from rice lands, a higher proportion than from any other area. Even in the rice fields, there was a great deal of labor that did not require specific knowledge of rice culture, or that could quickly be learned working alongside experienced workers. And in the beginning, for example, the principal industry in South Carolina had been the raising of cattle, and this continued for some time. Nor was rice the only crop. Each plantation endeavored to be self-sufficient, so that there was a good deal of more or-dinary farming: the raising of maize, wheat, vegetables, fruits, hogs, poultry, etc. In addition, there was need for various skilled artisans: car-penters, cabinetmakers, metalworkers, smiths, leatherworkers, coopers, boatmen, bricklayers, millers, weavers, tailors, seamstresses, potters, nurses, and midwives, for example, not to forget cooks and other workers in the Big House. Child care, an important aspect of slave life where women toiled in the fields all day, was the province of women too old or too young to work in the fields. In any event, children were put to work very early. (It is beyond the scope of this work to discuss the role of women in the production of rice except to note that they participated in all but the heaviest work. They were apt to have done most of the arduous pounding of the rice and, of course, almost all of the cooking. The cook-ing we shall examine further on.)[18]

Of particular interest to Littlefield is the area of the Southern Rivers, where the Bagas practiced a system of rice culture whose methods were "analogous to those in South Carolina"—and for good reason, because many of the physical conditions were similar; the lowlands were cut by numerous rivers with strong tidal movements; the mangrove swamps had to be cleared; the rice fields separated by dikes and levees, "furnished with sluice gates of hollow tree trunks," which could be opened or closed as necessary. All this is as described by Doar, including his finding long-buried hollowed-out logs used in the same way. And there was Madagas-car, where there were also parallels in production methods, according to Littlefield. This similarity assumes heightened significance when we learn that a slave trade existed between Madagascar and British America from the 1670s to 1698 and again from 1716 to 1721. (He notes that there is no evidence of direct importation into South Carolina for those crucial years, but the presence of slaves from Madagascar is documented; they may have been brought by way of the British West Indies, a common route.)[19] This significance is further enhanced when we remember that the seed for Carolina Gold is said to have come from Madagascar.

But most of the Carolina planters of rice came from the rice lands of West Africa. Wood movingly describes how the springtime motions of planting rice by pressing a hole with the heel and covering the seeds with the foot are similar to those used in West Africa. And in summer, when the slaves moved in a row through the rice fields, "hoeing in unison to work songs, the pattern was not one imposed by European owners but rather one retained from West African forebears." And in October, the threshed grain was "fanned" in the wind, using the "wide flat winnowing baskets" that were made by black hands using an African design.[20]

As late as the nineteenth century plantation owners were still aware of the technical prowess of African slaves in matters concerning the cultivation of rice. The historian Charles Joyner cites Elizabeth Allston Pringle, "a postslavery rice planter," who wrote: "Only the African race could have made it possible or profitable to clear the dense cypress swamps and cultivate them in rice by a system of flooding the fields from the river by canals, ditches, or floodgates, drawing off the water when necessary, and leaving these wonderfully [sic] rice lands dry for cultivation." Joyner also cites numerous awards won by African slaves on the Waccamaw River "for their masters." In two instances, the award was for "developing a new strain of big grain rice."[21]

The end of slavery was the end of rice culture in South Carolina. This was not immediately apparent, but the industry was doomed. There were other factors, such as increasing competition from new rice lands in Louisiana, which was aggravated by the fact that the wonderfully rich soil of Low Country South Carolina was too boggy and spongy to support heavy labor-saving machinery in the fields. Hurricanes and silting are often cited as contributing factors, but such disasters had always been part of the equation in the Low Country; so long as the African slave was on hand to repair the damage, the setback was only temporary. In 1927, according to John Martin Taylor, South Carolina food historian, the last documented commercial crop of Carolina Gold was planted by Theodore D. Ravenel. In 1935, drawing on nearly fifty years as a planter, Ravenel discussed the reasons for the long decline, writing that in 1881, "Labor was abundant and of good quality. Eighty per cent of the culture at that time was done by hand labor.... The younger ones were then being trained by the parents and the very efficient foremen, many of whom were former drivers, much respected by all the laborers." (Drivers had always been African-American.) But as time went on, the skilled ex-slaves left for higher wages in the phosphate mines and the saw mills, leaving the owners to do their own training of workers. "It is my opinion and the opinion of many of my friends who are forever gone that this lack of efficient labor was the biggest contribution to the slow but sure decline of rice culture in this section," he wrote.[22] That is, without the skills of the African-Americans that had been handed down from generation to generation, the proprietors were helpless, very nearly as helpless as they had been in the earliest days of rice culture before having been taught by Africans whatever they came to know about the culture of rice.

Panicle of Carolina Gold, as depicted by Betti Franceschi, grown on Turnbridge Plantation, South Carolina, by Richard and Patricia Schultz with Julius Bing, 1988.

CAROLINA GOLD

[Rice] is now Sown in *Carolina,* and become one of the great products of the Country: I have seen it grow, and flourish there, with a vast increase, it being absolutely the best *Rice* which grows upon the whole Earth, as being the weightiest, largest, cleanest, and whitest, which has been yet seen in the Habitable World.
— William Salmon, in *Botanologia,* London, 1710.

Varieties of Rice.—Of the varieties of rice brought to our market, that from Bengal is chiefly of the species denominated *cargo* rice, and is of a coarse reddish-brown cast, but peculiarly sweet and large-grained; it does not readily separate from the husk, but it is preferred by the natives to all others. *Patna* rice is more esteemed in Europe, and is of very superior quality; it is small-grained, rather long and wiry, and is remarkably white. The *Carolina* rice is considered as the best, and is likewise the dearest in London.
— Mrs. Isabella Beeton, in *Mrs. Beeton's Book of Household Management,* London, 1861.

In France, the most esteemed rices are: the rice of Carolina and of Patna, absolutely white, transparent, angular, elongated, odorless; the rice of Piedmont, inferior to the first, somewhat yellowish, rounded, opaque.
— Joseph Favre, in *Dictionnaire Universel de Cuisine,* Paris, [1894].[23]

The introduction into South Carolina of the specific strain of rice that was to become famed throughout the world as Carolina Gold is shrouded in legend, each "true" version of which differs from the others. (Before I go on, it should be explained that the name is due to the spectacular beauty of the ripe grain in the field, a sea of molten gold. To be sure, it could also be called "gold" in that it made the proprietors of the Low Country among the richest in the Colonies, but that came later.) As Daniel Littlefield says, "It is probable...that rice had various introductions into South Carolina from divergent sources...." One of the early secondary accounts is that of Mark Catesby (first published in 1731), who says that a new grain was introduced from Madagascar in 1696, but Littlefield cites letters written by John Stewart from South Carolina in 1690 to the effect that settlers were "already experimenting with cultivating rice in swamplands." (There is reason to believe that earlier efforts had been with "dry" rice, possibly borrowed from the Virginia experience alluded to earlier. The problem is that contemporary descriptions were all maddeningly vague, not only of the grain itself but also of methods of cultivation.) The version suggested by the Stewart letters would not be at variance with the account given by the historian A. S. Salley (1936), who maintains that it was Dr. Henry Woodward who "procured about a peck of gold seed rice which [Captain John] Thurber had obtained at Madagascar," and that "by 1690 the production of rice in South Carolina had so advanced that the planters asked that it be specified as one of the commodities of the province with which they might pay their quit rents," and that by 1700, its production was "so great that there had not been ships enough at Charles Town that year in which to transport it all." He also maintains that "The writer [Salley] has a sample each of rough and polished rice procured from Madagascar by Mrs. J. Palmer Lockwood and they are identical with South Carolina rice."[24]

The Rice Council agrees that rice was established as a major crop in South Carolina by 1700, citing the shipment of three hundred tons of rice, "referred to as 'Carolina Golde Rice,' to England in that year."[25] That is, once the proprietors found knowledgeable workers steeped in the lore of cultivating rice, meaning slaves from West African rice lands, things moved apace, especially considering the enormity of the venture, including a certain amount of experimentation with the seed rice as to optimal planting times, inundating and flooding times, etc., in a totally new environment. Littlefield suggests that it was those slaves who were responsible for the entire process. Africans "accustomed to the planting of rice" had been on the scene since 1685, as we saw. There may have been a small Malagasy presence from Madagascar, but conditions in South Carolina were far more like those in the West African rice lands, and he cites certain distinctive practices adopted in Carolina, such as thrashing techniques, which are characteristic of West Africa and not of Madagascar.

By 1710 William Salmon was able to write enthusiastically about the new rice. It must be noted that he was a bit of a mountebank, and he would not have found fault with the product of an English colony, but this does not detract from the fact that Carolina Gold burst on the world rice scene with éclat.

As noted earlier, *Carolina rice* came to be a generic term for long-grain rice of high quality and was frequently specified in cookbooks, not only in England but in France as well. This continues, in spite of the fact that commercial production effectively ended in the 1920s, so much so that Riviana Foods, Inc., appropriated the name as their trademark for long-grain rice, rice that may have been grown in any of a number of states but *not* in South Carolina. (When asked if there had been any connection whatsoever with the historical Carolina Gold, the spokesperson said, "No, they had simply liked the name.")

One of the boosters of Carolina Gold was Thomas Jefferson, who as ambassador to France worked to increase French imports of American products. It is true that he tried to interest the proprietors of Carolina in other types of rice, rice that could be grown on dry land, rather than "the kind they now [1789] possess, which requiring the whole country to be laid under water during a certain season of the year, sweeps off numbers of the inhabitants annually with pestilential fevers." However, when discussing an Asian strain of "dry" rice in this regard, there was no question as to which rice he thought was superior. He had some "dry" rice sent to South Carolina, but apparently nothing came of it.

Earlier, in 1787, Jefferson had also sent some rice from Piedmont to South Carolina, but it was not for the purpose of replacing Carolina Gold seed stores that had purportedly been pillaged by the British during their occupation (1780–1782), as maintained by a number of writers; if the perpetrators of that tale had bothered to read Jefferson, they could never have written such nonsense. First, he reports that both England and France were importing Carolina rice, precisely during that decade, so that some seed rice must have escaped notice by the British. More pertinent yet is the fact that the rice of Piedmont is the round rice familiar to us for its use in making *risotto,* and Jefferson describes both rices in some detail. According to him, Parisians preferred Carolina rice for making dessert dishes with milk because of "the superior beauty of the Carolina rice, seducing the eye of those purchasers who are attached to appearances." They complained, however, that "it crumbles in certain forms of preparation," that is, when cooked *au gras* [with meat]. In a letter to Jefferson from Charleston (1787), Ralph Izard, after noting that the rice from Piedmont "will bear no comparison with ours," makes this telling observation: "You say that our Rice dissolves when dressed with Meat: *this must be owing to some mismanagement in dressing it.* I have examined my cook on the subject, & find that as meat requires to be longer on the fire than Rice, they must be dressed separately, until each is nearly done, & then the combination is to be made. The water must boil before the Rice is put into it, or the grains will not be distinct from each other [emphasis added]." As I discuss later, Parisians generally have understood rice cookery very poorly. That said, I find in my own experience with the Carolina Gold of today that it does seem to require rather more flair in cooking than do some other rices; it is more delicate. And from Jefferson's discussion I gather that it was more fragile in the milling as well, certainly more so than the rice of Piedmont. This brittleness caused considerable loss, because the broken grades, or "small" rice, had to be sold at lower prices. (The special care that was necessary when cooking small rice can be seen on F 10). Jefferson wanted to interest the Carolina proprietors in raising Piedmont rice in *addition* to long-grain rice so that they could satisfy the French demand for the round rice of Piedmont, as well. Curiously, although the Italian round rice retained a certain following in France, Carolina rice increasingly became the more esteemed, as evidenced by Carême (1815, 1833–1835), Favre (above), and Escoffier (1921), and many others.[26]

Nothing came of the Piedmont rice experiment either, apparently. Carolina Gold belonged in South Carolina; it had been naturalized so thoroughly by the African slaves in the last years of the seventeenth century that so long as the knowledgeable African-Americans were there to cultivate it, it was top of the line. Charles Joyner cites records reporting that the slaves of Joshua John Ward and of John Hyrne Tucker "consistently earned silver medals for their masters" at the annual fairs of the Winyah and All Saints Agriculture Society, which had been founded in 1842. Medals were won for Carolina Gold in London (1851) and Paris (1855). And at least in the case of Ward, he and his slaves were "recognized for developing a new strain of big grain rice." (This must have been an improvement of Carolina Gold; no details are given, however.)[27] Its only serious drawback was that it required exceptionally labor-intensive methods of cultivation, due primarily to the boggy nature of the soil, which did not permit the use of labor-saving machinery, as mentioned earlier. But it was that same soil which nourished the Carolina Gold rice.

I have been unable to find any historical references to the *flavor* of Carolina Gold, that is, aside from Favre's noting that it had no aroma, and this may be telling. I find the resurrected Carolina Gold without any strikingly characteristic flavor, although alongside a dish of Carolina rice (a popular commercial brand of some repute), it is the commercial rice that seems dull, no matter how the two rices are cooked, Carolina style, Chinese style, or in pilau. So the Carolina Gold must have some subtle but real advantage, although I would find it difficult to describe. Furthermore, the soil and waters of South Carolina have changed over the past century or so, so that no matter how closely Richard and Patricia Schultz follow traditional methods in the'ı extraordinary venture, the rice is going to have changed in flavor, and not for the better. (I speak primarily of pollution, both offshore and upstream.) The textures of the cooked rices were more different than I would have expected, again with the edge going to Carolina Gold, which has an almost velvety quality. This was not a controlled experiment; for one thing, different rices require different timing; in addition, reactions to flavor and texture are highly subjective.

What cannot be considered a subjective reaction in the little experiment described above is the fact that the Carolina Gold cooked up snowy white, the whitest rice I can recall ever having seen, whiter than the com-

mercial strain. Whiteness is not necessarily a virtue with me, but historically it was perhaps its most dazzling characteristic, certainly the one that
was most remarked on. Jefferson, for example, referred to it as "the
white rice" whenever he compared it to other rices. And in addition to the
sources I cite above, there are other writers who remarked on its whiteness.

And now let us turn to the remarkable rice kitchen inspired by this
rice, a kitchen of myriad influences, including Persian, Arab, French,
English, and African, all executed by the African-American women who
did the cooking in South Carolina.

CHAPTER 2

To Boil the Rice

Leave rice in plain water to soak for about 25–30 minutes before cooking. Rince rice and drain off the water. For every cup of rice add 6 cups of water. Add salt to taste, and a few drops of fresh lime juice (if available). Let rice boil for 10–15 minutes till the same become tender. Drain off the excess boiled rice water in separate pan. You can use this water for soups as some of the vitamins and richness of rice will be there. Please do not stir the rice at this stage. Leave the pot on gentle heat for about 10 seconds [minutes?] with lid on till the rice get swelled and dry. DON'T STIR OR DISTURB THE RICE. Take the pot off the heat and Rice are now ready to serve....Each grain remains separate.

    —Sachdeva & Sons, Millers and Packers of Pari Dehraduni
    Basmati Rice, Amritsar, India, 1989 (1988 harvest).

             Vary Apang oro (riz sonnant)

    In Madagascar, we like the rice *"sonnant"* [resounding], that is, perfectly separate. In a manner of speaking, the rice must "resound" when poured on the plate....*Vary* means rice in Malagasy.

    ...First bring salted water to a boil. When it is boiling, throw in the rice (first well washed). Lower the flame. When the rice is half-cooked, drain in a sieve; put it in a pot, and allow it to cook and dry on gentle heat.

    —Maguelonne Toussaint-Samat, in *La Cuisine Rustique:*
    Afrique Noire [et] *Madagascar,* Forcalquier, 1971. (The
    author explains that the recipe is perfectly "orthodox"
    because it was given to her by her grandmother.)

Rice [*Chello,* when presented molded]

3 cups rice	4 tablespoons butter
6 tablespoons salt	

    Bring a large pot of water to a rolling boil. Pour in the rice and salt. Stir once. Boil hard for exactly 10 minutes. Drain in a large colander; rinse well under cold water and drain. Melt the butter in a saucepan over a medium heat. Pour in the rice. Place a dishtowel over the inside of the lid, bring the overlapping edges up over the wrapped lid. (The cloth absorbs the moisture, preventing the drops of water that ordinarily form on the inside of the lid from dropping back into the rice and making it soggy.)

Steam over a medium heat for 20 to 25 minutes, or over a medium-low heat for 30 to 35 minutes....

Always dish out the rice with a slotted spoon, fluffing it as you place it in a serving dish. A crust of *tah-dig* (literally, bottom-of-the-pan) will have formed on the bottom of the saucepan. To serve this in one unbroken piece, immerse the exterior of pan in cold water for a few minutes. Pry the *tah-dig* loose with a spatula.

—Nesta Ramazani, in *Persian Cooking,* 1974.

Fust t'ing yo' roll up yo' sleeve as high as yo' kin, en yo' tak soap en yo' wash yo' hand clean. Den you wash yo' pot clean, fill um wid col' wata en put on de fia. Now w'ile yo' wata de bile, yo' put yo' rice een a piggin [wooden pail] en yo' wash em well, den when yo' dun put salt een yo' pot, en 'e bile high, yo' put yo' rice een, en le' um bile till 'e swell, den yo' pour off de wata, en put yo' pot back o' de stove, for steam.

—Goliah, slave of Robert F. W. Allston, as cited by Charles Joyner.

Rice boiled to eat with Curry or roast Meats

Prepare as above [Wash and pick some rice]; then put it into a large quantity of water, boil it quick, throw in a little salt, and observe the very moment when it is swelled large, but not too much softened; then drain off the water, and pour the rice on the shallow end of a sieve: set it before a fire, and let it stay until it separates and dries. Serve it without sauce of any kind.

—Mrs. Maria Rundell, in *A New System of Domestic Cookery,* Exeter, New Hampshire, 1808.

To Boil Rice

To one pint of rice allow one gallon of cold water. Boil in an English-cast vessel. Let it boil slowly until the grains are perfectly swollen. Drain off the water carefully; add salt, stir and smooth it lightly with a spoon. Set back on the stove covered, and let it dry—one hour will not be too long. It will only be the richer if carefully done. Rice is more easily burned in a porcelain than in an iron, which also injures the vessel.... This is the Carolina mode of cooking rice. We but seldom see it in perfection.

—Theresa C. Brown, in *Modern Domestic Cookery,* Charleston, 1871.

Uncover as you walk along the banks of the fields, one of
their little three-legged iron pots with its wooden cover, and try, if
only from curiosity, the rice which they have prepared for their
midday meal.
>—Jacob Motte Alston, describing the cooking of rice by
> slaves at Woodbourne plantation, as cited by Charles
> Joyner.

[Rice is properly cooked only when it is] boiled till *done,* the
water "dreened" off, and set on the ashes to "soak." Around the
pot there is a brown rice-cake, in the center of which are the snow-
white grains, each thoroughly done and each separate. Unless one
has eaten rice cooked in this way, he knows nothing about it. The
stuff called rice—soft and gluey—may do to paper a wall, but not
to feed civilized man.
>—Jacob Motte Alston, as cited by Charles Joyner.

Chinese Rice
Take equal parts of rice and cold water. Wash your rice in
several waters, put it in a saucepan, salt, and let it boil. When
cooked put aside to soak until dry. Be careful, it burns easily.
Every grain of rice will be separate and dry.
>—Miss Eustis, *Mon Repos,* Aiken, South Carolina, 1904.

To Boil Rice
Pick out all discolored grains; wash it well in two waters;
soak an hour before boiling. Twenty minutes before serving, stir it
slowly into boiling water, previously salted. One pint of rice will
require four tumblers of water. When done, pour immediately into
a clean colander, and set it upon the coolest part of the stove. Toss
it up lightly with a silver or wooden fork. Every grain should
stand distinct. Boil it in an open stew-pan lined with tin or
porcelain. This is the way it should be cooked when eaten with
meats.
>—Mrs. A. P. Hill, Widow of Hon. Edward Y. Hill, of
> Georgia, in *Mrs. Hill's New Cook Book,* 1872.

To wash the Rice
Pour upon it water enough to cover; stir it round briskly with
the hand for several seconds; pour off the water, and add fresh;
stir as before, and repeat this several times. The whiteness of the
rice depends, in a great degree, upon the washing being thorough.
>—[Sarah Rutledge], in *The Carolina Housewife,*
> Charleston, 1847.

To gravel the Rice
After it has been washed, pour upon it water enough to cover
it; shake the vessel (a common piggin [pail] is best) containing the
rice, causing the gravel to settle; then pour carefully all the water,
with a portion only of the rice, into another vessel, (the vessels
being held, one in each hand;) pour back the water into the first
vessel, shake it again, and pour the water, with another portion of
the rice, into the second vessel. Repeat this until all the rice has
thus been transferred from the first to the second vessel. The last
of the rice being very carefully poured off with the water, the
gravel will remain.
—[Sarah Rutledge], in *The Carolina Housewife*,
Charleston, 1847.[1]

THERE ARE TWO MAIN SCHOOLS of thought on the proper
boiling of long-grain rice: the Indian method and the Chinese. Among
available Indian receipts I chose one given by Sachdeva & Sons because it
is more traditional than most and seems closer to those from which the
Carolina method was borrowed. It also gives interesting details. Note the
suggested use of the cooking water, which Maum Sarah also advises (F
50). Such use for soups and sauces must be an ancient practice; Apicius
of Rome gives a receipt from perhaps the first century A.D. in which he
calls for thickening a sauce with *oryzae sucum,* translated as "water in
which rice has boiled." Bearers of water down through the ages would
have been loath to throw away perfectly good water that had been obtained with such labor. (Note also the charming use of *rice* as plural, long
archaic in English.) Starting rice in cold water seems to have been an Indian practice; it appears in an "Indian" receipt given by Eliza Acton in
1845 and also in Miss Brown's South Carolina receipt (above). For early
examples of the Chinese method, I chose receipts by Miss Eustis of
Aiken, South Carolina, and by Mrs. Hill of Georgia, the latter being
somewhat modified.[2]

The classic Carolina method, recorded in 1756 by Eliza Lucas Pinckney, is presented at the beginning of this work. Receipts given by Sarah
Rutledge in *The Carolina Housewife* of 1847 (F 10) and the slave Goliah
(above) differ from the earlier one only in detail. The one attributed to
Alston (above), however, seems to hark back to Persian methods for
chello, in that a crust is considered desirable. This is the only South Carolina example I know, but it must have had some currency; I rather suspect
that it was the African-American field method he cites elsewhere in his
memoirs, one that almost surely was brought from Africa, particularly in
light of a slave trader's observation in 1788 that in Sierra Leone "the
Slaves...have their [midday] meal which consists of Rice cooked in y^e

fields." (That is, there is the Carolina dish known variously as rice casserole and rice pie, which is ultimately derived from the Persian *tah-dig* described above, but we are getting ahead of our story.) To be sure, the crust could have been serendipitous, at least originally, the result of field methods where the "soaking" would not have been as carefully tended as by an African cook in her kitchen. (*Soaking* is an old English term, most often used in regard to bread, for "cooking or baking thoroughly so that it not be soggy," so the word was aptly applied to rice cookery by English settlers in Carolina, all the more since previously they had known only soggy rice.)[3]

The Carolina method produces rice that is "white, dry, and every grain Separate," as promised in the 1756 receipt. It is a rare receipt, be it South Carolinian, Persian, or Indian, that does not make a point of this. When served, the grains tumble out like popcorn. The Chinese method, no matter how thoroughly the rice is scrubbed, produces grains that retain a certain stickiness, however distinct they may be. (This is as it should be, or the rice could not be picked up with chopsticks; most rice eaters who use the more ancient method of cooking eat with their hands, or did so historically.) In making composed dishes, this is of little consequence, since properly cooked Chinese rice separates immediately on saucing, and the loose starch is hardly sufficient to spoil things. It is also less fuss, and nutrients are better conserved, or so it is claimed, so that its use is threatening to displace the ancient method even in India, Iran, and Africa, to some extent, judging by the cookbooks.

Its presence in South Carolina is attested by the Eustis receipt as early as 1904 (above), and it is the method given by Vertamae Smart-Grosvenor, Geechee though she be. The popular *South Carolina Cook Book* (1954) gives both methods. And across the Savannah River the Chinese method is given by Mrs. Hill in 1872. But for the ceremonial standing dish of rice in old Charleston, all honors go to the traditional way. In this regard, Mrs. Ramazani notes: "Unlike *chello* and *pollo, kateh* [which she translates as "plain rice"] is not a fluffy rice, but is somewhat sticky. Thus it is never served to guests but is used for everyday family meals." Her receipt *"Kateh"* calls for steaming the rice Chinese style before adding butter and allowing the traditional Persian crust to form.

Regarding some of the points above, two receipts from Vietnam are illuminating. They were recorded by my daughter on a recent trip as given by her interpreters, one receipt from the North, one from the South.

Boil water first. Water [should be] two or three centimeters
over wet, washed rice. Boil to finish water. Then cover completely

to sit seven to ten minutes. Stir once with chopsticks. This is in the
North.
    In the South. Lots of water. Boil rice five or six minutes.
Pour out water, leave [rice] on very low [heat] ten to fifteen
minutes. If you want sticky rice, leave a little water.[4]

Rice has been the staple in Vietnam for millennia. What I find significant is that in the North, where there has historically been a certain
amount of Chinese influence, the method is Chinese, at least it is now,
largely. In the South, however, the older way is used, what I call the prototypical way, with the interesting detail of instructions for "sticky rice."
This last method produces rice of varying degrees of stickiness, depending on the amount of water left in the rice, ranging from just sticky
enough for the easy use of chopsticks to really sticky. Vietnamese rice, at
least that brought to me, is long-grain, although not as long nor as slender as are the premium rices of India. It is interesting to note that although in both cases it was the wife who cooked the rice, the husband
knew exactly how it was done, each making perceptive comments. This
was not a matter of being helpful in the kitchen but simply of knowing
the procedure of preparing the food of life.

THE BOILERS OF RICE

Promisin' talk don' cook rice.
    —Gullah version of an African Hausa proverb, as cited by
    Charles Joyner.[5]

So how did what are essentially Indian methods of cooking rice
come to South Carolina? The short answer is that the Africans brought
the secret of cooking rice with them. This is so self-evident that it should
require neither explanation nor documentation. That is, as Littlefield
writes in regard to the cultivation of rice, "Africans were on the scene."
And nobody else knew how. I do not suggest that they necessarily
brought the receipts for all or even most of the typical Low Country rice
dishes with them. It has often been said that only peoples who cultivate
rice love and respect it sufficiently to cook it well; it was this understanding that the African growers of rice brought with them. And it was they
who did the cooking.
    To appreciate how little the early English and French proprietors
knew about cooking rice, let us examine for a moment the history of rice
cookery in England and France. In both countries documented possession of rice dates back to the first half of the thirteenth century; actual
receipts appeared somewhat later. A French receipt "Blanc Mengier en

Caresme" [in Lent] from around 1300 calls for cooking rice in water, draining and drying it well [that is, "soaking" it, a distinctly Eastern touch], then pounding it and mixing it with almond milk; for serving, it is powdered with spices and decorated with whole cloves or fried almonds. Another from about the same time calls for cooking rice in cow's milk with saffron, then adding fatty bouillon.

English manuscripts from the fourteenth century include an inordinate number of receipts calling for *flower of rys;* even receipts that start out with whole rice often call for one to "bray [t]hem rygt wel in a mortere," before or after cooking. One receipt, "Blomanger of fysch," calls for washing a pound of rice, seething it till "they breste [burst]" before further cooking it with perch or lobster and sugar with milk of a lavish two pounds of almonds. Another receipt "Blomanger" calls for substantially the same procedure but substitutes chicken for fish, is colored with saffron, and decorated with blanched almonds. In both countries, rice continued for some time to be associated with these "white" dishes and with such flavorings as almonds, rosewater, saffron, etc., a taste for which had been acquired at the time of the Crusades.[6]

The Saracen fragrances of these dishes notwithstanding, neither the French nor the English ever learned to do anything much with rice but make porridges and puddings, some of them very elegant indeed, but they constitute a minor aspect of rice cookery. In 1894 Joseph Favre noted that Indian and Chinese cooks "justly consider rice cooked *à la française* a profanation," adding that French receipts call for cooking rice till it bursts *[faire crever],* resulting in an "insipid, gluey porridge," whereas the grains should remain perfectly whole and separate. Madame Saint-Ange (1958) sadly comments: "To cook rice till it bursts *[faire crever]* is the only goal sought." There is evidence that things were quite different in Provence, that is, with regard to pilau; I find no evidence that the secret of properly boiled plain rice was known there, however. We shall examine this further in chapter 3, "Pilau," where we shall also meet up again with the *blanc manger.*

The instruction to "seethe till it burst" continued as a ritornelle in English receipts. In 1669, Sir Kenelme Digby (who was something of an exoticist, having also given the earliest receipt in English for brewing tea that I know of) gave a receipt entitled "Boiled Rice dry," pure Chinese in method, but I find no echo of it in works following him. Not until 1747 do I again find an acceptable English receipt for boiling rice, this to accompany "A Currey the Indian Way," given by Hannah Glasse in *The Art of Cookery.* The receipt seems to have continued in all succeeding editions (except, curiously, the American editions), with little suite. In 1807, however, Maria Rundell's *A New System of Domestic Cookery* broke out with an astonishing twenty-one receipts for rice, one of them a proper Indian method for boiling it, again to be served with what was becoming the sempiternal English curry. (The work appeared in Boston the same year, so that the first *published* receipt in this country for properly boiled rice seems to be this one, an ironic note.) Unfortunately, the secret of beautifully boiled rice seems not to have caught on in the same way, although a few perceptive nineteenth-century writers did give receipts, always to accompany curry, the best of which was a very detailed one by Eliza Acton in 1845, which appeared in an American edition the same year, continuing to appear in an astonishing total of nine editions here. But this English infatuation with curry was not the route of the Carolina method for boiling rice, which must have long antedated 1747. More compelling is the fact that curry has never historically become a South Carolina dish. (Mrs. Stoney included a receipt in her compilation [F 63], but it was from Mrs. Parker, who was not, I believe, a South Carolinian.) Nor do receipts alone teach people how to cook rice; if such were the case, the English would know how to cook rice perfectly, as would Americans of the northern Colonies, all of whom had access to detailed classic methods in popular cookbooks. It is an understanding that comes only with an intimate knowledge of, and respect for, rice.[7]

If evidence of the African role in South Carolina rice cookery be required, we have but to turn for a moment to areas of the United States where there were either only few Africans or some among whom any rice traditions had died out, or to put it another way, where the culinary heritage was that of northern Europe. Cookbooks written by Northerners demonstrate this graphically. Only a handful give acceptable receipts, some patently, even proudly, borrowed from South Carolina sources: Eliza Leslie gives "a Carolina receipt" in 1837; Sarah Hale gives "To Boil Rice Carolina Fashion" in 1873; and Mary Lincoln gives one in 1883. Sarah Rorer gives a passable one in 1886, but two perfectly wretched ones in 1902, one calling for cooking the rice thirty minutes; the other, entitled "Boiled Rice, East India Fashion," calls for boiling one cup of rice in a quart of water for ten minutes, "tossing the rice with a wooden fork almost constantly," then pushing the kettle to the back of the stove, continuing to "toss every few minutes," until "cooked and dry." There is no mention of draining. She announces that "this method requires very much more care and knowledge than the preceding one." This last example points up the fact that there was a demonstrable decline in quality beginning around the turn of the century, which I attribute to the baleful influence of the burgeoning home economists and to the fact that there was no cultural foundation for good rice cookery in the North. Things got no better, as illustrated by a ludicrous receipt given by Irma Rom-

bauer in the popular *Joy of Cooking* (1936) that calls for cooking one cup
of rice in two quarts of water "until it is tender (about 25 minutes)...
Continue to cook the rice until the water is absorbed." The dear lady assures the reader that "its entire nutritive value is retained." (In context it
is clear that "two quarts of water" is *not* a misprint for "two cups.") With
such teachers, it is small wonder that few Northerners can cook a decent
pot of rice. With the recent surge in popularity of Chinese cuisine, there
has been some small improvement, but it is by no means widespread.[8]

As might be expected, Southern receipts tend to be on a higher level
because of the continued African-American presence. Veronica Walker,
for example, says that her grandmother in Georgia washes the rice well,
puts it to boil "in a *lot* of water," never stirs it but does lift off the scum
that rises—a nice touch—then drains it and lets it "soak" at the back of
the stove, all in accordance with the ancient way. (In this regard, John
Taylor, food historian of South Carolina, tells me that this is still pretty
much the custom among African-Americans in the Low Country but that
most whites nowadays use what he says is often known as the *Charleston
steamer,* something of a cross apparently between a double boiler and a
couscous steamer. (Moroccans steam rice much as they do couscous in
such a utensil, so that the method has the weight of history behind it.)
The system is "foolproof," he says. There is what appears to be such a
steamer, called a *rice boiler,* pictured in *Mrs. Parker's Complete Housekeeper* (1891), from which work Mrs. Stoney gleaned over twenty receipts,
but no directions are given for using it. Mrs. Rorer mentions in passing in
1902 that rice may be "steamed in a 'cooker,'" specifically differentiating it from a double boiler but giving no directions.[9]

But in 1885 Mary Stuart Smith of Virginia wrote: "Rice being a
South Carolina staple, to South Carolinians we are indebted for the best
modes of preparing it. In Virginia they used generally to cook it into a
mush paste that was anything but appetizing." Mary Randolph had given
excellent receipts in *The Virginia House-Wife* in 1824; it is clear, however,
that they were not always followed, at least not in the period following
the end of slavery, when a great many white women all over the South
were suddenly thrown on their own resources or had to make do with unskilled immigrant help. The problem of having to cope with practical
kitchen matters is the underlying theme of most Southern cookbooks
published in the 1870s and 1880s. "A crisis is upon us which demands the
development of the *will* and *energy* of Southern character [emphasis ori-
ginal]....As woman has been queen in the parlor, so, if need be, she will
be queen in the kitchen....*The race of good cooks among us is almost ex-
tinct* [emphasis added]." (This last was the only reference, and that somewhat oblique, to the cause of the "crisis," the emancipation and

subsequent departure of the African-American cook.) So wrote E. W. Warren of Macon, Georgia, in his introduction to *Mrs. Hill's New Cook Book* (1872), a work from which Mrs. Stoney collected nineteen receipts.[10] Mrs. Hill, it must be said, was one of a small number of Southern ladies who seem to have been well versed in cookery, even though it may be supposed that they never had to actually toil in the kitchen.

It is my belief that the Indian method is the prototypical method for cooking long-grain rice common to the areas of origin and early dissemination. (The apparent exception is China, but rice came to China relatively late. The Chinese method I attribute to the general dearth of fuel that has shaped the entire concept of cookery in China. That is, using the Chinese system, rice requires little more than five or ten minutes on high heat, depending on the quantity of rice and intensity of heat, after which it is left to "soak" on retained heat while accompanying foods are being cooked. Not requiring the preliminary heating of a large pot of water, this most efficient system was very likely already in use for the earlier millets.) That is, *I think that so long as Africans have cooked rice they cooked it in the manner they brought to South Carolina: The Indian way. The Madagascar way. The African way.* This is not susceptible to proof; it matters little for this study whether the method had been known to them for millennia or merely for centuries. The point was to cook rice in such a way as to eliminate any loose starch so that the cooked grains would be perfectly separate and fluffy.

The cooking of short-grain rice is another matter. The development of *japonica* strains seems to have taken place in relatively recent times in far-flung places of relatively temperate climate, and cooking methods tend to be idiosyncratic, that is, peculiar to an area and its rice, varying from the steamed rice of Japan to gruels of varying consistency, always making a virtue of the greater absorbency and starchiness—or stickiness—of short-grain rice as compared to the long; one of the more brilliant examples is the Italian *risotto*. (*Pudding rice* is an English cookery term for short-grain rice as differentiated from Patna rice, for example.) As might be expected, the cooking qualities of medium-grain rice fall between the two extremes. It is not that shorter-grain rices cannot be boiled the Indian way—they can be and are—but they require greater care in order to achieve separateness of grain. The botanists say that in general the starchiness of rice varies inversely with the length of grain, and this is true in practice. I further find that it is the *relative* length that is particularly relevant. That is, prime basmati rices run about the same length in grain as American rices touted as "extra long-grain" but are so much more slender as to appear needlelike in comparison and are correspond-

ingly less starchy in their cooking qualities. To put it somewhat simplisti-
cally, it is as if texture and flavor were concentrated in the skinnier grains.

PRACTICAL NOTES ON BOILING LONG-GRAIN RICE

As can be seen, traditional receipts, even South Carolina ones, vary
surprisingly in detail. What this means is that so long as certain basic
principles are understood and respected, precise procedure in certain details may be subject to cultural and even personal preferences, not to
mention differences in the quality of rice, etc.

The single most serious danger is overcooking; it is certainly the most
common error in the American kitchen. No matter how carefully a receipt is followed in other respects, rice will burst and become pulpy and
gluey if overcooked. When done, the grains are slightly swollen and tender, but just tender, that is *al dente.* While the outline of the grain does
soften a bit, perforce, it must remain clean, or all is lost, and one might
just as well call it porridge and be done with it. It is perhaps an illusion,
but the grains seem to lengthen rather more than they fatten, at least with
good rice; indeed, the degree of lengthening is one criterion of quality
among Indian cooks.

While the cooking time varies with the rice, I have never yet cooked
white rice longer than ten minutes using the traditional method. When I
cook basmati rice Indian style, that is, presoaked for thirty minutes, it is
done in less than five minutes; Julie Sahni says *two* minutes from the moment the water comes to the boil again.[11] This is due in part to the presoaking and in part to the thinness of grain. *Better underdone than over;*
it must be remembered that rice continues to cook somewhat during the
"soaking" even as it is losing surface moisture.

I remind the reader that in rice cookery, the term *presoaking* refers to
an operation which involves soaking the rice before cooking it, the chief
virtue of which may be that the cooking time is dramatically shortened, a
matter of some importance. The term *soaking,* on the other hand, refers
to the operation conducted after boiling for the purpose of assuring separateness of grain, as explained earlier.

I have tried the cold water methods, and they work fine. However, I
prefer throwing the rice into boiling salted water so that I can more easily
determine when to start checking for doneness.

Authorities agree that *rice must not be touched during the "soaking,"*
because it is especially vulnerable to damage until that operation is complete. Rice seems to compose itself, to become almost resilient, during
"soaking," after which it may be fluffed up with a fork or incorporated
into a composed dish with little danger so long as it is done with care. It

may even be subjected to further cooking in a composed dish with far less danger than if done before "soaking." (In this sense, the process serves a function similar to the icy bath that follows the scalding of green vegetables in French cuisine, in that it "sets" texture.) It is not necessary to "soak" rice for an hour, as some receipts insist, although it is good to know that it can sit for that long and longer without damage, so long as the heat is gentle enough, always taking care that the rice not dry out. I often conduct the operation over simmering water, or in the lowest possible oven, or in one that has been turned off. Or it may be done on very low heat over a flame-tamer. If you want a crust to form, you may raise the heat somewhat, but watch it, as it burns easily. Sarah Rutledge's directions (F 10) regarding the amount of residual water and length of "soaking" time are perceptive. I also use the system of placing a towel— actually paper towels—under the lid to avoid the problem of condensed vapor dripping on the rice, which would make it soggy. Interestingly, the wooden lid noted by Alston in his description of African-American rice pots (above) would serve the same function.

The "middlings" and "small rice," for which receipts are given (F 10), are grades of broken rice which did not fetch as high a price as perfect long grains. Flavor is unimpaired, but special pains must be taken in the cooking, or it will end up as mush.

Miss Rutledge's system for unmolding the "soaked" rice (F 10) is related to the pyramidal or domed form of the Persian *chello*.

Authorities also agree that American rice need not be presoaked, even for Indian or Persian receipts where soaking is the rule. They are referring to standard packaged brands available today, of course, but it is true that I have not encountered such instructions in any South Carolina receipt; however, Mrs. Hill of Georgia (1872) says to "soak [the rice] an hour before boiling," and we may suppose that she was dealing with Carolina Gold. Nowadays growers and nutritionists emphasize that it is not necessary to wash American rice because of cleanliness of packaging, nor desirable, because washing would remove vitamin additives. They are opposed to traditional cooking methods for the same reason.[12] (My own feeling is that such vitamins are so minimal that I prefer the beauty of the classic method, and that those who are concerned about vitamins would do well to use brown rice. The use of brown rice would be an anomaly in any traditional dish where beauty or delicacy of flavor is paramount—the classic standing dish or fragile custardy dishes, for example. However, although it would be rank heresy, it would be delicious in some of the earthier dishes, such as hoppin' John or certain breads.)

As to the choice of rice, the most authentic is Carolina Gold. It should be tried by anyone who has an interest in re-creating tastes and textures of the past, be it by so little. According to John Taylor, it is available from Turnbridge Plantation, P. O. Box 165, Route 1, Hardeeville, SC 29927. It is a highly labor-intensive rice as compared to commercial rices, and is correspondingly costly. (It should be noted that proceeds go to local charities.) At best, the rice is in short supply and the hurricane of 1989 took its toll. I have sung the praises of this rice elsewhere.

I use Dehraduni basmati rice, the finest commercially available in this country, but the Patna rices are also very good. The Dehraduni rice has incomparable aroma and an almost nutty flavor, and cooks up beautifully. It is not exactly cheap, but in lots of ten kilograms it runs less than $1.25 a pound and is well worth it. Indian rices are available in Indian stores and specialty shops, including some health food stores. Basmati strains are being grown in Texas and California. Those I have tried are very good rices but do not have the aroma of those from India and, curiously, the grains do not lengthen in cooking as with Indian basmati rices. They are available in specialty shops and even some supermarkets. Brown basmati rices are also becoming available.

All Indian sources say that rice improves with aging. It turns a beautiful ivory color which further deepens with time. Flavor is said to improve and, perhaps more strikingly, so do the cooking qualities. That is, aged rice is said to be less likely to present problems of stickiness than that which has been recently harvested. Premium rice is sometimes aged for decades; Julie Sahni tells me that when the first son is born, rice is traditionally set aside for use at his wedding festivities when the time comes.[13] I have not heard of such aging practices elsewhere; indeed, it is often newly harvested rice that is prized. Perhaps, as with wines, some are improved by aging and others are best consumed young. I must say that if one uses proper technique, there is no problem with stickiness, even with less exalted grades of rice. All imported rices must be washed, by the way, and I follow the Indian practice of soaking it, partly because it then cooks so quickly and partly because I believe that Indians know a thing or two about their own rice.

Standard American long-grain rice, available in any supermarket under any of several names—*Carolina,* for one—will be the choice of most Americans, and it is perfectly acceptable, if a trifle dull. Some authorities suggest the use of "converted" rice, but others disapprove.

What is *not* acceptable is instant rice, or any preflavored rice. Nor is medium-grain rice, which food writers often tout as "all-purpose," which it is not. It does not answer for long-grain rice nor for making a *risotto,* for example, no matter what American authorities may claim. The correct choice of rice is a question not only of culinary perceptiveness but also of courtesy.

Leftover rice can be reheated fairly successfully. Sprinkle it lightly with water, the amount depending on how dry it has become, and "soak" it once again; it will not have the charm of freshly boiled rice but is perfectly acceptable, especially if enriched with a little butter and seasoned with salt and a few twists of the pepper mill. Or use it in various composed dishes, breads, or puddings.

I see that I have not discussed the Chinese method in these practical notes. It is not quite as straightforward as it might seem, in that the standard proportion of twice as much water as rice is not always correct. The ideal *proportion* of water varies with the amount of rice (lowering somewhat as the amount of rice increases), with whether the rice has been washed or presoaked, with the type and age of rice (surprisingly in some cases), with the weight and shape of the cooking pot, the intensity of the heat, etc. But in a general way, I find the standard proportion of water on the high side, because all too often the rice has to cook too long in order to use it all up. *I find three cups of water ample for cooking two cups of dry rice.* Once the characteristic steam holes appear on the surface, the pot must be covered and the heat turned down very low, because the rice is "soaking," and all the usual rules apply. For this amount no more than twenty minutes from start to finish is required. I should perhaps note that although I am Danish and was thus reared innocent of properly cooked rice, I was taught by Chinese cooks how to cook it some fifty years ago. They taught me to presoak the rice, by the way, an instruction I do not recall having seen in Chinese cookbooks in either English or French.

CHAPTER 3

Pilau and Its Kind

A dish of Pelo, which is rice boyled with Hens, Mutton,
Butter, Almonds and Turmerack.
—Sir Thomas Herbert, in *A Relation of Some Yeares
Travaile Begunne Anno 1626, into Afrique and the
Greater Asia* [Persia], London, 1634.

To make Pullow, the Meat is first Boiled to Rags, and the
Broth or Liquor being strained, it is left to drain, while they Boil
the Rice in the same; which being tender, and the aqueous parts
evaporating, the Juice and Gravy incorporates with the Rice,
which is Boiled almost dry; then they put in the Meat again with
Spice, and at last as much Butter as is necessary, so that it
becomes not too Greasy or Offensive, either to the Sight or Taste;
and it is then Boiled enough when it is fit to be made into
Gobbets, not slabby [that is, not sloppy], but each Corn of Rice is
swelled and filled, not burst into Pulp.
—John Fryer, in *A New Account of East India and Persia.
Being Nine Years' Travels, 1672–1681,* London, 1698.[1]

PILAU IS THE MOST CHARACTERISTIC DISH of the Caro-
lina rice kitchen, where its name is pronounced either *PUHR-LOE* or *pi-
LOE.* Word and dish come from Persia; the Persian word *pilau* took
various forms in the countries to which the dish spread, such as *pullao* in
India, *pilaf* in Turkey, and *pelau* in Provence, this in addition to various
transcriptions of these forms and changes with time; the modern form in
Iran today is transcribed as *pollo* or *polo,* for example.
   The journey of pilau from Persia to South Carolina was a long one,
so long and so scantily documented that its precise itinerary may never be
known. I have unearthed a number of tantalizing nuggets of historical
data; the ultimate source is not in doubt, but without certain data down
through the centuries, some aspects must remain speculative. No matter
how beguiling, every construction presents certain difficulties. Linguistic
evidence and basic technique might suggest a direct connection with Persia; the borrowing of the then contemporary Persian word, rather than
the *pullao* of Moghul cuisine or the far better-known Turkish form *pilaf,*

is not without some significance. Yet the more I consider the question of direct contact with Persia, the more complex the problems become. It is difficult to attribute the successful naturalization of an alien culinary concept to ephemeral contacts of the sort provided by trade relations, even supposing that the Colonies flouted the Crown's interdictions on such trading. Surprisingly, there is a French connection—surprising because the French, in spite of their culinary genius, cook rice indifferently, which is a polite way of saying badly. (I am not alone in this; Favre and Madame Saint-Ange are as critical as I; even Escoffier unhappily admits as much.)[2] Actually, I should say a *Provençal* connection, which is altogether a different story. There are problems here, as well. Perhaps there were many paths, crossing and recrossing in such a way as to obliterate many footprints. And it was all so long ago. History is rarely tidy. What can be said is that dishes of such sophistication are not transmitted by a simple exchange of receipts alone; much as with the cultivation of rice, the African-Americans who did the cooking in South Carolina had to have had long experience in rice cookery, or the pilau would never have taken root and flourished as it did.

Let us begin by defining a pilau. In its most basic version, *long-grain* rice that has been washed and presoaked is added to simmering aromatic broth, usually in the proportion of two parts of liquid to one of rice by volume, then covered and cooked until "nearly dry," an instruction that is repeated over and again in many ways and in many languages. When writers say "nearly dry," they in no way mean dried out. But *there must be no residual liquid, and the grains, while glistening from the requisite fat, should* seem *dry and, above all, be perfectly separate.* On rare occasions, further liquid is added at this point to form a sauce, but the effect is quite different from that obtained by simply not finishing the cooking properly. The rice has to "soak," to compose itself, just as with plain rice, after which it becomes more resilient and better able to retain its integrity when liquid is added or additional ingredients are forked in, always providing that it be done with great care. Although the method superficially resembles the Chinese method of steaming rice, the presence of fat, be it so little, assures a separateness of grain that is otherwise unobtainable. The meat that provided the broth is traditionally arranged on top of the rice. *The classic pilau is not so much a receipt as a culinary concept,* one infinitely adaptable to featuring various ingredients but always true to the basic concept here outlined. There are other categories of pilau, to which we shall come in due time.

THE PILAU COMES WEST

Isfānākyīya [Spinach and Rice Dish]

Take fat meat [mutton] and cut into medium-sized pieces.
Slice the fresh tail [sheep tail fat], dissolve [render], and remove
the sediment. Put the meat into this oil *[alya]* and stir until
browned: then cover with water that has been heated separately.
Add a little salt: boil, and remove the scum. Throw in a handful
of chick-peas that have been soaked and peeled. Take fresh
spinach, wash, remove the lower roots, and cut with a knife into
fingers [strips], then pound in a stone mortar, and put into the
saucepan. When nearly cooked, add dry coriander [seeds],
cummin, brayed [pounded] pepper, mastic [aromatic gum of
Pistacia Lentiscus], cinnamon-bark, and a little garlic bruised fine.
Now fill with water as required, letting the water be lukewarm.
When it has boiled for an hour, add clean, washed rice as
required, placing it over the fire until it is set firm and smooth:
then leave over a slow flame for an hour, and remove. Meanwhile
prepare red meat [raw meat] minced fine and made into cabobs,
and fry these in oil with the usual seasonings. When the
concoction is ladled out, strew over it this fried meat, together
with the oil as required, sprinkled with fine-ground cinnamon, and
serve.

  —Muhammad ibn al-Hasan ibn Muhammad ibn al-Karīm
  al-Kātib al-Baghdādī, 1226. Translated from the Arabic as
  A Baghdad Cookery-Book by A. J. Arberry, 1939.
  Material in brackets added by K. H. altogether
  independently of Arberry's translation.

For *Blanc Mengier*

If you wish to make *blanc mengier,* take the wings and feet of
gelines [hazel grouse or fattened pullets] and put them to cook in
water; then take a little rice and soak it in that water, then let it
cook on a low fire, then cut the meat into thin strips, and set it to
cook [with the rice] with a little sugar.... And if you wish, use
whole rice [that is, instead of pounded rice] in the bouillon, or
almond milk; it is then called *angoulée.*

  —*Traité de Cuisine Écrit vers 1300.* [Instructions to pound
  the rice were inadvertently omitted by the scribe; it was
  this pounding that differentiated *blanc mengier* from
  angoulée in French medieval cuisine.]

Ris Engoulé

Aliter [another way], RICE. Pick it over, wash it in two or
three sets of hot water until the water runs perfectly clear, then

half cook it *[demy cuire]*, drain it and place it in plates on trays to
finish draining and to dry before the fire; then cook it till nearly
dry with fatty beef bouillon and saffron, if it is a day when meat
is permitted; and if it is a fish day, do not use meat broth, but
instead use well pounded almonds *sans couler* [that is, pounded
almonds and water as for almond milk, but without straining it as
is customary]; then add sugar but no saffron.
    —*Le Ménagier de Paris,* about 1393.[3]

    The travels of the pilau started long ago, perhaps sometime after the
Arab conquest of Persia early in the seventh century, when the Arabs set
about emulating the brilliant cuisine of the Persians, as is shown by the
manuscript collection of 1226 in Baghdad cited above. It includes several
receipts which outline perfectly classic pilau technique: washed rice is
added to a simmering aromatic broth, cooked until "set firm and
smooth," that is, "nearly dry" and not burst, after which it is left to settle, or "soak," for an hour. Aside from the use of *alya* [rendered sheep's
tail fat], the ubiquitous cooking medium of the Middle East, these pilaus
would not be too far out of place in a modern Persian cookbook; slightly
archaic touches may well reflect Persian practice of the day. The meat is
mutton; chicken is called for elsewhere, as are lentils, beans, leeks, saffron, dill, "Persian milk" [yoghurt], and macaroni; and the occasional
and rather curious combination of various forms of pasta with rice is still
characteristic of the cookery of Persia and the Middle East.
    From then on, *it may be said that the pilau followed Islam;* it was the
Moghuls who brought it to India, where the *pullao* is regarded as a Muslim dish, for example. Nor was it necessary that Islam prevail as religion,
as is demonstrated by Armenia. Usually the name accompanied the dish,
but not always, as can be seen in the Baghdad manuscript, even though
many products kept their Persian names in Arabic. This is still true in
modern Arab cookery: the *sayyadieh,* featuring fish, the *ghadous bi'l-
arouzz,* featuring salt cod; and the *makloubeh,* one of the molded pilaus,
featuring chicken, for example. And there is *jambalaya,* defined as rice
cooked with meat or shellfish in *Al-Mawrid* by Munir Ba'albaki (1984).
(*Pilau* does appear in Arab dictionaries as a borrowing from Persian, but
descriptive Arab names are more usual for pilaus.) We shall return to the
jambalaya.
    There are a number of dishes that started out as pilaus, most notably
arroz con pollo [chicken with rice] and the variously composed *paella* of
Spain. (*Arroz* comes from Arabic *aruz,* variously transcribed, which in
turn is thought to have come from India, probably from the same word
that gave Greek *oryza. Paella* refers to the outsized, shallow cooking pan,

from Latin *patella,* like French *poêle.*[4] It is not beyond the realm of possibility that *paella,* referring to the previously known utensil, replaced *pilau* in the way that so often happens, as I discuss in chapter 5, "Hoppin' John"; that is, a known word of similar sound could have been substituted for an unknown one, but there is no direct evidence that this occurred.) It was the use of the short-grain rice of Valencia that changed the character of the pilau in Spain. To keep the grains separate, the entire point of a pilau, it was necessary to resort to a different technique, that of briefly sautéing the raw rice before adding liquid, an operation that sets the exterior starch. Separateness of grain is further assured by cooking the *paella* in a very thin layer; even when sautéed, the favored rice tends to stick together otherwise.

Sautéing the raw rice is also the starting point of the Italian *risotto,* using the round rice of the Po valley, but the subsequent addition of liquid by degrees and all but constant stirring are peculiar to this dish, I believe. The grains are separate, but only by virtue of a creamy sauce formed by the stirring in of the loose starch as it cooks; it is thus too "slabby" to be a proper pilau, but the historical relationship is evident nevertheless. The preliminary sautéing of raw rice is not confined to short-grain rice; it occurs even in parts of India and is customary in Turkish *pilaf. It was developed as a foolproof method of assuring separateness of grain in a pilau,* even when using starchier grades of rice; the method may well antedate the cultivation of rice in Spain, a development attributed to the Arabs. (Starchiness is a fault in long-grain rice; in short-grain rice it is simply a characteristic, although there, too, is a wide range of quality, with those rices containing a resistant nugget, the "pearl," being the most esteemed for *risotto.*)

Joseph Favre claims that the pilau, name and dish, came to France at the time of the Crusades. As to the name, I do not find it in old texts, and the earliest citation by Robert is 1654, citing travel memoirs from the East. Maddeningly, Favre claims that the word signified "a *ragoût* of rice, peas, and mutton"[5] (perhaps not all that different from the receipt for *Shūrbā* given at the beginning of chapter 5, "Hoppin' John"?), all without offering a scrap of documentation. Nor does he refer to the history of pilau in Provence, altogether another story, one to which we shall shortly turn.

Certainly the receipts given above for *angoulée* show that the pilau was known in Paris by around 1300; the broad characterizing aspect is present, that of rice cooked whole in broth (or in almond milk for fast-day versions). The use of long-grain rice is also a requisite characteristic; the dish evolved around its use. We are not told what rice was used, but since both receipts use classic long-grain methods from the East, it could well have been long-grain, indeed almost surely was, since rice was imported and the receipts came from long-grain sources. Note in particular the instruction to "half cook" the rice in the 1393 receipt. The name is properly *ris en goulée,* in which form it occasionally appears, and it may be loosely translated as "mouthfuls of rice," recalling the *Gobbets,* meaning bite-sized morsels, in Fryer's description of *Pullow* (above), referring to the fact that the rice is cooked until "nearly dry," an instruction that also appears in the 1393 receipt.

In classic French cuisine the *angoulée* did not last long, and by the time it seeped down to more popular levels as *poule au riz,* it had become a homey, rather soupy affair that remains almost an institution in northern France, pleasant enough but bearing little relationship to a pilau, except in the broadest historical sense; the rice is cooked until it is *bien crevé,* or "thoroughly burst and pulpy." In a separate line of development, the name *blanc manger* came to be applied to a gelatin-based sweet dish made with almond milk, harking back to medieval fast-day versions. It has now pretty much fallen into disuse.

In English medieval works there are many receipts for *blanc manger* calling for the then-distinguishing pounded rice or rice flour; one for "Blawmanger" calls for cooking rice "til thay breke." Receipts parallel to that for *angoulée* are somewhat rare, but one from the fourteenth century, "To make blaumaunger gros," calls for mixing picked, presoaked rice with "good almound melk," then mixed with the flesh of hens or capons cut into *gobetes* and all cooked together with sugar and fat until *charchaunt* [heavy, stiff]; one is to "serve it forth" studded with fried almonds and strewn with sugar.[6] The Saracen aromas are strong; it is clearly an Eastern receipt. But this tradition of rice cookery faded. I find no evidence of a strong tradition of chicken-and-rice dishes in England such as exists in France, for example. The history of sweet *blanc manger* in England more or less parallels that in France, except that it continued to evolve into debased versions using nothing but sweetened cow's milk and starch, typically arrowroot rather than the earlier rice flour; American versions tend to use cornstarch. In neither country is there so much as a memory of almond. In our South there was a revival of rice *blanc manger,* to be discussed in chapter 8, *"Sweet dishes."*

This is perhaps the place to note what may be the earliest published receipts in English using the name *pilau,* that is, aside from Fryer's lovely description cited earlier. In *The Art of Cookery* (1747) Hannah Glasse presents "To make a Pellow the Indian Way" and "Another Way to make a Pellow." Both are hopelessly garbled versions of a putative Indian *pulau;* as given, neither shows the least comprehension of the principles of rice cookery. One calls for three pounds of rice cooked in three-quarters of a pound of butter with no mention of liquid except for warning that

"You must put in a little Water to keep it from burning, then stir it up very often. . . ." The other calls for making a gargantuan broth with three gallons of water, "wasted" to a gallon, all for only one pound of rice [a scant two and a half cups]. The meat is cooked separately. Beyond the fact that they contain rice and meat, neither remotely resembles the Carolina pilau, nor any other, and those who suggest that the Carolina pilau came by way of Mrs. Glasse or earlier putative common sources simply have not studied the receipts. The Indian *pullao* and the Carolina pilau had evolved quite differently after leaving Persia, with the Carolina pilau, by whatever path it took, having become far *less* elaborate, always retaining classic Persian technique. Mrs. Glasse gives one more receipt in this regard, "A Pillaw of Veal" (see chapter 4, *"Casseroles"*).

Since the above was written, I have found an earlier receipt of great interest, "To make a Poloe," given by E. Smith in *The Compleat House-wife* (Williamsburg, 1742, and ostensibly in the fifth London edition of 1732, on which the American edition is based). It calls for boiling "a Pint of Rice. . .in as much Water as will cover it; when your Rice is half boiled, put in your Fowl, with a small Onion, a Blade or two of Mace, some whole Pepper, and some Salt; when 'tis enough, put the Fowl in a Dish, and pour the rice over it." But surely *it is "your Fowl" that should be "half boiled. . .in as much Water as will cover it* [emphasis added]." Such was the understanding of rice cookery in eighteenth-century England that one could call for cooking rice *twice* as long as fowl, not to mention the alarming insufficiency of liquid with which to complete the operation, or absence of the requisite fat for proper cooking of rice in a pilau. An error, certainly, but an error of concept, not a simple nod, one which lasted as late as the eighteenth London edition of 1773, although *Compleat* had been modernized to *Complete*. Indeed, it persisted for yet a century, appearing in *Mrs. Hale's New Cook Book* (1873), where it is listed in the index as "Turkish pillau," although in the text it is simply "To make a Pillau." It is copied verbatim from Mrs. Smith's receipt, with only a bit of modernization of language, except for a caboose sentence suggesting that "A small piece of salt pork or bacon boiled in the rice, and then taken out, adds to the flavor." It all shows that Philadelphians were no more knowledgeable than were the English in terms of rice cookery.

Where did this receipt come from? *Poloe* might seem to be a variant of modern Irani *pollo,* but I believe that Mrs. Smith erred in the transcription of the title much as she had in the text. In any event, spelling was often highly erratic, and I suggest that she got her receipt from South Carolina. (It will be noted that Mrs. Smith did not claim an exotic origin for the dish, as writers were so prone to do; Carolina was an English colony, not really "foreign." It was only much later when Mrs. Hale appropriated the receipt, not knowing its true provenance, that she felt compelled to fabricate one, entitling it "Turkish pillau," *Turkish* having been a popular designation for anything "foreign." To be sure, it is Turkish neither in concept nor detail. Nor in name.) Had it been presented correctly, it would conform to classic Carolina practice in every detail of method, seasonings, and proportions, as may be seen by comparing it with Mrs. Blake's Low Country receipt for "Carolina Pilau" (F 54), which differs only in the presence of bacon, a typical but not invariable ingredient. While she starts rice and fowl together, it is *"in as much water as will cover the whole* [emphasis added]," and this is the crucial point. "Stew for about half an hour, or until...done," she adds; for a less tender fowl, partially cooking it before adding rice would be good procedure, presumably the intent in Mrs. Smith's source receipt. Seasonings are identical: Onion, mace, and pepper. No saffron.[7]

If Mrs. Smith did indeed get her receipt from Carolina, and I find no other reasonable answer given the culinary evidence, it would tend to support my thesis, discussed further on, that the pilau had been known in Carolina from the early days of rice cultivation, having been brought by French Huguenots towards the end of the seventeeth century. This is hardly susceptible to proof, but I find no contrary indications. What can be said is that Carolinians would never have been able to make a successful pilau Carolina style, or any other, for that matter, following Mrs. Smith's dyslexic directions. But they would not have needed them; I am convinced that they had had the original long since.

THE CAROLINA PURLOW

To make Purlow
It is a dish made with whole rice, thus: —instead of plain
water boil a piece of bacon, or sound salted pork, and one or two
fowls, in the usual way. Take them out, and set them by the fire.
Then reduce the water in the pot to the proper quantity for boiling
[the rice]. Add a little salt, spice, and black pepper to the taste,
and when boiling put in the rice after well washing. Boil from
twenty to thirty minutes. Put the pot then to soak or steam over a
few coals, and in twenty minutes the rice will be done. Serve it on
a large dish, the bacon or pork and fowls side by side on the top
of the rice.
—Phineas Thornton, of Camden, South Carolina, in
The Southern Gardener and Receipt Book, 1845
[copyright 1839].

A Pilau

Take a large fine fowl, and cover the breast with slices of fat
bacon or ham, secured by skewers. Put it into a stew-pan with two
sliced onions. Season it to your taste with white pepper and mace.
Have ready a pint of rice that has been well picked, washed, and
soaked. Cover the fowl with it. Put in as much water as will well
cover the whole. Stew it about half an hour, or till the fowl and
rice are thoroughly done; keeping the stew-pan closely covered.
Dish it all together, either with the rice covering the fowl, or laid
round it in little heaps.

You may make a pilau of beef or mutton with a large quantity
of rice; which must not be put in at first, or it will be done too
much, the meat requiring a longer time to stew.

—Eliza Leslie, in *Directions for Cookery,* 1837.[8]

There are surely earlier mentions of pilau in Carolina, but the earliest I find appears in the notes of William Bartram, the great naturalist
who led a scientific expedition through South Carolina, Georgia, and
Florida in the years 1773 to 1777. He noted that they took "three young
raccons...which are excellent meat; we had them for supper, served up
in a pillo." On another occasion, they had squabs, "made into a pilloe
with rice." This was in what was still wilderness in east Florida, but significantly, the expedition had been outfitted in Charleston. He had
friends in Charleston and corresponded regularly with Martha Logan,
the writer of the gardening calendar. And he had accompanied his father
on much the same itinerary beginning in 1765, so that there is every reason to suppose that he had long been familiar with the pilau of South
Carolina, as evidently his bearers, who must have been African-
American, were, and they knew how to cook it. I have no further evidence, but I am convinced that pilau was a feature of South Carolina
cookery practically from the beginning.

The lag between practice and the printed word is one of the most
frustrating aspects of work in the discipline of culinary history. Just for
example, we know that flat hearth cakes of maize, variously called *johnny
cake, hoe cake, pone,* etc., were made by the Colonists virtually from the
beginning. Yet the earliest extant receipt appeared in 1796, a lag of some
175 years. Many receipts were never written down, and most of those that
were have been lost. There are examples of even published works that sur-
vive in a unique copy. This appears to be the case with *The Carolina Receipt Book,* By A Lady of Charleston (1832), a work listed by Anna Wells
Rutledge, who suggests that it may have been written by Harriott Pinckney. To date I have not been able to locate this work, so that I am unable
to say whether it includes a receipt for pilau. For that matter, its omission

would be inconclusive; *The Centennial Receipt Book,* Written in 1876 By A Southern Lady [Miss Mary Joseph Waring], has no receipt for pilau, for example. Such an omission could be an oversight or result from a feeling that "everybody" knows how to make it. But I present Thornton's receipt "To Make Purlow" of 1845 above to show that the dish was known even in the pine barrens. Keeping in mind that there were few African-Americans around Camden and that Thornton's wife was from Massachusetts—for that matter, Thornton was not a native South Carolinian himself—it shows that pilau had become a signature dish for all of South Carolina. I believe that Miss Leslie's earlier receipt came from Carolina, as had her way of boiling rice.[9]

Before we continue, let us pause to make certain observations concerning the pilau of Carolina. The first concerns technique: the rice is not sautéed, and it is added to simmering, seasoned liquid, or with water to a prepared aromatic base. When specified, the proportion of twice as much liquid as rice by volume is usual. The rice is steamed until "nearly dry." The method is entirely classic, as are the methods for the molded pilaus, a category we shall come to in due time. That is, the technique that evolved around the use of long-grain rice of high quality in Persia also worked with Carolina Gold; it was not necessary to resort to methods developed elsewhere for inferior grades of rice.

If the technique is classic, the composition is not. Most strikingly perhaps, it tends to be characterized by the presence of *bacon,* a term which historically did not necessarily refer to a product that involved curing nor even to any particular cut of pork. Even in the United States, as late as 1806, Noah Webster defined *bacon* as "hog's flesh cured with salt and dried." In South Carolina practice, the use of *smoked* pork seems to have been frowned on, at least by some. Theresa Brown of Anderson wrote in a postscript to a receipt "Chine Pileau" (1871): "Use fresh sausage, smoked ones would impart an unpleasant flavor to the rice." Mrs. Hill of Georgia wrote much the same in her receipt "Sausage Pilau" (F 55), which originally also appeared in 1871. There could have been a touch of affectation here, not typical of popular taste, but my impression is that these writers were defending an older tradition that had begun to erode; that is, previously it had not been necessary to specify that pork used in pilau should not be smoked. (I should note that South Carolina receipts for curing bacon known to me call for smoking; perhaps it was not considered necessary to explain how to cure bacon in brine, hardly a complicated process. It is also to be noted that smoked pork keeps better than that cured in brine, an important consideration in a semitropical climate.)

Pork is anathema to Muslims, so that in the lands of origin and early dispersion of the pilau the most refined versions used butter, often clari-

fied, as the fatty element. But the versions featuring mutton were liable to
be enriched with the creature's own fat, as we saw in the receipt from
Baghdad. So it is clear enough how pork came to be used by non-Muslim
peoples, a practice I believe to have been initiated in Provence. Miss
Brown, for example, calls for butter in her receipt "Chicken Pileau"
(1871) but notes: "A small piece of fat pork in lieu of butter." In truth,
South Carolinians seemed to prefer the added savor given by fatty cured
pork, enough to make it virtually a characteristic of Carolina pilau. And
it is a felicitous addition. Also, Miss Brown and Mrs. Hill were right;
smoked pork does overwhelm the delicate flavor of a pilau; it takes beans
to stand up to smoked pork.

Perhaps just as striking is the virtual absence of spices and aromatic
herbs in the pilaus of Carolina as compared with those of Persia. Just
scanning Persian recipes for *pollo* and other rice dishes, I find saffron,
cinnamon, fresh dill weed, coriander, lemon juice, dried Persian lime, onions, turmeric, peppercorns, and one lovely receipt calling for three cups
of parsley, leaf fenugreek, and scallions, finely chopped; this in addition
to almonds, walnuts, pistachios, hazel nuts, peaches, apricots, dates,
prunes, currants, and yoghurt, as well as numerous pulses and vegetables
used as principal ingredients or in combination with meat. I hasten to
add that they are not used pell-mell, but artfully chosen and blended to
enhance the main ingredients. This is contemporary practice, to be sure,
but judging by such medieval receipts as we have, I have the impression
that spicing has not changed dramatically down the centuries.

Similar scanning of the receipts for Carolina and Georgia pilaus included by Mrs. Stoney in her work gives us pepper, "a little mace," red
pepper [cayenne], "some spices," curry powder, Madeira, "a sprig of
parsley," two tablespoons of "mild grated cheese," bacon, tomatoes, and
onions. And that about does it for aromatic seasonings.

What happened to all those Eastern spices in this Eastern dish? For
that matter, what happened to those "all kinds of aromatick herbs" that
were to be planted in February and dried in June, according to Martha
Logan's eighteenth-century garden calendar for the Charleston area?
While she is disappointingly unspecific, all the herbs listed above were
cultivated elsewhere in the Colonies, even in the North, and surely were in
South Carolina. They also had the requisite spices, as shown by this receipt from *The Carolina Housewife* (second edition, 1851):

A Curry Powder
Take of mustard seed (scorched and finely powdered) one and
a half ounces, four ounces coriander seed in powder, four and a
half ounces turmeric seed in powder, three ounces black pepper,
one and a quarter ounces cayenne pepper, one ounce lesser

cardamums, half ounce ginger, one ounce cinnamon, half ounce
cloves and half ounce mace. Mix these powders well, and put them
into a wide mouth bottle for use.

But no receipt for curry is given, nor did the dish enter traditional
Carolina cookery, at least not in the classic works. (There is a receipt in
Mrs. Stoney's collection, but it is not of Carolina provenance.) Nor do I
find any receipts in *The Carolina Housewife* even calling for curry powder. Are we to suppose that it was simply a convenient blend of spices to
be used at discretion? It is true that Miss Taft calls for curry in her
"Shrimp Pie" (F 68), for example. All of the spices appear in various receipts of Miss Rutledge—although not in any given one—as well as many
herbs, including what she calls *fines herbs,* including chopped shallots,
parsley, tarragon, thyme, bay leaf, majoram, and lemon peel simmered in
butter.

It thus becomes more difficult to explain the dearth of seasonings in
Carolina pilau recipes. Elizabeth Verner Hamilton writes in her foreword
to *Two Hundred Years of Charleston Cooking* (1976), answering a complaint by Lettie Gay, the dietician in New York who had "corrected mea-
surements, and sometimes changed them [the receipts] beyond
recognition," in this regard: "What Miss Gay didn't know, but what every
. . .Charleston cook knows automatically, without having to be told by
the receipt, which is used only for proportions, is that one puts in onions
and a bay leaf, parsley and thyme—a *bouquet garni*—. . .and then the
dish is far from flavorless."[10] Certainly this is part of the answer, but it
does not explain why Miss Rutledge listed aromatics in all *but* the receipts
for pilau, all of which are seasoned pretty much with only salt and pepper. Are we to suppose that Mrs. Huger's "some spices" (F 56) are in fact
a few pinches of a curry powder similar to that detailed by Miss Rutledge
in 1851? If this was Low Country usage, it represents a debasement of
Persian practice, by which spices are selected and blended for a specific
dish, then pounded before being used.

> There was a time when folks had cooks,
> Who never did depend on books
> To learn the art of cooking.
> The help knew all the tunes by ear,
> And no one dared to interfere;
> They brooked no overlooking.
> —A. J. S., from the forward
> to *Charleston Receipts,* 1950.[11]

I have some difficulty accepting the idea that African-American
cooks made their pilaus as plain as the receipts seem to indicate. I suggest

that their ways of seasoning them may have remained the "secret" of those women. Cooks, through the ages and round the world, have always been jealous of their domain, gifted cooks in private homes notoriously so. They do not easily give away their little culinary tricks, whether in the French provinces or South Carolina Low Country. Such accounts as we have, while scanty, do not contradict such an attitude on the part of the African-American women who did the cooking for the aristocracy. The kitchen staff in great houses was self-perpetuating; apt youngsters among the helpers were taken in hand by the cook and trained to take over eventually. And in spite of being slaves, they guarded their domain as cooks have always done. The new young bride of the heir of the plantation, almost invariably inexperienced in domestic management, would rarely have been able to face down the cook, who would have been infinitely more experienced, not only in kitchen lore but also in dealing with people, including the previous mistress. Traditionally the mistress occupied herself with the making of bread, desserts, pickles, preserves, ratafias, cordials, etc., at least to the extent of actively supervising their production. And this practice accounts for the continuing English or French character of those receipts. Those departments of cookery were conducted in a separate workroom in an establishment of any importance, so all was well. And a great number of English or French receipts were orally transmitted to the African-American cooks as they were in households all over the South, thus assuring a certain measure of continuity with the mother cuisine.

But the pilau was outside the culinary traditions of England and northern France. That is, the pilau that had been brought back from the Crusades soon deteriorated into porridges and puddings, as detailed earlier. The story of pilau in Provence is altogether another matter, one to which we shall turn in due course.

THE RECEIPTS

Let us quickly scan the pilau receipts of South Carolina. The combination of chicken and bacon with rice may be said to constitute the archetypical pilau in the Low Country, at least historically. Sarah Rutledge's receipt "Carolina Pilau" (F 51), Mrs. Blake's "Carolina Pilau" (F 54), Phineas Thorton's "To Make Purlow" (above, p. 43), and Mrs. Hill's "Rice Pilau" (F 55) from across the Savannah River are of this type; they differ only in minor details, chiefly in seasoning, with Miss Rutledge's being the most sober.

There are, to be sure, chicken and rice receipts without bacon. Mrs. Huger's "A French Pilau" (F 56) is seasoned with Madeira, "some spices," an onion, and butter in lieu of bacon, and is surely a family heirloom, a bit fancied up, perhaps; the technique is flawlessly classic. In her receipt "Pilaff" (F 52) it is not, which may account for her calling it *pilaff* rather than *pilau;* that is, the rice is properly cooked, but the suggested mixing in of leftover stewed turkey is not traditional.

There is a curious unattributed receipt "Chickens Stewed with Tomatoes" (F 62), presumably of Low Country provenance, that has this notation: "It must be a moist stew," which explains why it is not called a *pilau,* since it is otherwise fairly classic. Mrs. Hill of Georgia, in her receipt "Tomato Pilau" (F 54), which differs from the previous one primarily in being less rich with butter, cautions the uninitiated that "this should not have gravy." (Her original work had been published in New York for a general readership.)

Up in Maryland Mrs. Howard's receipt *"Poulet au Riz"* (given twice, F 51 and F 64) calls for sautéing the rice before it is cooked with the previously sautéed chicken. Again, this is not Carolina technique.

There are surprisingly few vegetable pilaus aside from those where tomatoes are a supplementary ingredient. Receipts like "Tomato Pilau" (unattributed), nowadays more likely to be called "Red Rice," and Mrs. Blake's "Okra Pilau" (both F 56) call for bacon; neither receipt mentions seasoning, not even salt and pepper. It is to be noted that okra, or gumbo, plant and names, are of West African origin; *Nkru-ma* comes from the Twi language of Ghana, according to Jessica Harris; *kingombo* comes from Angola, with *kin-* being the "usual Bantu prefix," according to the *Oxford English Dictionary.* Okra and rice have an affinity for each other and the combination is popular not only in Africa but also in Persia and India, as well as in the African diaspora. The technique of frying the okra before cooking with the rice is one that I find in Indian receipts. Mrs. Howard of Maryland gives a receipt "Rice and Tomatoes" (F 52) which also calls for onions and green [bell] peppers, with an optional addition of chicken. As with any proper pilau, it is to be cooked until "almost dry."

I hardly know what to say about Mrs. Blake's "Bubble and Squeak" (F 61). The name properly belongs to an old English dish of slices of leftover beef fried with cooked cabbage and is attributed to its cooking sounds. A receipt for it appeared in American print by 1808;[12] I have never before seen one that calls for rice, and it must be peculiar to the Low Country. The instruction to "boil until rice is swollen and soft" could be construed as indicating that it was not intended to be a proper pilau, being perhaps a bit on the mushy side, but this is by no means certain, as I note that she does not employ the consecrated instruction to "cook until almost dry" in her other receipts.

Roast Squab with Rice Pilau

4 squabs	2 cups rice
6 slices bacon	4 cups of chicken stock
1 onion	4 eggs
¾ cup chopped celery	Salt and pepper
Mustard pickle juice	

Dress the squabs as usual. For the stuffing use a rice pilau made as follows: Dice the bacon and cook until crisp. Remove the bacon and add the chopped celery and onion to the bacon drippings and let them brown. Cook the rice in the chicken stock until tender and add the bacon and onion and celery mixture. Beat the eggs and add to the rice, stirring well so that the heat of the rice may cook the eggs, and season to taste with salt and pepper. Stuff the squabs with the mixture and make mounds of the remainder on which to lay the squabs. Bake in a hot oven (425 degrees F.) for about twenty-five minutes, basting the squabs frequently with mustard pickle juice. The mustard pickle adds a piquancy to the squabs and combines well with the pilau stuffing.
    —Blanche S. Rhett, as edited by the dietician Lettie Gay, in *Two Hundred Years of Charleston Cooking,* [as first published in 1930].

Two sorts of pilau that must have been popular in the Low Country are scantily documented: those featuring game and those featuring fish, Elizabeth Hamilton makes the same observation concerning game receipts in general in her foreword to *Two Hundred Years of Charleston Cooking,* remedying the lack with receipts for wild duck, marsh hens, shad, and shad roe.[13] Mrs. Hill of Georgia does note that "birds are as good in pilau as chickens" (F 56), and she must have been referring to game birds. The incomparably delicious thieving rice birds, for which Mrs. Stoney includes a receipt signed by Eliza Peronneau Mathewes (F 4), must have been served with rice, perhaps on occasion even bedded on a pilau. And I cite Mrs. Rhett's receipt for squabs (no longer wild, alas), served with a pilau that was far more elaborate than the *pilloe* made with squabs mentiond by Bartram back in the 1770s. (The squabs are baked atop the mounds of enriched rice so as to produce a crisp crust on the rice. The technique is thus related to that for the casserole; see chapter 4, "Casseroles.")
    Bartram also mentioned raccoon "served up in a pillo," and this sort of game pilau I have not found in the cookbooks, but surely all such creatures, including squirrel, rabbit, possum, etc., must have been made into tasty pilaus, even occasionally for the table of the plantation owner.

There is only one receipt for fish pilau in our work, and that is given almost as an afterthought to Mrs. Hill's receipt "To Hash Fish" (F 68) and is really just a way of using leftover fish. But fish makes wonderful pilau. Mrs. Blake, in her "Rice Pie" (F 59–60), does suggest "hot stewed oysters or birds" with which to fill. Mrs. Huger gives a receipt entitled "Shrimp Pilau" and another "Shrimp Pie" (F 67), and Miss Taft also gives "Shrimp Pie" (F 68). These last four receipts are discussed in chapter 4, "Casseroles."

French Pilau
1 3-pound fowl
Salt and pepper
2 cups uncooked rice
$1/4$ cup butter
1 cup blanched almonds
1 cup white raisins
$1/4$ teaspoon curry powder

Have the chicken cut into pieces for serving and boil it gently in water to which salt and pepper have been added. When the chicken is tender, remove it from the broth. There should be about four cups of the chicken stock. To this add the rice, cover it tightly, and let it cook until the rice is tender—about half an hour.

Add the butter to the hot rice and then stir in the other ingredients.

In serving, put the rice first upon the dish and then lay the fowl, which has been kept warm, upon it. This is a delicious dish for Sunday night supper served with Virginia ham, hot biscuits, French peas and coffee, with charlotte russe for dessert.

—Mrs. Charles Cotesworth Pinckney, Runnymede on the Ashley, as edited by the dietician Lettie Gay, in *Two Hundred Years of Charleston Cooking*, [as published in 1930].[14]

As explained elsewhere, one traditional pilau of Persia that never became popular in the Low Country is the sweet pilau, typically using various dried fruits and nuts, such as apricots, peaches, currants, dates, almonds, pistachios, walnuts, etc., usually in combination with meat or fowl. Mrs. Pinckney's receipt above is the only one of this type that I have found attributed to a South Carolinian. In this sense, the attribution is impeccable, but I note that the editing is suspect, and in spite of the Pinckney name, the receipt, as given, has suffered twentieth-century alterations.

(The Sunday night supper sounds delightful. I trust that awkward writing accounts for coffee apparently being served with the meal rather than with or after the dessert.)

There are two receipts included by Mrs. Stoney that list fruit among the ingredients; Mrs. Parker's "Pillau—The Turkish Soup" (F 46) calls for raisins, currants, and cherries, but it is neither *pillau* nor is it Turkish, as evidenced by the presence of pork. (Also, the Turkish name is *pilaf*.) Had she been a South Carolinian, surely she would have known better. It is to be noted that not one receipt in her own earlier work is for a proper pilau. And Mrs. Howard of Maryland contributes a receipt "Indian Pilau" (F 53) which suggests that "Malaga raisins are often boiled with the rice." This is indeed a *pullao*, if not perfectly classic. None of these receipts reflects traditional South Carolina practice.

LOU PELAU

Pilau...in the Midi of France, rice that is scarcely done [à peine crevé], served nearly dry and mixed with meat or shellfish....
   —*Nouveau Petit Larousse*, 1931.

"Qu vòu faire lou pelau, lou couquihage!" cri des *poissonières de Marseille et d'Aix.* ["For you to make a pilau, shellfish!" cry of the fishmongers of Marseilles and Aix.]
   Tian de sardino, pilau de sardines. [Sardine pilau.]
   Lou gros pilau, cataclysme social. [Social cataclysm.]
   —Frédéric Mistral, *Lou Tresor Dóu Felibrige* [1878-1886].

Un pilau tel qu'au ciel en mange Mahomet. [A pilau such as Mohammed eats in heaven.]
   —Joseph Méry [1798-1865]; closing line of the Provençal poet's receipt for pilau.

Cassolo...[a dish] cooked in the oven in a terrine of that name, composed of rice or other whole grain, seasoned with *petit salé* [pickled pork] or *andouille* [tripe sausage]...."
   —Maximin d'Hombres et Gratien Charvet, *Dictionnaire Languedocien-Français*, 1884.[15]

Riz en pilau

Cook a capon, which has been trussed as for an *entrée*..., in a good bouillon; when it is done, strain the bouillon through a very fine strainer into a pot; add a little saffron, and put it on the fire.
   Then add one or two pounds of rice. There should be nearly two and a half times as much bouillon as rice by volume; take

care that the bouillon is extremely rich; once it has started to boil, turn down the heat and continue to simmer till done; the rice should be nearly dry and scarcely cooked *[peu cuit];* a few minutes before serving, take a casserole of suitable size, or a turk's-head mold, and coat the inside well with fat skimmed from the bouillon; place part of the rice in the mold, spreading evenly; lay the capon thereon, breast down; fill the mold with the rest of the rice and place it between two sources of heat or surround it with hot coals; unmold it onto a great platter, and serve, accompanied by a terrine of bouillon so that the rice may be moistened with it if desired.

    —*Le Cuisinier Durand,* Nîmes, 1837.*

Pilau de Cailles [Quail]

    When the quail have been cleaned and trussed, allow them to become golden brown in a pan, using either fat or butter, then season with salt; cover them completely with bouillon, skim, cover the pan, and cook for twenty-five minutes; lift them out and keep them warm [with a little reserved bouillon].

    Strain the bouillon through a fine strainer; into it throw a handful of rice per person, and let it cook on a gentle fire; dress the rice in a mound, slightly flattened on top, on which arrange the quail, spooning over them the reserved juices.

    —Marius Morard, in *Manuel Complet de la Cuisinière Provençale,* Marseilles, 1886.

Pelau de riz au muscle [Mussels]

    Put into a pan 2 spoonfuls of olive oil, an onion and a leek, chopped; let it take color, then add a chopped tomato, and when well colored, throw in 250 grams of rice; give a few turns with a spoon and add half a liter of water; add 2 dozen mussels from rocky waters, well washed and scraped with a knife, a crushed clove of garlic, a *bouquet garni* composed of thyme, bay leaf, fennel, and celery; season with salt, pepper, and saffron; cover the pan and allow to cook gently and without stirring till done, a

---

*I have not seen the first edition of 1830. In context it is clear that a certain amount of bouillon is reserved for use at table, also that the bouillon should be measured to gauge the amount of rice. What is less clear is when the fat for coating the mold is to be skimmed from the bouillon; since he stresses that the final bouillon must be extremely rich (in order to provide the fat necessary for proper crusting of the casserole—see chapter 4, "Casseroles"), I suggest that the fat used is that skimmed from the already-prepared bouillon in which the capon is to be poached. Either chicken fat or butter may be used, if more convenient. A brisk oven will do the trick of supplying heat top and bottom.

matter of 20 minutes. When it is served, take out the *bouquet garni.*

It is to be observed that one should not cook the mussels in the rice thus if they do not come from clean, rocky waters, free of any silt or mud. Above all, they must be well cleaned. If there is the least doubt as to their provenance, they must be opened separately by putting them over high heat with half a glass of water in a covered pot [just until the shells open, a matter of a couple of minutes, discarding any that do not open]. They must not be added to the rice until taken from their shells, and the cooking liquid not until it has been carefully strained and decanted so as to leave behind any mud or impurities, which sink to the bottom. [This liquid should be figured into the total amount.]

    —J.-B. Reboul, *La Cuisinière Provençale.* Marseilles, no
       date [first published in 1895].

                  Ris ai fava [Rice with fava beans]

Rice, 500 grams / young fava beans for shelling, 1 kilogram / onions, 150 grams / 2 cloves of garlic / *petit salé* [pickled pork], 120 grams / olive oil, 3 tablespoons / water / salt.

Chop the garlic and onion fine, cut the *petit salé* into lardons. Shell the fava beans.

Allow the onion, garlic, and lardons, with the olive oil, just to take color in a *cocotte* [cooking pot of cast iron]. Do not let them brown. Take off the fire.

Measure the rice, take double the amount of water by volume, heat it, and pour it into the *cocotte,* salting lightly.

When the water boils, throw in the beans and cook them gently for about twenty minutes.

Carefully drain the onions, garlic, lardons, and beans, reserving the water the beans were cooked in, and put them in the *cocotte.*

Place the *cocotte* on the fire, add the rice, and warm it [for a moment, stirring].

Bring the cooking water to a boil and pour on the rice one and a half times as much liquid as rice, by volume [which should amount to that reserved from cooking the beans].

Cover the *cocotte;* cook for seventeen minutes on a gentle fire; turn off the heat; allow to rest for ten to fifteen minutes.

Before serving, you may add a few pats of fresh butter.

    —Raymond Armisen and André Martin, *Les Recettes de la
       Table Niçoise,* 1972.[16]

Caesar's *Provincia,* one of the three parts of ancient Gaul, has always been a country unto itself, and so remains to a surprising degree. In a general way, it can be said to have designated the lands where various forms of *langue d'oc* were spoken, rather than the northern *langue d'oïl,* which gave rise to Modern French. In other words, the Midi. (Actually, the use of *langue d'oc* extended well beyond the present political borders of France, into Catalonia, which is cut in two by the French-Spanish border; for example, the ancient Catalan province of Roussillon, whose capital was Perpignan, became part of France only in the seventeenth century. Catalan is still spoken there.) What came to be called *Provence* was the heart of the Midi, one of its several provinces. Its great seaport of Marseilles was founded by Phocaean Greeks about 600 B.C. as Massilia and is the oldest city of France. Down through the ages the Midi has been overrun by Romans, Visigoths, Franks, Arabs, Crusaders bent on extirpating the Albigensian heresy, and the Catholic kings of France bent on extirpating the Protestant heresy, whose adherents, popularly called *Huguenots,* held a number of strongholds in the Midi. (In the Cévennes, for example, entire areas were virtually depopulated because of massacres of Huguenots or their flight in face of danger.) That is, the history of the Midi has been quite separate from that of northern France; indeed, they were separate nations by all usual criteria—language, contiguous territory, etc.—and were often at loggerheads. Finally the kings of France prevailed and the Midi became part of France, at least politically. After the Revolution, the republic gerrymandered the ancient provinces and prohibited use of the *langue d'oc* of the troubadours of old, whose brilliant use of the vernacular in poetry is said to have influenced Dante. (All provinces and non-French languages in France suffered the same fate, but we are here concerned with Provence.)

All this has its importance. The pilau became naturalized in Provence as *lou pelau,* at what I believe to have been an early date; so thoroughly that the word entered the popular language in the form of street cries, in phrases of figurative meaning, some of which were recorded by Mistral (above). Such usage presupposes long acquaintance. In addition, pilau is associated with a number of Provençal words, such as *jambalaia* (which see), *tian, cassolo,* and by extension, even possibly *gratihoun,* at least in some instances, as can be seen by cross-references in various lexicons. In this light, the entry of *las specias de la gratonaya* [spices for the *gratonaya*] in communal accounts of Sisteron, cited by Louis Stouff in *Ravitaillement et Alimentation en Provence aux XIVe et XVe Siècles* (1970) could be of interest. A *gratonaya,* is, of course, a *gratin,* as is a *gratihoun,* references to and receipts for which abound in medieval manuscripts under such names as *Gratunée, Cretonnée d'Espaigne* (it is often attributed

to Spain), etc. I find no receipts calling for rice, and they vary considerably, but they are generally characterized by the formation of a surface
crust—as are all *gratins*—although it is not necessarily formed by baking.
A *tian,* named for its shallow baking dish, is a *gratin* by definition, and it
occasionally involves rice, as can be seen above. In that sense, the *cassolo*
is also a *gratin,* as are the rice pies and casseroles of Carolina (see chapter
4, "Casseroles").

We get little assistance from lexicographers concerning culinary
terms, above all those on a popular or regional level. To this day standard
French dictionaries do not list the *tian* of Provence or the *cotriade* of Brittany [a fish stew], although neither dish is obscure. Because of a growing
interest in regional cuisines, both are now amply documented in regional
cookbooks, although receipts for *tian* are more often given under *gratin*
for the benefit of the general French reader. What I am saying is, that I
can give no documentation on the date of introduction of the term *pilau*
into Provençal. *Tian* and *cassolo,* receptacles often associated with the
making of pilau, are frequently cited by Stouff, however, as occurring in
medieval kitchen inventories.[17]

> But let us proceed. Hypotheses about past events are not
> susceptible to scientific proofs, and the historian can never hope
> to have a hypothesis certified as anything better than reasonable.
> We must lope along where scientists fear to tread. It seems
> reasonable to say that human beings, in matters of diet, especially
> of the staples of diet, are very conservative, and will not change
> unless forced.
> —Alfred W. Crosby, Jr., *The Columbian Exchange* (1972).[18]

My hypothesis is that the pilau was brought to Carolina by Huguenots fleeing Catholic persecution. The presence of the pilau in Provence
is established—not securely documented until the nineteenth century, it is
true, but popular dishes have always been ill-recorded—and I shall discuss shortly why and how its naturalization there must have occurred
long before the flight of the Huguenots from Provence in the late seventeenth century. To paraphrase Littlefield on the cultivation of rice, other
peoples knew about the pilau, but the Huguenots were on the scene.

It has been objected that most Huguenots in Carolina did not come
from Provence, or even the Midi. Considering that some of the most important Huguenot strongholds were in the Midi, particularly in the
Cévennes, adjacent to Provence, it seems reasonable to suppose that there
must have been at least a few. Nor does the objection take into account
the compelling presence of rice in South Carolina. That is, the early pro-

prietors must have been avid for receipts, all the more since most of them, English and French alike, knew little to do with rice beyond making porridges and puddings. Even a single family from Provence could very nearly have introduced such a concept into the new rice lands. And there were such families, that is, judging by a peculiarly Provençal receipt given by Sarah Rutledge in *The Carolina Housewife* (1847), *"Boeuf a la Gardette,"* actually an old receipt for *daube*. The name comes from the Camargue; the Provençal form is *la gardiano,* sometimes translated into French as *à la gardiane,* which may be loosely translated as "cowboy stew," that is, stew or pot roast as made by *les gardiens de boeufs* [tenders of steers]—or rather, their wives—the raising of beef cattle having traditionally been a major industry in the Camargue, going way back. *Gardette* could be a corruption of what might have become an all-but-forgotten word, but I suggest that it was prompted by the mistaken notion that *gardette* was better French, inasmuch as the elliptical term *à la* requires that a feminine form follow. The tenderizing technique of marinading in vinegar was usual because the dish was traditionally made from the tough meat of elderly bulls. Indeed, the *daube* is of Mediterranean origin, formerly always calling for larding, then marinading in vinegar and long slow cooking, precisely as directed in Miss Rutledge's receipt. The dish came to be picked up by establishment cuisine in France, undergoing considerable refinement, substituting wine for vinegar, for example, and often being served cold as a decorated *entrée;* the vinegar was no longer as necessary because the meat was presumably of higher quality. Several such receipts appeared by 1715 in *Dictionnaire Pratique du Bon Ménager de Campagne et de Ville* by L. Liger. It was these later refined versions that came to England and the Colonies, as represented by the receipts in *The Virginia House-Wife* by Mary Randolph (1824), for example. So that Miss Rutledge's receipt suggests a direct Provençal provenance, an old one. There are other intimations of a Provençal presence in Carolina, the use of Provençal forms of *casserole,* as in Harriott Pinckney Horry's receipt for *cassorol,* as well as other forms, discussed below in chapter 4, "Casseroles."

I believe that it was the serendipitous meeting of Carolina Gold and Provençal receipts for pilau that enabled pilau to flourish as it did in South Carolina; that, and the skill of the African-American cooks who had long known rice cookery, almost surely including certain versions of pilau (see chapter 5, "Hoppin' John").

In addition, the pilau was *regarded* as French in Carolina, and surely this is significant. That is, entitling receipts "French Pilau" would seem to indicate that they had come from France by way of the Huguenots. There are two such receipts in Mrs. Stoney's collection; Mrs. Huger's "A

French Pilau" (F 56) and Sarah Rutledge's "To Make a French Pilau" (F 51). The Huger family was of French lineage, and Miss Rutledge may have gotten her receipt from a Huguenot family; as noted elsewhere, she gratefully acknowledged that family receipts had been made available to her. It will be noted that while her receipt is for a molded pilau, or rice pie (see chapter 4, "Casseroles"), that of Mrs. Huger is for the simpler, more basic version. That is, the appellation *French* refers to origin, not to type. (The "French Pilau" attributed to Mrs. Cotesworth Pinckney [given on p. 51] has been fancied up with almonds and raisins, but this must have been a twentieth-century debasement, perhaps due to her having heard tell about Eastern pilaus that contained fruit and nuts.)

At this point the only serious question is this: How did the pilau find its way to Provence? There are a number of possible scenarios, but before we discuss them, let us study for a moment the pilau in Provence, particularly as compared to that in South Carolina. The name itself is telling. As noted earlier, not all transplanted pilaus bear the name, but those of Provence and Carolina do, except for certain variations, particularly molded versions. As to pronunciation, there is no accounting for that of *PUHR-LOE,* except to note that the consonants *l* and *r* have a confused historical relationship, especially with word borrowings. But the South Carolina alternative pronunciation of *pi-LOE,* with its unaccented first syllable sounding like *pill,* is that of Provençal *pelau* with the same indeterminate, unaccented first syllable. (Proper French pronunciation of *pilau* is *pee-LOE.)*

Classic Provençal cookbooks all give receipts for *pelau,* sometimes *pilau,* sometimes simply listing principal ingredients. In addition to the classic receipt *"Riz en pilau"* (see above, pp. 52–53) given in *Le Cuisinier Durand* (1837), considered to be the earliest Provençal cookbook, other pilaus are presented under descriptive names. In addition to the receipt cited above, Morard also gives receipts for pilau under other names, such as *"Saucisses au Riz,"* which seems to have been a popular version in Carolina.

Although it is a bit of a digression to discuss them, Morard's receipts for *rizotte* are particularly interesting. In spite of the name, variously spelled, *le rizotte* has little or nothing to do with Italian risotto; that is, the rice for *le rizotte* is specifically cooked *en pilau,* a common Provençal designation, to which he devotes an entire section, making a point that each grain be "well detached," and that one not disturb the rice during cooking, in contrast to the characteristic constant stirring of rice during cooking of the *risotto.* He also specifies the use of *riz caroline,* indicating that historically both pilau and *le rizotte* were made with long-grain rice in Provence, while *risotto* evolved around the round rice of Italy. (The existence of *le rizotte* may explain in part the fact that classic French cuisine hopelessly confuses pilau and Italian *risotto.* Chefs of Provençal origin are more knowledgeable. Durand perceptively notes that rice is "more pasty. . . when one adds the liquid little by little.") What is particularly interesting about *le rizotte* is its kinship to the molded pilaus of Persia and Carolina, in that an aromatic *ragoût* (one of chicken, another of mussels, in Morard's work) is encased in cooked rice and unmolded for serving; they differ in that *le rizotte* is not baked in the oven in order to produce the characterizing crust. (This may simply reflect a historical lack of individual home ovens, because the Durand receipt given above is a perfectly classic crusted rice casserole; see chapter 4, "Casseroles.") Reboul also gives several receipts for *rizoto* in *La Cuisinière Provençale* (1895) which follow the procedure outlined by Morard for *le rizotte.* The dish seems to be associated with Toulon.

Perhaps the most classic Provençal receipt for pilau is that given in poetic form by Joseph Méry, the closing line of which is cited above (p. 52). It calls for cooking rice in a wonderfully rich broth, including ham (which would have offended Mohammed, to be sure, but shows the historical presence of cured pork in Provençal pilaus), and chicken "that has been nourished on wind-blown grain in the meadows," all perfumed with saffron, to be sure. In addition to the presence of cured pork, the most interesting detail from a historical point of view is his insistence on *"riz du Levant, vierge de la poussière* [rice from the East, with no trace of starch dust]," that is, specifically not the short-grain rice of Italy or Spain but translucent long-grain rice of high quality, what the French call *riz glacé;* he even tells the reader where to buy it. And the technique bears this out in that there is no preliminary sautéing of raw rice. It is a perfectly lovely receipt; if only I were a poet, I would translate it all. André Castelot (1972), in presenting Méry's receipt, makes a point of the fact that the rice is *"à peine crevé* [scarcely cooked]," this for the benefit of the general French reader, who is brought up to think that rice is not cooked unless it is *burst.*[20] He gives neither source nor date, but it would be from before 1865, so that it is an early recorded receipt, roughly from the period of Durand's receipt of 1837, perhaps, but more revealing in certain details as well as being more telling in that it is not given by a professional cook. That is, Méry was a poet singing praises of a beloved Provençal dish, just as he also sang praises of the legendary *bouillabaisse* of Marseilles. The pilau was a part of daily life, not the creation of a chef who might have come into possession of an Eastern receipt.

Going on to more modern works, C. Chanot-Bullier, in *Vieii Receto de Prouvençalo* (1972), gives *"Li limaço au ris"* [snails with rice] among other receipts for pilau; Jean-Noel Escudier, in *La Véritable Cuisine Provençale* (1964), gives a receipt *"Poule au riz au safran,"* a classic pilau; and Maguelonne Toussaint-Samat, in *La Cuisine Rustique: Provence* (1970), gives *"Pelau de riz de favouio"* [crabs] and *"Pourprion au Riz"* [octopus]. These examples by no means exhaust my sources; Escoffier gives sixteen receipts for *pilaw* in *Le Riz* (1927), for example, and there are others, but these suffice to show the extent to which the pilau flourished in Provence.

These examples also serve to demonstrate the extraordinary kinship between the pilaus of Provence and of Carolina. The classic long-grain technique for both is mentioned earlier (p. 37). And in composition they are both characterized by the elegance of simplicity; there is but one principal ingredient in addition to the rice; all else is added to enhance that combination. I do not find a single Provençal receipt that calls for fruit or the slightest suggestion of sweetness, and this accords with Carolina practice, at least traditionally. I find little use of spices except for black pepper. (While I suspect that the use of fruits, nuts, spices, and sugar may have characterized the medieval court cuisines of the Midi, as they did the court cuisines of Paris and other countries, including Catalonia, this practice had fallen into disuse pretty much by sometime in the seventeenth century. People who know their wines eschew sweetness and heavy spicing in their cuisine; very few wines can stand up to either, so sweets are served only when the meal is over. If anything, Provençals are stricter in this respect than are the French north of the Loire.)

Even on the subject of other aromatics, I find Provençal receipts remarkably restrained. The most common instruction is to add a *bouquet garni,* occasionally spelling it out as including thyme, bay leaf, celery, and parsley, occasionally leeks or garlic—and saffron, said to be the legacy of the Phocaean Greeks in Provence. (In this regard, there is a striking passage in *Les Delices de la Campagne* (1662) by Nicolas de Bonnefons concerning the seasoning of rice: "In the Villages they add saffron to give it the color and taste to which they have been accustomed since ancient times *[de toute ancienneté],* even though it is bad." It is not clear just what he meant by "Villages." The author was valet to the young Louis XIV and thus reflected aristocratic attitudes of northern France in matters of cuisine. But I find no trace of the use of saffron north of the Loire; even in the Saintonge, its presence in *la mouclade* [a creamy mussel stew] is considered as something of an aberration, and this place is below the Loire. He may have meant to qualify those villages as having been in Provence, in which case his comment would be accurate insofar as usage of saffron is concerned, particularly as it concerns a receipt for rice, a rather poor one, it must be said, although the general level of his receipts is high.) If we accept Mrs. Hamilton's suggestion that an onion and a *bouquet garni* were always added to Carolina receipts for pilau, they are very like those of Provence, always excepting the mysterious absence of saffron from those of Carolina. Saffron must have been grown in South Carolina, if only for medicinal use. Martha Ballard, a midwife of Hallowell, Maine, for example, recorded in her journal for August 14, 1787: "Clear & hott. I pikt the safron." Bernard McMahon, seedsman of Philadelphia, listed it for sale in 1806, and Jefferson ordered it. Perhaps in the early days growing saffron had seemed a luxury. (It is to be remarked that the *jambalaya* of New Orleans, discussed further elsewhere, also lost its note of saffron when it was transplanted to America.)[21]

Aside from the disappearance of saffron, the most interesting differences in composition between the pilaus of Provence and Carolina involve the infinitely greater use of seafood in Provence—mussels, in particular—and the use of African okra in Carolina. To be sure, shrimps are a common element in Carolina pilaus, so they may have taken the place of mussels.

Perhaps the most telling similarity between the pilaus of Provence and Carolina is the characterizing use of *bacon,* a practice I believe to have been initiated in Provence. *Bacon* was the term in both Old French and Old Provençal; the most common forms in the various *langues d'oc* are *bacoun* and *bacou,* designating what is better known elsewhere in France as *petit salé,* various lesser cuts of pork cured and stored in brine. The American term of *salt pork* does not adequately translate *petit salé; pickled pork* would be more accurate, with the understanding that there is no question of vinegar, only a certain characteristic fermentation that takes place. (In Modern French, *bacon* has been retrieved, as it were, from English and refers to *smoked* bacon, *à l'anglaise,* but this was not the original meaning. Neither French *lard* [a cut corresponding to American bacon] nor *petit salé* is smoked; for that matter, ham rarely is.) In terms of providing the fatty element of daily diet, *petit salé* was the mainstay of French country cooking. Even in Provence, the fabled land of olive oil, it was valued because of the savor it imparted to all sorts of dishes, beginning with *la soupe,* often eaten thrice daily; the further inland and the further back in time one goes, the less important olive oil becomes. (Obviously, distance from the olive groves was part of the story, as was the fact that olive oil was a cash crop; so were hogs, but with these the idea was to sell the "noble" parts and make the rest up into *petit salé,* etc.) In the Vivarais, just across the Rhône from the upper reaches of Provence, Père Menfouti is cited as saying: *"Lou lard—faî la soupo—e maîlo part* [bacon makes the soup—and the better part of it, meaning of the meal]," as given by Charles Forot in *Odeurs de Forêt et Fumets de Table* (1964).

Historically, cured pork had become a characterizing element of the pilau in Provence. In a lengthy discussion of *"Le pilaf aux moules"* [mussels], Austin de Croze gives what he claims to be the true receipt *[la bonne et véritable recette]*, which calls for 250 grams of salt pork or *lard* [unsmoked bacon], which amounts to half a pound of cured pork for two pounds of mussels, much of whose weight is accounted for by shells, a remarkably substantial proportion of pork. It is to be emphasized that this receipt of 1928 was "correcting" the earlier one by Reboul (given above, pp. 53–54), who was a fellow Provençal.[22] It is not that the presence of cured pork is invariable in Provençal receipts, but I get the impression that it was the *old* way. De Croze uses the term *pilaf*, explaining for the general French reader that in Provence it is called *pilau*. The Provençal connection that I propose would certainly explain the lingering preference for *unsmoked* cured pork evidenced in some Carolina receipts.

In available Provençal works I find only one receipt for pilau featuring pulse (given above, p. 54), and it is contemporary. Such combinations may not have been common, or they may have been ill-recorded, but considering how popular chick-peas have long been in Provence, it is curious that that I do not find receipts for combining them with rice in pilau, a classical version in the East, for example. (In practical terms, fresh baby lima beans, while not at all Provençal, may be substituted for fresh favas, which are hard to find.) In any event, the only recorded bean pilau of Carolina known to me is associated with African-Americans (see chapter 5, "Hoppin' John").

There are other popular rice dishes in Provence, notably *la soupe courte,* an ancient festival dish, calling for mutton, *petit salé* or other cured pork, onions, aromatics, saffron, and rice; it is not a soup but a very thick stew or a rather wet pilau. (Several sources, including Amelia Wallace Vernon, formerly of Florence County, South Carolina, have described what sounds like a similar dish using chicken instead of the mutton of Provence; it is called *chicken bog* and is made outdoors in wash tubs to serve large crowds. The function of the dish is thus the same; it is difficult to make very large amounts of a proper pilau, so it ends up being "boggy," not a bad description of *la soupe courte,* judging by the proportions given in the receipts and its name.

I find no trace of the Carolina or Indian way of cooking plain rice in Provence. (This method is seldom referred to by French writers, but when it is, the term used is usually *riz créole,* an allusion to French West Indian, African, or Malagasy methods, a telling association.) However, *riz en pi-*

lau [rice cooked as if it were a pilau] is very popular. Morard devotes an entire section to it, calling for using "bouillon that has not been skimmed," further fortifying it with butter if indicated, observing usual proportions and procedure. But it is often cooked simply with water, with either butter or olive oil added for the requisite fat, and perfumed with saffron. (See *"Riz au Safran."*) This is the Provençal version of "plain rice" and is used as an accompaniment to the main dish. (Durand uses the term for chicken pilau [above, p. 52], but that is highly untypical.)

I recognize that these receipts were recorded no earlier than the third decade of the nineteenth century. But popular cuisine has ever been poorly recorded; even the picturesque *bouillabaisse* was not recorded until 1837, and that is thought to go back to antiquity; legend attributes its invention to Venus, which may be dismissed but does suggest that it has been considered to be ancient for long centuries. The receipts have surely evolved somewhat down through the ages in their secondary ingredients—tomatoes strike an anachronistic note, for example—but the basic structure seems to have remained constant, that of a humble fisherman's stew composed of what remained of the day's catch. It is always seasoned with saffron, a legacy of the Phocaean Greeks. (In truth, there are innumerable fish stews, all seasoned with saffron, all over the Mediterranean, some say wherever Greeks colonized. And contrary to the food writers, *bouillabaisse* does not mean "boiling lowered"—which is nonsense, being contrary to culinary procedure, where rapid boiling is necessary to amalgamate oil and broth—but is a corruption of *bouillir* [to boil] and *peis* [the Provençal word for fish]; a *bouillabaisse* is a fish boil.)[23] So lack of documentation previous to 1837 should not be regarded as necessarily indicating that the pilau did not have a long history in Provence before then.

In *haute cuisine,* a highly codified and artificial art whose beginnings were in the court kitchens of the Île de France—that is, around Paris—a unique development that has little to do with French family cuisine anywhere in France, receipts were written by, or dictated to scribes by, professional male cooks, so that on that level new culinary ideas spread somewhat more rapidly; it was a question of professional pride and dazzling the jaded palates of the nobility. (Even so, there are no extant culinary manuscripts from much before 1300 in France.) But on the popular level, the level on which the pilau survived in Provence, people were far more conservative in matters of food. New ideas did not take root easily. Nor were receipts recorded. Who would have recorded them? Who would have read them? Only rarely did popular dishes make the leap to *haute cuisine.*

As for dishes of the Midi, more than class was involved; I was told time and again in France that "there is no cuisine south of the Loire."

When asked about such wonderful dishes as *cassoulet* and *bouillabaisse,* the response was categoric and invariable: "That is not cuisine." What they really meant to say was, "That is not French," because they were perfectly willing to accept popular dishes of northern France as "cuisine."

A digression: The disdain of the French culinary establishment for popular dishes of the Midi has its parallel in the United States with regard to Southern cookery. A few colorful dishes came to be known in mainstream American cookery—jambalaya comes to mind, and that is recent, historically speaking—but the Carolina pilau remains all but unknown elsewhere. *Webster's New International Dictionary* (second edition, 1961) defines pilau as "an Oriental dish." Fannie Farmer in 1896 gives two receipts entitled "Turkish Pilaf" but not a hint of our own Carolina pilau, which is revealing but hardly surprising, given her parochialism. The completely revised edition of 1979 again gives receipts entitled "Turkish Pilaf" but none for pilau, and the same ignorance of the very existence of Carolina pilau is evidenced in *The Joy of Cooking* by Irma Rombauer (1975), the encyclopedic *American Cookery* by James Beard (1972), and *The Dictionary of American Food and Drink* by John F. Mariani, who attributes the pilau to ten different countries in addition to Louisiana and Florida in the United States, all without mentioning South Carolina. And it would have been better had Evan Jones, with Judith B. Jones, *not* mentioned it in *American Food* (1973); their receipt calls for bacon fat, chopped scallions and green pepper, canned red pepper, crab meat, oysters, minced clams, okra, and diced ham, all for a pathetic one-half cup of rice.[24] *But the Carolina pilau is characterized by an elegant simplicity of composition, featuring a single ingredient, that is, in addition to rice which is the point of the dish.* All else is added to enhance that combination. The Jones receipt is a mess. To borrow Churchill's possibly apocryphal complaint about an offending pudding: "It has no theme." My point is that establishment writers, whether in France or the United States, are woefully ignorant of regional cookery, and this explains in large part why the pilau of Provence, for example, was not documented in a cookbook until 1837 and the *jambalaia,* its alter ego, came to be regarded as a wisp of folklore.

JAMBALAIA, JAMBALAYA

*Jambalaia, Jabalaia, Jambaraia (mot arabe)...*voir *pelau* [see *pelau*]...
—Frédéric Mistral, *Lou Tresor Dóu Felibrige* [1878–1886].

Jumballaya a la Creole
Add to a cupful of rice, which has boiled five minutes, a rich

brown chicken fricassee, put it in a saucepan, not closely covered, let it dry slowly, turn with a fork. The Carolinians make different perlous prepared in the same way by adding cooked tomatoes and butter. Green peas with a little butter is delicious. Okra and tomatoes fried together and added to rice. Oysters a little fried in butter. Hopping John is made in the same way with small pieces of fried ham, fried sausages, to which you add some cow peas that have been partially boiled. Season highly. The St. Domingo Congris is like the Hopping John.
 —Célestine Eustis, *Cooking in Old Créole Days,* 1904.

Jambalaya of Rice and Shrimps
 Boil two dozen of large shrimps; when cold, peel and set aside. Fry in hot lard a chopped onion and a cupful of rice washed in cold water. Let the onion and rice fry well, add the shrimps, stirring constantly. When browned add enough water to cover the whole. Season with salt and pepper, a bay leaf, thyme and chopped parsley. Let boil slowly, and add water until the rice is well cooked. When done let it dry and serve hot.
 —*Mme. Begué and Her Recipes: Old Creole Cookery,* 1900.

Jumballaya
A Spanish Creole Dish
 Wash 1 lb. of rice, and soak it an hour; cut up a cold roast chicken or the remnants of a turkey and a slice of ham, which fry in a tablespoonful of lard; stir in the rice, and add slowly, while stirring in a pint of hot water; cover your pot and set it where it can cook slowly. Jumballaya is very nice made with oysters or shrimp.
 —*The Creole Cookery Book.* Edited by the *Christian Woman's Exchange* of New Orleans, 1885.[25]

The *jamablaia* of Provence is now only historical. René Jouveau describes it in *La Cuisine Provençale de Tradition Populaire* (no date, by 1972), giving a detailed list of ingredients for a classic pilau, including chicken and saffron rice cooked in the broth, but no proportions. Escoffier, a good Provençal, does not mention it by name in *Le Riz* (1927), for example, and I find no receipts in any works I have consulted. The northern disdain for the cuisines of the Midi, referred to earlier, is responsible for the abysmal ignorance of all but the most picturesque meridional dishes on the part of establishment. Receipts for pilaf do appear, but it is regarded as an exotic dish, a dish from the Orient; no mention is made in *Nouveau Larousse Gastronomique* (1967) of pilau being a Provençal dish. Indeed, the ignorance of the editors is such that they are able to give a lu-

dicrous receipt *Jambalaia de Poulet (Cuisine indienne),*" flagrantly unaware that the name applied to a dish long known in Provence. It is
described as "a sort of pilaf," which is true enough, but the receipt as
given is simply diced ham and leftover chicken reheated with leftover rice.
Neither name nor receipt is Indian. Nor yet a proper pilaf.

But the *jambalaia* of Provence lives on in the *jambalaya* of New Orleans, at least in name. Conventional wisdom has it that it is a Spanish
Creole dish, derived from the *paella* of Spain, carrying in its wake pop etymology suggesting that *jam-* (from French *jambon,* "ham") had been
prefixed to a corruption of *paella* on the premise that ham had not been
an ingredient of the *paella* but was an original stroke of genius that had
occurred in New Orleans. This, however, is not borne out by the receipts
on either side of the Atlantic. Some form of pork is a usual ingredient in
the *paella* and, as we have seen, cured pork is a characteristic of the pilau
of Provence. "Jambalaya of Fowls and Rice" appears in Lafcadio
Hearn's *Creole Cook Book* (1885), with a note that it is "said to be an Indian dish." It is, however, a perfectly classic pilau, which does indeed include ham, but several receipts from the turn of the century do *not,*
among them the one given by Mrs. Eustis (above), the three given by
Mme. Begué (one of which appears above), and two of those in *The Picayune Cook Book* (1901). (The receipts in the *Picayune* work are for atypi-
cally soupy mixtures, excepting *"Jambalaya au Congri,"* effectively a
hoppin' John [see chapter 5].) Also, the *paella* evolved around the use of
short-grain rice, as explained earlier, and requires a very different technique from that of jambalaya, which is based on long-grain rice.

In *Creole cookery,* in addition to "Jumballaya" (above), there appears "To Make A French Pilau," copied word for word from that given
by Sarah Rutledge in 1847 (F 51); it is repeated in a mangled form in the
Picayune work as *"Pilou Français."* Perhaps because it concerns a molded
pilau, or rice pie, the relationship between pilau and jambalaya seems not
to have occured to anyone but Mrs. Eustis (see above), and she had Carolina connections. I cannot account for the name *jambalaya* in New Orleans for what is historically the same dish as the pilau in Carolina.
Certainly the French of New Orleans were of a different milieu in that
they were largely Catholic, which could be more significant than it might
seem. However, I wonder whether it is not possible that the term *jambalaia* was current in Catalan, a *langue d'oc,* at one time, thus accounting
for the persistence of the idea in New Orleans that it is a Spanish Creole
dish. There is no evidence of this, I must stress, but words do have a way
of completely disappearing from view—occasionally having been recorded only once, apparently—only to mysteriously reappear far away,
much like rivers that go underground to reappear in a cascade with no im-

mediately apparent source. As for the possibility of this dish having come from Spain, I noted earlier that the techniques involved in making the *paella* and the jambalaya are quite different. That objection is not insurmountable. For example, in her receipt *"Riz a la Valencienne"*—what is manifestly intended to be a *paella*, a dish of Valencia—Mrs. Eustis takes considerable liberties with the basic technique, adapting it to her specified "best Carolina rice," which is long-grain, whereas the rice of Valencia is short-grain. She does not seem to notice its kinship to a receipt entitled "Jumballaya" given by her on the very same page. However, she does bake *Riz a la Valencienne* in the oven in line with makeshift practice for *paella*, but contrary to practice for jambalaya. The internal evidence of receipts shows that jambalaya is more akin to pilau than to *paella*. Catalonia and Provence had ties of long standing, both political and linguistic, and it would not be surprising if there were at one time parallels in their cuisines. If there was a *jambalaia* in Catalonia, I suspect that it resembled a pilau more than the *paella* of Valencia. All of this is highly conjectural, but it fits such evidence as we have and would help to explain some puzzling aspects concerning the jambalaya.

In addition, *jambalaia* was recorded in Provençal by Mistral, citing variant forms of *jabalaia* and *jambaraia* used by other Provençal writers. *Webster's Ninth New Collegiate Dictionary* (1983) defines *jambalaya* as a Louisiana French word from Provençal *jambalaia*. On the other hand, *Webster's New International Dictionary* (second edition, 1961) speculates that it is "per[haps] a Negro corrup[tion] of F[rench] *jambon,* ham," by which is meant a word of Gombo origin, perhaps, although that is not clear. This is hardly more justifiable than the pop etymology noted above, nor does it answer how *jambalaia* came to be recorded in Provençal as an Arab word.

Because the word appears in only one Arab lexicon, questions have been raised as to whether it is actually an Arab word; also, the form is somewhat irregular, it seems. However, it seems no more irregular to me than are so many of the dish names recorded in the Baghdad manuscript of 1226 referred to earlier, such as *jurjānīya, tabāhaya,* for example, not to mention *alya,* the Arab name for rendered fat of sheep's tail, which is a very slightly altered form of *-laia,* or *-laya,* the ending of *jambalaia,* by metathesis, or simple transposition. Considering that Arab pilaus were so often started off with *alya,* precisely as in the receipt *"Isfānākyīya"* (given earlier, p. 38), this seems like a promising approach to identifying the word.

Also, it may have changed form on introduction to Provençal. For example, Arabic *iskebêȳ,* referring to a way of keeping food, usually fried fish, in seasoned vinegar, variously became *escabeig, escabeyg, esquabey, scabeig,* and *esbeig* in Catalan (early fourteenth century, according to Rudolf Grewe), as well as *escabetx* (fourteenth century, according to Corominas); *espimbèche* and *espinbesche* in French (*Ménagier de Paris*, 1393); *escabeche* in Spanish (1525), according to Corominas); and surviving popular forms in Italian are *scapace, scapece,* and *scabeccio,* not to mention surviving colonial forms of *seviche* and *caveach* in Spanish and English, respectively. Although recorded in medieval Paris, the *espimbèche* is for *rougets,* fish peculiarly associated with the Mediterranean, strongly suggesting that the receipt came from there, particularly in light of the Arab connection. There is also a listing of *une espinbesche de un bouly lardé* [meat that is larded, simmered, then marinated in seasoned vinegar], which by reversing operations may figure in the evolution of the *daube,* a dish particularly identified with Provence.

In addition, culinary terms are notoriously ill recorded, as I noted earlier with *tian* and *cotriade,* neither of which appears in modern French dictionaries. *Bahaṭṭa* (a Persian loan word from Hindi *bhat*) appears in Arabic in 1226 but not since, apparently. By whatever name it was known, pilau was an Arab dish—if only by adoption, as was *iskebêŷ,* both borrowed from the Persians.[26] And the fact that Mistral thought that *jambalaia* was an Arab word must have some significance.

A note on historical method in culinary history. While lack of early citations must be taken into account, it is not necessarily conclusive. One cannot prove a negative, particularly where early documentation is so sparse. Just so, while first citations must be considered, they too are not necessarily conclusive in determining chronological order of appearance and dispersion of a dish, nor even its origin. Usage antedates the written word, particularly at a time when most people were illiterate; the only question is by how long, and this can vary enormously. This is assuming that a given term or receipt was recorded and, if so, that it survived, and that it came to the attention of scholars with some knowledge of culinary matters for evaluation. A lot of ifs.

These citations, scanty as they are, suggest that there was an unexpectedly pervasive Arab influence in France, particularly in the lands of the *langue d'oc* and that it has been little studied. It should be remembered that the *langues d'oc* of Provence and Catalonia are far closer to each other than either is to French or Spanish, respectively. And there have been political and other ties down through the centuries, as discussed earlier (p. 55). That is, while shifting political realities forced certain allegiances, they were never as deep as those of cultural identity, as most obviously exhibited by linguistic identity. The very use of *langue d'oc,* whether in France or Spain, came to be regarded as an expression of separatism, as indeed it was. So that there is little mystery about the dispersion of ideas and customs, including culinary customs, within boundaries of such linguistically cohesive areas. When, as here, a vanquished nation's culture comes to be known only in the language of its conquerors, if at all, certain aspects are often dismissed as myth or folklore. But we are the poorer for such losses, and it becomes the duty of historians to ferret out these lost histories as best we can, given the paucity of documentation.

One such historian is Louis Stouff, who in *Ravitaillement et Alimentation en Provence aux XIVe et XVe Siècles* [food and provisions in Provence during the fourteenth and fifteenth centuries] (1970), points out that there has been "a nearly total absence of writing on the subject of food in medieval Provence," meaning that serious research has only just begun. His work is prodigious, as prodigious as it is frustrating in some respects. (For one thing, it is 507 pages long and has a strangely inadequate index.) It supplies the answer to the question of how many butchers there were in Arles in 1306—fifty-two—and how many of them were kosher—an astonishing fourteen, or 27 percent. However, if you want to know about the pilau, there is not a word, nor of the *bouillabaisse* of antiquity, although there is an entire chapter on seafood. This may well reflect the state of surviving data, but it also reflects a point of view. He is a historian who knows so little culinary lore that he is able to write concerning the *lardadoyra* (variously spelled), an item in a fourteenth-century kitchen inventory, that "if one is to believe Honnorat [*Dictionnaire. . . de la langue d'oc ancienne et moderne,* 1846-1847], it is a metal instrument. . . for inserting lardons into meat." If he so mistrusted Honnorat, he had but to look up modern French *lardoire* [larding-needle] in any dictionary. Likewise, he gives *"Sinamomus* (?)" [parentheses and question mark original], clearly baffled as to its identity. Today it is better known as *cannelle* in French, but even *Petit Robert* (1967) gives modern *cinnamome* [cinnamon], defining it as *cannelle*. (The question of the ill-differentiated cinnamon and cassia is not at issue here.) None of this is arcane.

We all nod from time to time, but such an attitude on the part of a food historian can be likened to that of a musicologist who cannot read music. It is bound to have affected what he was looking for, hence, what he found. That is, bean-counting clerks of yore did not tell us how the beans were cooked, and total reliance on such sources imposes a bean-counting mentality on the historian. Still, being a serious researcher, Stouff does note some strange lacunae; in medieval records from Provence he finds mention of oysters only once and of mussels not at all, yet in the sixteenth century a work by "a gentleman of Arles" described supplies of oysters as being "very abundant," he says. The widespread use of oysters and mussels in the Mediterranean has been recorded since early classical time. The question is thus: If the use of mussels is not so much as mentioned in the collected records of two long centuries in Provence, *what else is missing?*

This mystery of the missing oysters and mussels illustrates the inherent dangers of the school of food history which maintains that official and semiofficial records from markets, abbeys, hospitals, etc., are the only admissible sources for study. These records are invaluable, and we must be grateful to Stouff for having made them available to us. But the very paucity of records after all these centuries is bound to give an incomplete, hence misleading, picture. What is typical about hospital food? Or that served in the archbishop's palace? Above all, such bean counting does not take into account the vast and varied resources of *individual* family sustenance activities: kitchen gardens, fruit trees, *clapiers* [rabbit hutches], poultry, hunting, fishing, snails, wild mushrooms, even tiny vineyards producing only enough wine for an extended family, and a hog or two. All of this is *undocumented food.* Even after centuries of "progress," it goes on; I have witnessed it myself. And in spite of the much-vaunted "scientific" nature of evidence from official records, not even the most assiduous researcher is going to find documentatuon of such activity, because it was never written down. Incomplete as they are, Stouff's scattered references to produce from "documented" gardens show how rich a resource they were: in addition to such items as grains, olive oil, wine, nuts, and fruits, I find twenty-five different vegetables listed, among them *lugumina* [various pulse], *brocoli, rapa, insalata* [lettuce, in addition to other salad greens in context], *spinargium* [spinach], and *cogorda* [*courge,* an Old World gourd resembling pumpkin, a word now applied to squash], among the expected *caulis* [cabbage], *alh* [garlic], etc.

An aside. Gardening and other subsistence activities were common all over France, as is evident from early and continued publication of gardening and horticultural manuals. The English had similarly great traditions. All of this lore was brought to Carolina. (Indeed, the humble collard, almost a symbol of soul food, was brought by the English; the word is a phonetic corruption of *colewort,* which designates a cabbage that does not head. It may have taken the place of certain African greens in the slave diet.) In addition, there were the new products and gardening lore of the slaves from Africa and the Native Americans. Contrary to popular wisdom, vegetables of all kinds were highly regarded and widely cultivated in the South, as elsewhere in the Colonies, for that matter. (It is true that many white Southerners may have lost touch with the land during the centuries of slavery, forgetting the arts of cultivating vegetables and cooking them, but that was later.)

One problem in my research concerns the provenance of rice in sufficient quantity to support what became a fairly broad base for the pilau. There never developed in Provence an authentic rice kitchen. But the base was broad enough for the pilau to have become a popular dish, a dish of the people. I do not propose that the poor were necessarily part of this base, at least not historically; if rice was imported, they would not have been able to afford it. As to possible cultivation of rice, Alfred Franklin in *La Vie Privée d'Autrefois: Cuisine* (1888), notes that attempts to acclimatize rice in the Midi started in the sixteenth century; Waverley Root reports an attempt in the seventeenth century; and *Nouveau Larousse Gastronomique* (1967) says that attempts were made in the Auvergne by Cardinal Fleury (1653–1743), giving no date. I find no record of success until rice was planted once again in the Camargue, the brackish marshlands of Provence, early in this century.

Such evidence as I find from the eighteenth and nineteenth centuries indicates that rice was imported, and that in Provence, long-grain rice was preferred over short-grain rice from nearby Italy or Spain. (This was contrary to the situation in Paris, where Italian rice came to be preferred by many; see the section above in chapter 1, "Carolina Gold.") All this information is extremely scanty. Could there have been successful but unrecorded attempts to cultivate rice on a subsistence level, much as happened among African-Americans in our own South? (These latter instances have been little known, as I discuss in chapter 5, "Hoppin' John.") I think it most unlikely, and even if so, it could hardly have been decisive; I think that we must conclude that rice was imported, and from long-grain rice lands. Stouff mentions rice several times, once as having been imported "by sea," specifically along with spices, which would suggest an Eastern source.[27]

Charles the king, our mighty emperor,
has been in Spain for all of seven years,
has won that haughty land down to the sea.
There is no castle still opposing him,
nor town or wall remaining to be crushed,
except the mountain city, Saragossa.
Marsilla holds it; he does not love God,
but serves Mohammed, and invokes Apollo.
No matter what he does, his ruin will come.
  —Opening lines of *Le Chanson de Roland,* as
   translated by Robert Harrison under the title
   of *The Song of Roland* (1970).[28]

At last we return to the question of when and how the pilau came to
Provence. As we have seen, nineteenth-century versions of pilau in Provence and South Carolina, as recorded in the cookbooks, are parallel versions, remarkably similar in all basic respects: in technique, by definition,
and more tellingly perhaps, in general character and sobriety of composition as contrasted with the elaborate versions of the East; the most important difference was the disappearance of saffron when it crossed the
Atlantic. So the pilau had to have come to Provence early enough to permit the naturalization of this Muslim dish in a then militantly Christian
land, to the point of becoming a popular dish, complete with pickled
pork—*lou bacou,* mainstay of the popular diet, particularly in *la soupe,*
along with bread.

Remembering that on a popular level peoples do not easily change
their food habits—we speak of a time before they read cookbooks—such
acceptance entails a compelling presence over a period of some time.
Also, any thesis should explain the retention of the Persian word *pilau,* or
in Provençal, *pelau.* Let us discuss the historical events susceptible of ful-
filling these requirements.

> *Lo Pelau de Crancas* [Pilau of She-Crabs]
> *Se ditz qu'un Dagtenc qu'èra tornat de las Crosadas*
> *n'importèt la recèpta al país.* [It is said that an Agathois returning
> from the Crusades brought the receipt of his homeland.]
>   —Paulona Duconquéré, in *Cosina Occitana del País d'Agde.*
>   *Picapol, 1987.* *

The influence of returning Crusaders is the romantic answer to explain the changes that took place in the food habits of northern Europeans during that period, and certainly these warriors played an
incalculable role in this regard. The use of all manner of produce that had
hitherto been unknown in northern latitudes—almonds, dates, dried currants, saffron, rose water, pomegranates, peaches, apricots, lemons, or-

---

*Agde is a port city in the ancient province of Languedoc, about sixty kilometers west of
Montpellier, the great medieval center of medical learning. Whether or not it was a returning Crusader who brought the receipt to Agde, the tale indicates that *lo pelau* was considered to be very old, and that it had come from the Levant. The receipt calls for pork—and
needless to say, saffron—so that the dish evolved in the Languedoc much as it did in adjoining Provence. In this and other receipts, Mme. Duconquéré makes a point of *crancas* [fe-
male crabs], *"subretot pas de crancs* [above all no male crabs]," evoking South Carolina
insistence on she-crabs.

anges, and rice, for example, not to mention sugar and most spices other than black pepper—can be attributed to that influence. (Many of those very names are from Arabic or by way of Arabic from the East.) But as regards our particular thesis, there are objections. First, this answer applies to *northern* Europe. Provence is a Mediterranean land and had long been exposed to Eastern influences for that reason, as well as to certain African influences from across the Mediterranean. In addition, there is class. Returning Crusaders who were kings and noblemen were delighted with these Eastern delicacies, enough for them to show up in surviving culinary manuscripts from around 1300 and in royal accounts before that. Even the pilau came to Paris, as we saw earlier, but it soon deteriorated into porridges and puddings, even before it finally seeped down to the popular level. *But this did not happen in Provence; there the pilau not only survived in a classic form but also retained its Persian name.* That is, as I said earlier, I believe that receipts for *angoulée*, effectively a pilau, such as appeared in Parisian manuscripts around 1300 and 1393 (given earlier, p. 38), were also known in aristocratic households in Provence.

But whatever contributory influence returning Crusaders had in this respect, beginning around 1100 with the end of the First Crusade, there were other forces at work there. For one thing, this scenario alone would not explain how pilau became a popular dish; returning foot soldiers, I suspect, were happy to get back to their Christian bread and *la soupe*. (I do not mean to imply that the Arabs did not have wheat bread. Certain wheats originated in Arab lands; others have been cultivated there since early antiquity, and the purposeful making of *raised* bread is believed to have originated in nearby Egypt. But among the Arabs the usual bread was in the form of thin, flat loaves, *pita* bread, still popular all over the Middle East today, not at all like any of the historical breads of France.)

The Arab invasions of France during the eighth century offer an attractive solution to the problem. As noted earlier, there are Arab traces in the various patois of the Midi and in its regional cuisines, particularly in ancient Septimania, a term which by the time the region was occupied by the Arabs referred to a large area of the Midi. The Arabs were stopped in their northward sweep by Charles Martel in 732, when they were actually threatening Tours on the Loire, a historical boundary between northern France and the Midi. I have not studied these invasions, but from the earliest incursions until their armies were ousted from the Midi, the Arabs spent considerable time there. And who knows how many stayed behind?

Nor was that the end of it all. The threat from the south to Frankish domination of greater France continued, not only from the Arabs who had been driven back to Spain but also from "the separatist Christian dukes of Aquitaine, Narbonne, and Provence" (against whom Martel had led a punitive expedition), as put by Robert Harrison in his introduction to *The Song of Roland;* this all led to endlessly convoluted, and finally treacherous, alliances involving the Gascons and the Abbasids of Barcelona (rivals of the Amayyads, who held Saragossa under Marsilla), with the laying waste of parts of Spain, including Christian cities such as Pamplona in Navarre. This particular escapade concluded with the retreat of Charlemagne through the pass at Roncesvals in 778, an event celebrated in *Le Chanson de Roland,* and serving to remind us that history is ever written by those who are finally victorious.[29] That is, Charlemagne, who wreaked havoc in much of the Midi, and Roland, his favorite, are considered *national* heros in France today. The peoples of Provence, Aquitaine, Narbonne, and Gascony may have different ideas on the subject; certainly they did at the time.

In addition, the political borders between Provence and Catalonia shifted back and forth; as noted elsewhere, the Provençals and Catalans had more in common with each other than with either France or Spain, respectively. And, of course, the Crusades dragged on and on, nearly to the end of the thirteenth century, with time out for a bonus crusade to stamp out the Albigensian heresy in the Midi, including Provence, which finally was concluded in 1229 with victory for Paris. (I note that the principles of that movement were formulated by Mani, a Persian born in the third century near Baghdad; not that I think there is any connection with our pilau, but to demonstrate that there were Persians in Baghdad of ancient Mesopotamia, and that there was a great deal more exchange of ideas than many moderns realize. If Manichaeism could take root in the Christian lands of the *langue d'oc,* why not the pilau?)

It is impossible to say with any degree of certainty that the pilau was introduced to Provence as a result of the Arab invasions. There remain certain difficulties with such a construction, among them the use of the term *pilau.* (There is the beguiling term *jambalaia,* discussed earlier, but that is troublesome, although not materially impossible.) What can be said is that such preoccupation with the Saracens—beginning with the invasions and lasting through the Crusades—has to have left its mark from a culinary point of view, preparing the way, as it were, for the adoption of the pilau as a Provençal dish. The composition of the pilau in Provence is not at issue; obviously, pork was not an ingredient at the beginning, whenever and however it was introduced, but otherwise the composition of modern pilaus in Arab lands, as recorded in cookbooks and in practice, at least as I have encountered them in homes and restaurants in the Middle East, is not so different from that found in nineteenth-century Provençal cookbooks. And none of them is all that different from certain versions of the *angoulée* of the fourteenth century, receipts for which appear earlier in this section; that is, they are classic in technique and sober in composition.

PILAU AND THE JEWS OF PROVENCE

Pillau
One pound mutton, three tomatoes,
half pound rice, salt.

Cut up the mutton which must be raw and rather fat, add a little water, and put the stewpan on a slow fire till the meat absorbs the water and is a light brown. Put the tomatoes in a pan without water, and stew till soft. Strain the pulp through a sieve and add one [and?] a half pints of water. Pour this over the mutton, add salt to taste, and boil it up. Wash and dry the rice, put it in the stewpan, let it boil five minutes, and then simmer half an hour.
    —*The Little Book of Jewish Cookery,* London, [1912].

Stewed Rice
Four ounces rice, four tomatoes, a
tablespoonful of oil, salt, pepper,
saffron.

Slice the onion and fry it in the oil till brown, then add a pint of water, salt, pepper, and saffron. Wash the rice and add it with the sliced tomatoes and let all simmer at the side of the stove till the water is absorbed and the rice dry.
    —*The Little Book of Jewish Cookery,* London, [1912].

Riso del Sabato Sabbath Saffron Rice
Risi Gialli [literally, yellow rice]

1¹/₂ cups long-grain rice	¹/₁₆ teaspoon dried saffron
6 tablespoons oil from a roast	salt
3 cups hot broth	pepper

Place rice in a saucepan with the oil and cook, stirring with a wooden spoon, until rice begins to make a sharp, dry noise— approximately 3 minutes. Add 1 cup of hot broth and cook, covered, over high heat for 5 minutes, or until almost all liquid has evaporated. Add a second cup of broth and continue to cook on high heat until rice is almost dry again. Add saffron and the last cup of broth and cook another 5 minutes. Add salt and pepper to taste. Mix well. Remove from heat and spread over a

large flat dish to cool as quickly as possible. Serve at room
temperature.   Serves 6.
—Edda Servi Machlin, in *The Classic Cuisine of the Italian
Jews,* New York, 1981.

Riz au Safran
For 6 people:
a large pinch of saffron
2 tablespoons of olive oil
1 large onion, finely chopped or grated
1 cup raw rice
2 cups hot water
$1/2$ teaspoon freshly grated nutmeg
2 bay leaves
salt
Freshly ground black pepper

Crush the saffron into 2 tablespoons of hot water and let it
stand.
Heat the olive oil in a heavy-bottomed pan. Add the onion,
cover and cook slowly for 3 to 5 minutes, or until the onion
becomes transparent. Add the rice and stir over a low flame until
all the grains are coated with oil. Add the dissolved saffron and 2
cups hot water and stir. Add nutmeg, bay leaves, salt, and pepper.
Bring to a boil, then reduce the heat and simmer, covered, for 15
minutes. All the liquid should be absorbed and the rice tender.
Fluff the rice with a fork and remove the bay leaves. Just before
serving, add a dash of olive oil and check the seasoning again.
You can keep this warm over simmering water until ready to
serve.
—Mireille Johnston, *The Cuisine of the Sun: Classic Recipes
from Nice and Provence,* New York, 1976.[30]

It was not until I studied the work of Louis Stouff that I learned just
how extensive and how important the Jewish presence had been in medieval Provence. His figures on kosher butchers in Arles for 1306—*27 percent of all butchers*—as well as figures for Aix, Avignon, Carpentras,
Grasse, Manosque, and Marseilles, sent me scurrying to the *Encyclopedia
Judaica.* According to that source, their presence in Arles is documented
by A.D. 508, and legend dates it back to the time of the Diaspora, towards
the end of the first century. From our point of view, it is not these early
dates that are so interesting as the fact that there had long existed large
stable communities to which new exiles kept coming. Exasperatingly, few
details are provided on their points of origin, beyond noting that at the

beginning of the twelfth century "a large part of Provence was incorporated into Catalonia, bringing [Jewish] Provençal scholars into contact
with those of Barcelona," and that "many Spanish thinkers [fled] to Provence when Jewish centers in Spain were destroyed" in mid-twelfth
century.

But it is not unreasonable to suppose that many of the Jews of Provence came there directly from the Levant. The presence of Jews in Eastern lands has been known since the Babylonian Captivity (beginning in
the sixth century B.C.) in some instances, and Josephus in the first century
A.D. is cited as saying that, "Jews beyond the Euphrates are an immense
multitude and not estimated by numbers." And, according to the *Encyclopedia Judaica,* "The *Book of the Maccabees* alludes to the existence of
Jews in 'the cities of Persia and Medea.' " Elsewhere, Baghdad, Ahwaz,
Isfahan, and Shiraz are specifically mentioned as having important Jewish centers, and that intermittent waves of repression caused the Jews pe-
riodically to flee to "other parts of the Islamic world." Why not
Provence as well? It is not that there were not periods of repression there
as well, but on the whole, the authorities were relatively tolerant, and
there were long periods of flowering of Jewish culture.

The Jews of Provence were Sephardim, a term loosely designating
not only Spanish Jews but also Oriental Jews, that is, those of the Islamic
world. The *Encyclopedia Judaica* notes that in Provence "a great deal of
effort was expended on the translation of literature from Arabic to He-
brew," particularly in Arles, which would seem to indicate that they had
come from Arab lands. It is often forgotten that historically Arabs and
Jews have always had close—if often troubled—relations, particularly in
the learned professions, medicine above all.

As to food, the same source says that "Sephardi cookery makes
much use of spices, olive oil, rice, pulses, and lamb," noting a penchant
for mint, saffron, garlic, cumin, coriander, and cinnamon. And specifically, "Persian Jews eat rice foods (pilaw) [parentheses original]." In
short, the foods of the Islamic world, and while dietary laws of Jews and
Muslims differ on details of ritual slaughtery—both proscribing pork
however—and the use of shellfish, for example, the fact is that the character of most dishes borrowed by Jews from Muslims would not have
been materially altered. (There is one notable exception, that of certain
molded pilaus, where yoghurt is mixed with the rice and used in conjunction with meat [see chapter 4, "Casseroles"]. But for the most part, it was
simply a matter of avoiding proscribed foods.)

As I wrote earlier, the pilau followed Islam; by extension, this includes those who lived in Islamic lands. I propose that Jews from Persia
played a particular role in the history of the pilau in Provence. But we can

see that there were other contributory forces as well. The pilau was recorded in Paris around 1300 under the name of *angoulée,* a variant of
"Blanc Mengier" (p. 38). (A parallel receipt, *"Manjar Blanch,"* right
down to the wings and feet of *gualines* [the *gelines* of the French version],
appears in *Libre de Sent Sovi,* a Catalan manuscript of the early fourteenth century, as edited by Rudolf Grewe. So the dish could well have
been known in neighboring Provence, particularly considering the historical and linguistic ties.) But in northern France, the *angoulée* soon deteriorated, as noted earlier, while in Provence it took root and prospered,
maintaining a classicism in structure down through the centuries that is
remarkable. Also very telling is the fact that in Provence the old Persian
name of *pilau* was attached to the dish, and so remains to this day in spite
of centuries of effort to abolish the language of Provence.

I have no scientific evidence, but internal evidence is compelling, and
there is a certain amount of corroborative material in the receipts from
modern Jewish cookbooks (given above). The "Pillau" is interesting in
that it is, finally, a pared-down version of the *"Isfānākyïya"* from Baghdad (given earlier, p. 38); that is, there is an inversion of browning and
stewing operations of the meat, and the supplementary ingredients are altogether different, but if one were to substitute spinach for the anachronistic tomatoes, the basic structural relationship would immediately
become evident; even the instructions for taking raw, fat mutton cut into
pieces evoke the instructions from the Baghdad receipt. The lack of saffron in the modern receipt is baffling; I believe that it was inadvertent because it characterizes so many other receipts in the book, including
"Stewed Rice" (above) as well as yet another pilau, "Sausage and Rice."
(Obviously the sausages would not have been of pork.)

I have included three modern receipts for saffron rice to show the extraordinary kinship between two Jewish receipts of different provenance
and what is usually called *riz en pilau* in Provence. "Stewed Rice" is the
least classic in that tomatoes have been added, but that is a detail. I suggest that the pilau receipts in the London work passed by way of Spain.
Mrs. Machlin has been influenced by Italian *risotto* technique in adding
the liquid by degrees, but she specifies long-grain rice in the land of
round rice and does not stir the rice once liquid has been added. She tells
a revealing story involving a Jew of Ferrara in order to "emphasize the
'Jewishness' of *risi gialli"*: a Jew who forgets *risi gialli* is "a person who is
trying to forget his past and his heritage—such as a *nouveau riche* or a
renegade—[hence] is called *risi gialli."* She says that saffron "is said to
have been brought there [to Italy] from Asia Minor by the Jews for their
Sabbath rice." But the dish itself was brought from the East; saffron had
come to the entire Mediterranean in early antiquity. (*Risi gialli* is served at

room temperature in Jewish homes because of Sabbath cooking restrictions.) I find it remarkable that the tradition of saffron rice, as brought by Jews from the East, is found in such close parallel forms in London (ignoring the essentially extraneous tomatoes), Italy, and Provence, the last no longer peculiarly Jewish; indeed, I suspect that its Jewish association in Provence has been largely forgotten.

To show that the days of emigration of Persian dishes with Jews fleeing persecution are not over, I note a receipt *"Persian Rice,"* in *Jewish Cooking from Around the World* (1986) by Josephine Levy Bacon (a book acquired only after the present work had been sent to the publishers). The receipt is prefaced thus: "Many Iranian Jews have come to live in Los Angeles, and this recipe belongs to Hannah Fereydoun of Beverly Hills. Also called *chello,* it is unique." The receipt is essentially the same as that of Nesta Ramazani (cited earlier, pp. 22–23), including the traditional Persian way of soaking the rice overnight and, above all, that of purposefully making a lovely crust on the bottom, "a delicacy," as the writer of the receipt describes it; it differs really only in that oil is used rather than butter so that it may conform to dietary restrictions concerning meat with milk products. If enough Jews from Iran were to settle in Beverly Hills, *chello* and *pollo* could well become local specialties in that region, as I believe happened in medieval Provence, the difference being that we have no such documentation in the case of Provence.

Besides being Sephardim, who were the Jews of Provence? Again drawing on the *Encyclopedia Judaica,* they were "involved in most transactions of wheat and wine. They also traded in spices....[They] cultivated vineyards...as well as market gardens....The number of Jewish physicians in Provence was particularly great." (This is not surprising considering the celebrated medical school, founded in the tenth century, in nearby Montpellier, which was to become a major Huguenot stronghold.) They were also active in money lending. In other words, they must have constituted a fair proportion of the professions and the wealthy merchant class in the cities in which they were numerous. Their having been traders in spices goes far to explain how they got rice and saffron from the East for their pilau.[31]

One can only speculate on how long it might have taken for the pilau to have become a popular dish in Christian Provence, or precisely what the process involved. If the *angoulée* was known in aristocratic households in Provence, as I believe it was, this could have facilitated disperson and eventual popular acceptance of pilau, but I believe that the tradition of the pilau brought by the Jews from Persia was responsible for the historical continuity of the dish and its name. All of this may have taken some time; pilau was not Christian food. Indeed, rice itself was an alien corn.

The following is a digression, but there is a certain parallel between the histories of pilau and of *escabeche*—like pilau a dish borrowed by the Arabs from the Persians—which is illuminating. Hannah Glasse, in *The Art of Cookery* (1796, and perhaps somewhat earlier editions as well), gives a receipt "The Jews Way of preserving Salmon, and all Sorts of Fish," a classic escabeche in all but name. And indeed, she also gives a receipt "To pickle Mackerel, called Caveach," which originally appeared in 1847. There is no reason to doubt that this dish had been brought to England by Jews fleeing the Spanish Inquisition. But the dish had been known in England long before Mrs. Glasse belatedly attributed it to the Jews. Sir Hugh Platt, in *Delightes for Ladies* (1627, and earlier), gives a receipt entitled "Fish kept long, and yet to eat short and delicately" [as compared to salt fish], noting that some would use "the sweetest civill [Seville] oile that you can get," suggesting a Spanish origin, or rather a path by way of Spain. (It should be explained that *escabeche* differs from ordinary pickled or soused fish in that it is fried in olive oil before seasoned vinegar and fresh olive oil are poured over it for keeping.) Receipts for it appeared in manuscripts—the early seventeenth-century English aristocratic family manuscript collection, transcribed and annotated by this writer under the title of *Martha Washington's Booke of Cookery* (1981), for example—and in most popular cookbooks well into the nineteenth century, when its popularity seems to have waned. (Curiously, the *OED*, after duly noting that *caveach* is from Spanish *escabeche*, implies a West Indian origin for the dish, clearly unaware that it had been known in England early enough to have been published before English colonization in the West Indies began, certainly long before a distinctive cuisine would have had time to develop there, let alone be recorded. It is possible, even likely, that *caveach*, the word, was a charming West Indian corruption, perhaps from Spanish-speaking neighbors. That is, I find the dish in the first years of the seventeenth century in England but no form of the word until well into the eighteenth century, when *caveach* appeared. A receipt "To pickle Mackrel," a perfectly proper escabeche, appears in *The Compleat Housewife* by E. Smith in the Williamsburg edition of 1742, so the dish early came to the Colonies. A receipt "To Pickle Mackerel Call'd Caveech'd," an all but verbatim copy of the 1747 receipt by Mrs. Glasse, appears in the receipt book of Eliza Lucas Pinckney, dated 1756, and was duly copied by her daughter Harriott Pinckney Horry when she started her own collection in 1770. This last receipt was copied word for word for inclusion in *The Carolina Housewife* (1847); only spelling and punctuation were tidied up a bit.[32]

What I have been trying to say is that even a tiny minority can introduce a dish to a larger community if conditions are propitious. In the case
of escabeche, the receipt provided a palatable way of keeping fish for
some time, a matter of incalculable interest in the days before refrigeration. (I might note here that the first time I encountered escabeche was in
the home of a Jewish neighbor whose mother had come from Romania,
so that the dish survives among Jews on a traditional level. It also came to
be adopted as a bit of exotica in the United States some decades ago.)
Reasons for the adoption of pilau in Provence are less apparent, and certainly less compelling than those that obtained later in the Carolina rice
lands, where new receipts for rice would have been eagerly sought after.
Still, the dish did historically become popular in Provence, and I believe
that it had been brought by Jews from Persia, either directly or by way of
Barcelona.

> *"Ris a l'amelo,"* plat traditionnel que mangent les juifs du
> *Midi dans leur carnaval qu'ils appellent Pourim.* [Rice with
> almonds, the traditional dish eaten by Jews of the Midi during
> their carnival, which they call Purim.]
> —Frédéric Mistral, *Lou Tresor Dóu Felibrige* [1878–1886].[33]

As noted earlier, Stouff does not mention the pilau, at least not by
name, nor any dishes peculiarly associated with the Jews except in the
narrow sense of kosher butchering and making of wine. He does, however, mention a number of rice dishes, one of which is *"rissum cum lacte
amicdalarum et puluere cynamomi* [rice with almond milk and powdered
cinnamon," translated by him simply as *"riz au lait d'amandes,"* or "rice
with almond milk"], served at a convent in Avignon in the fourteenth
century, and at the table of the archbishop of Arles in the fifteenth century. This is, of course, one of the fast-day versions of *blanc mengier* or
angoulée for which I earlier gave receipts (pp. 38–39), one from around
1300, the other about 1393. It will be recalled that *angoulée* is a pilau.

"Rice with almonds" is also a dish specifically associated with Sephardic Jews, a highly useful one in that it provides a rich, creamy, sweet
dish that is permitted in conjunction with meat because the "milk" is
from almonds. (There is a receipt for such a dish, "Almond Rice," in *The
Jewish Manual,* London, 1846.) It is particularly associated with Purim, it
would seem, at least in Provence, a nice touch, since Purim is a spring
feast commemorating Esther and her having contrived to have the Jews
of Persia delivered from a general massacre planned by Haman, the villain of the story, all this back in the sixth century B.C. Certainly the dish
has to have originated in a land of rice and almonds. The fact that it

graced the table of an archbishop in medieval Provence suggests long acceptance, however the dish was brought to Provence, whether by returning Crusaders or by Jews from Persia.

Another entry, *"In safrano ad ponendum in riso"* [loosely, "saffron for putting in rice"], dated 1383, from a convent in Avignon, definitively documents the addition of saffron to rice in medieval Provence; it is otherwise uninformative, but considering that saffron characterizes the fourteenth-century receipts earlier given for *angoulée*, a pilau, it seems reasonable to suggest that the entry concerns such a dish.

Although, I cannot say when the pilau became sufficiently naturalized in Provence to acquire its characteristic note of *petit salé*, or pickled pork, it had to have happened well before the last quarter of the seventeenth century, before the Huguenots fled France for South Carolina. The pilaus of Provence and Carolina as recorded in cookbooks, beginning in 1837 and 1845, respectively, are parallel receipts in all basic respects; only in details of composition do they differ, the only one of importance being the disappearance of saffron. (It also disappeared from the jambalaya of New Orleans, as noted earlier.)

I should note that Harriet McDougal, granddaughter of our own Mrs. Stoney, tells me that there is speculation in some circles in South Carolina that among the original Huguenot proprietors there had been some who were issue of *conversos,* that is, Jews who had converted to Christianity in Spain under the Inquisition but who finally fled to neighboring Provence after all, as the ruthless extirpation of *conversos,* and suspected *conversos,* continued down the centuries. Many, perhaps most, of them had come from the East originally, including Persia, and they could well have provided a link to the Christian population of Provence with regard to the pilau. Certainly it is not unreasonable to suppose that the *conversos* would have tended to gravitate toward the dissidents who became Protestants rather than toward supporters of the church militant. However, I believe that this would have been too late to have had much influence beyond reinforcing, perhaps, that of the Jews of Provence in this regard. That is, I believe that the pilau had long been a naturalized Provençal dish by that time. I recount this because I find it intriguing that South Carolinians have considered the possibility of *conversos* having been among their Huguenot forebears.

The story of Huguenot involvement with rice would not be complete without mentioning their role in seventeenth-century attempts to grow rice in the Camargue of Provence. It was the duke of Sully, finance minister to Henry IV, and Olivier de Serres, the king's agricultural advisor, who were responsible for those efforts, all three Huguenots. (That is, Henry of Navarre had reneged in order to become king of Catholic

France with his celebrated decision that, "Paris is well worth a mass.") As Waverley Root remarks, "Huguenots must have had a special affinity for rice...." I have not done independent research on this aspect of the question, but the Protestantism of the principals is a matter of record, and Root cites a decree of August 23, 1603, directing that such a project be undertaken.[34] The connection may not be significant, but it is interesting. Be it also noted that Henry and de Serres were of the Midi, although not of Provence.

CHAPTER 4

The Rice Casseroles of South Carolina

To make a Cassorol or rather a rice pye
In the first place you must have a copper Pan well tined. A Tin pan will not do —Boil 3 pints of rice rather softer than you do rice in Common. grease the pan well with Butter and press it (the rice) well into the pan round the sides and bottom and top and put to Bake at the fire turning it round constantly as it will burn. When it is of a good light brown turn it out on a Dish and cut out in the middle in the middle [sic] sufficient to make room for a rich Fill or veal or anything you please.
> —*The Receipt Book of Harriott Pinckney Horry,* 1770, Hampton Plantation, South Carolina, transcribed by Richard J. Hooker, 1984. (Parentheses original; editorial *"[sic]"* added by Hooker.)

Castrole
Braise whatever meat you desire; after having drained it, dress it on a platter, and place around it rice that has been nicely cooked in a bouillon further fortified with [unsmoked] bacon. Pour over all a little rendered back fat; smooth it nicely with a knife so that it has the form of a nice round cake. Bake in a good hot oven so that a golden crackling crust will form; drain off the excess fat, and serve dry.
> —*Dictionnaire Portatif de Cuisine,* Paris, 1772.

A Pillaw of Veal
Take a neck or breast of veal, half roast it, then cut it into six pieces, season it with pepper, salt, and nutmeg; take a pound of rice, put to it a quart of broth, some mace, and a little salt, do it over a stove or very slow fire till it is thick, but butter the bottom of the dish or pan you do it in; beat up the yolks of six eggs and stir into it; then take a little round deep dish, butter it, lay some of the rice at the bottom, then lay the veal on a round heap, and cover it all over with rice, wash it over with the yolks of eggs, and bake it an hour and a half; then open the top and pour in a pint

of rich good gravy. Garnish with a Seville orange cut in quarters, and send it to table hot.
—Hannah Glasse, in *The Art of Cookery,* London, 1796.

Carrole of Rice

Take some well-picked rice, wash it well, and boil it five minutes in water, strain it, and put it into a stew pan, with a bit of butter, a good slice of ham, and an onion. Stew it over a very gentle fire till tender; have ready a mould lined with very thin slices of bacon: mix the yolks of two or three eggs with the rice, and then line the bacon with it about half an inch thick; put into it a ragout of chicken, rabbit, veal, or anything else. Fill up the mould, and cover it close with rice. Bake it in a quick oven an hour, turn it over [on a serving plate], and sent it to table in a good gravy, or curry sauce.
—Maria Eliza Rundell, in *A New System of Domestic Cookery,* New York, 1817.

Rice Edging, for a Currie, or Fricassee

After soaking and picking fine Carolina rice, boil it in water, and a little salt, until tender, but not to a mush; drain, and put it round the inner edge of the dish, to the height of two inches; smooth it over with the yolk of egg, and put it into the oven for three or four minutes, then serve the meat in the middle.
—Maria Eliza Rundell, in *A New System of Domestic Cookery,* New York, 1817.[1]

THESE RICE CASSEROLES AND PIES of Carolina constitute a particular category of pilau, an important one as shown by thirteen receipts in Mrs. Stoney's collection. Although poorly differentiated by their names in the cookbooks, as can be seen in the title of Harriott Horry's receipt, there are three types that are actually rather different one from the other. In its most elaborated form, the casserole is a crisp golden shell which serves as an edible container for an elegant presentation of a *ragoût,* much in the manner of the *timbale* and *vol-au-vent* of *haute cuisine.* Judging by its name and history, I believe that this particular version was developed in France. There are early French receipts for *casserole* made of bread; such a receipt is given by L. Liger in 1715, for example. And in 1815 Carême gave a receipt *"Casserole au Riz à la Moderne,"* suggesting that versions of it had long been known, perhaps on the order of that earlier recorded by Mrs. Horry. He described it thus: "The rice casserole is an *entrée* as elegant as it is rich; its form and especially its appetizing aspect give it a distinctive character.... [It] is the very model of beautiful

golden-crusted *entrées."* The receipt for the crust alone is more than three
pages long, not including plates showing decorative designs. In brief:
Carolina rice is cooked in bouillon until it bursts, then worked and
shaped, using a suitable form of four to five inches in height and seven in
diameter. It is then decorated, brushed with clarified butter, and baked
until it becomes a vibrant gold in color, when it is ready to be filled. He
calls for Carolina rice, he says, because "it alone is suitable for this sort
of work...as the rice of Piedmont does not have enough consistency."
      Certainly Mrs. Horry's receipt of sometime after 1770 is less elabo-
rate than that of the greatest pastry chef in French history, but it shows
that the rice casserole must have been in significantly wider use in France
than would be evident from purusing French cookbooks. (The Horry
family was of French Huguenot lineage, so that there is no mystery
there.) I find no vestige of this particular casserole in either French or
Provençal cookbooks, but that is not necessarily conclusive. I dare not
speculate as to how prevalent it was in Carolina, nor how long it lasted.
Sarah Rutledge did not include a receipt for it in 1847 and, again, while
this absence is not conclusive, it is suggestive. She noted in her preface
that her work was "a selection from the family receipt books of friends
and acquaintances," making a point of the fact that "nearly a hundred
dishes in which rice or corn form part of the ingredients" had been included. Directions for roasting, boiling, frying, etc., had not been included, she said, because they "are found in Miss Leslie's excellent
'Directions for Cookery.' " In short, Miss Rutledge recognized the peculiar genius of South Carolina cookery and set about to record it. Some
fifty-three receipts include rice as the characterizing ingredient, and it
would have been strange had she not included one for such an imposing
dish if it was still in fashion.
      Even in France the days of Carême's *"Casserole au Riz à la Moderne"*
of 1815 were numbered; I do not find it in Escoffier, for example, and the
Nouveau Larousse Gastronomique (1967) discusses it under *"Casserole au
Riz à l'ancienne."* But I did find a receipt for it, "Rice Casserole," in a
highly unlikely source, *The Cook's Own Book* (1832), by "A Boston
Housekeeper," that is patently a somewhat shortened translation of the
Carême receipt.[2]
      With all its éclat, Carême's casserole has more to do with the art of
making pastry than that of making pilau. Yet there is a historical relationship, particular to Mrs. Horry's receipt. This becomes evident with the
version given by Mrs. Blake, which she calls "Rice Pie [1]" (F 59-60); it is
this version that resembles *Kateh Ghalebi,* a molded rice dish of Persia,
for which Nesta Ramazani's receipt calls for lining a ring mold with a
mixture of cooked rice, melted butter, raw egg yolks, and yoghurt, then

dribbling butter over all before baking. The golden-crusted rice is unmolded, and serves to present an aromatic stew. There are certain differences in detail, but the kinship is striking.

Mrs. Rundell's receipt "Rice Edging" is something of a variation on
the above; its importance to us lies in its structural similarity to one given
by Mrs. C. N. West, which she calls *"Cassereau"* (F 69). The composition
is different, but the two versions serve the same function, that of a
crisped edging for the presentation of a stew.

There are eleven more receipts for molded rice dishes presented in
Mrs. Stoney's work; I would like to call them *pies* but, as I noted, they are
poorly differentiated. These pies differ from Mrs. Blake's version discussed above in that the baking dish is lined with cooked rice which has
been enriched with butter, and usually egg or egg yolk as well; a seasoned
stew or fricassee is placed therein, then all is covered with more of the enriched rice before being baked to a golden brown in the oven. The top is
occasionally gilded with egg yolk. This type harks back to the *Tah-Chin*
[literally "arranged on the bottom of the pan," according to Mrs. Rama-
zani] of Persian cookery, where the boiled rice is enriched with egg yolks
and yoghurt, as before. The most elaborate versions, such as the receipt
"Dami Ghalebi ba Morgh," call for scenting the enriched rice with saffron, alternating layers of this rice with cooked chicken, soaked dried
apricots, peaches, prunes, currants, dates, and walnuts, all covered with
the same rice, and melted butter dribbled over; the whole is then baked in
the oven for about an hour. The idea is to have as much crusty *tah-dig* as
possible, top and bottom.

The *Carrole, Castrole,* and *Pillaw* (above) are versions of this type, as
is Durand's Provençal receipt *"Riz en pilau"* of 1837 (given earlier, pp.
52–53). The one for *Carrole,* I believe, comes from a Carolina source;
Mrs. Rundell gives a number of receipts from American sources (for
breads, in particular), including receipts for rice. I also believe that Mrs.
Glasse got her receipt for *pillaw* from Carolina; that is, there are absolutely no Eastern touches whatsoever, not even saffron—the orange being
simply a garnish—and the technique is in line with practice in Carolina.
Nor does she call it Indian. (The wonder is that she was able to set it
down straight, considering her ludicrous receipts for Indian *Pellow* described earlier.) While the usual term in Carolina for this preparation was
either some form of *casserole* or *pie,* there is Miss Rutledge's "French
Pilau" (F 51), as well as the "Shrimp Pilau" (F 67) of Mrs. Huger; both
receipts I believe to have come from Carolina Huguenot families. This is
also in line with Durand's Provençal receipt for *"Riz en pilau."*

The *"Castrole"* I believe to be a receipt from Provence and its frac-
tured spelling an error in interlingual transmission, a misreading by the

Parisian editors of the dictionary of a Provençal form of *casserole*, the proper French term. (Much the same also happened with Mrs. Rundell's *Carrole*, but here I believe the Provençal form to have come by way of South Carolina.)

It will be helpful to examine the use of the term *casserole* for a moment. In the culinary jargon of the French establishment a *casserole* is a stewpan *à queue*, meaning "supplied with a single straight handle"; its use to designate an edible container is rare and quite specialized; to use it referring to a baking dish or its contents is rarer still. This is in Paris. In the Midi, things are different. Mistral defines one form, *cassola*, as an earthenware pot, but also as "a dish that one cooks in a baking dish in the oven; it is composed of rice or groats [*gruau*, which in context can refer to virtually any whole grain], seasoned with tripe sausage or *petit salé* [pickled pork], and is held in high esteem in the Cévennes." (The Cévennes, be it remembered, is adjacent to Provence and constituted one of the most important Huguenot strongholds.) He also refers the reader to *"Tian de sardino, pilau de sardines."* That is, *tian* and *cassola* both have a strong connection with pilau and with rice generally. (Both pots are earthenware, but the *tian* is larger and shallower than the *cassola*.) He cites, for example, a Provençal proverb *"I'a de ris au tian."* It is of more than passing interest in this regard that the etymologist Joan Corominas says that forms of *cazo* and *cacerola* (alternative Spanish forms meaning a "stewpan") are common to the Iberian languages and the many *langues d'oc;* the origin, he says, is uncertain, but he suggests Arabic *qasca,* translated as *gamella* [pan], among other meanings. One *langue d'oc* form is *casso,* parallel to Spanish *cazo,* for example, and there are myriad variants. Considering the historical Arab presence in those two areas and the unfixed vowels in Arabic, I find Corominas surprisingly cautious in his proposal. (I note that American use of the term *casserole* is closer to that in the Midi in that we always use it to designate a baking dish or its contents rather than a cooking pot with a handle.)

It will be seen that the *Castrole* is related to *le rizotte* of Toulon, referred to earlier (p. 58), except that the *Castrole* is gratinéed, as are, of course, most of these molded pilaus, whether they be Persian, Provençal, or South Carolinian. As noted earlier, Miss Rutledge's receipt for "French Pilau" (F 51) is perhaps the classic Carolinian type. There are important differences in detail, but the historical kinship with the Persian type is close, in that the rice is well buttered after being cooked in broth, as for pilau, and the top is further gilded with egg yolk. (This receipt is repeated, wrongly attributed to Mrs. Hill [F 55].) Again, in her receipt "Rice Pie [1]" (F 57), she suggests adding a raw egg yolk to the rice mixture, echoing Persian practice, and the presence of hard-cooked eggs harks back to a similar use in *A Baghdad Cookery Book.*

Mrs. Hill gives a receipt "Rice Chicken Pie" (F 57–58) in which the top layer of rice is not enriched in any way, a culinary error in that it will dry out rather than develop a nice crust. Mrs. Stoney's "Walworth Chicken and Rice Pie" (F 58) is a layered rice pie; here the rice is enriched by pouring the juices of the chicken, fortified with butter if indicated, over the top of the rice so that it will become "crisp." Mrs. Huger's receipt *"Cassereau"* (F 63) differs from these receipts essentially only in that the rice is enriched with "a rich tomato sauce" and additional butter. (I suggest that *cassereau* is a "French" spelling of *cassoro,* a *langue d'oc* form recorded by Mistral, of which it is a homophone. This is interesting, because it shows that the *langue d'oc* was fading, so Carolinians, even French Huguenot Carolinians, came to use what they considered to be proper French spellings of all-but-forgotten words. That is, the *Cassorol* of Mrs. Horry (above) is not a misspelling of *casserole* but a *langue d'oc* variant.)

Miss Rutledge's receipt "Rice Pie [2]" (F 59) calls for enriching the rice with butter, eggs, and nearly a pint of milk, a technique that seems to be reserved for use with pieces of raw, rather than previously cooked, chicken or meat. The use of milk in the rice mixture is not structurally different from the use of yoghurt in Persian receipts of the same type; the difference in flavor, however, is great. Obviously, extra fluid is needed to compensate for evaporation due to longer cooking time, and milk improves the quality of the crust. (I note here that Jewish law forbids the use of milk with meat, a question that must be addressed in light of what I believe to be Jewish association with the pilau in Provence; however, this stricture applies only to the meat of mammals, so that milk products may be used with chicken. As for the shrimp dishes of this type, shrimps are not permitted at all. In Carolina, shrimps effectively replaced the mussels, so popular in Provençal pilaus.)[3] The directions in Mrs. Dill's receipt for "Rice Pie" (F 59) are highly elliptical; I must suppose that they were understood to follow the procedure more completely outlined in the previous receipt on the same page and again in Mrs. Blake's receipt for "Rice Pie [2]" (F 60).

Mrs. Huger uses the same technique of enriching the rice in her receipt "Shrimp Pilau" (F 67), in which the shrimps are used raw. This is a layered pie. (One plate of shrimps equals one pint, according to *Old Receipts from Old St. John's* [1920s, according to John Taylor].) Concerning her receipt "Shrimp Pie" (F 67), I must again suppose that her directions are elliptical and that the usual procedure for rice pie is understood. Miss

Taft gives a receipt "Shrimp Pie" (F 68) in which she enriches the rice with a pound of butter, three eggs, and both tomato juice and milk, thus not only acidulating the milk but also enhancing the rosy color of this shrimp dish. This is one gargantuan pie; most of us would halve the amounts, or even quarter them, for ordinary use.

I find no evidence of any of these splendid casseroles and pies having spread from the Low Country, at least not sufficiently to have made a lasting impression. Even in *The Picayune's Creole Cook Book* (1901) I find only an inept receipt "A French Pilou," calling for only one-half cup of rice for two chickens, pathetically little; this in addition to an undistinguished "Rice Border." Elsewhere in the United States historical receipts for rice casserole or rice ring are mushy concoctions with no relationship to the rice casseroles of South Carolina, certainly not an Epicurean one. I have the feeling that rice pie is not as popular in South Carolina as it used to be. There is no receipt in *Charleston Receipts* (1950) and only one in *The South Carolina Cook Book* (copyright 1954), that attributed to Mum Rosie and perfectly classic, as well it might be since she is presumably African-American. Use of the old slave names died hard.[4]

Practical Notes: I strongly urge the use of yoghurt in place of milk when making the rice pies involving the use of raw meat or fowl, as in Miss Rutledge's "Rice Pie [2]," Mrs. Dill's "Rice Pie" (both F 59), Mrs. Huger's "Shrimp Pilau" (F 67), etc. Not only is it Persian practice, but also I believe that in the early days of those Carolina rice pies the milk was more often clabbered than not, given the climate and state of refrigeration. This is strongly supported by the statement of Anna Pinckney in the interview cited in an earlier chapter (p. 4) to the effect that as a child she "drank clabbered or slightly soured milk from the family cow." Naturally clabbered milk—that is, milk that has been neither pasteurized nor subjected to immediate chilling—is delicious, with a taste and texture not all that different from the yoghurts in the Middle East, which are incomparable. Modern milk has a flat taste that gives rice pies the taste of unsweetened rice pudding, really rather dull, and this fact might account for the decline in popularity of these scrumptious and imposing dishes. They are made with surprisingly little effort. So try using yoghurt, *plain* yoghurt and the most natural you can find, and taste the difference. At the least, add a spoonful or so of lemon juice to each cup of milk to approximate the delightfully tart note of the rice pies of yesteryear.

In these same pies, those calling for chicken are more successful than those calling for shrimp, because the shrimp tends to get overcooked by the time the rice has developed a lovely golden crust; I have made them successfully, but this factor must be taken into consideration; chicken is more forgiving in this regard. In this day of chicken parts, I suggest using pieces all of a kind for even cooking.

Some of the rice mixtures are not buttery enough; Mrs. Dill's receipt calls for rather a lot, but Miss Rutledge's "spoonful of butter" for a quart of raw rice is simply not enough for nice crust formation, even assuming that it was a large heaping spoonful.

CHAPTER 5

Hoppin' John and Other Bean Pilaus of the African Diaspora

Shūrbā

Cut fat meat into middling pieces. Dissolve fresh tail [sheep tail fat], and throw away the sediment. Put the meat into the oil, and stir until browned. Cover with lukewarm water, and add a little salt, a handful of peeled chick-peas, small pieces of cinnamon bark, and some sprigs of dry dill. When the meat is cooked, throw in dry coriander [seeds], ginger and pepper, brayed fine. Add more lukewarm water, and put over a hot fire until thoroughly boiling: then remove the dill from the saucepan. Take cleaned rice, wash several times, and put into the saucepan as required, leaving it over the fire until the rice is cooked: then remove from the fire. Sprinkle with fine-brayed cummin and cinnamon. Wipe the sides of the pot with a clean rag, leave over the fire for an hour, and then remove. Do not leave so long that the rice becomes hard set [dried out]. If desired, add some cabobs of minced meat.

—Muhammad ibn al-Hasan ibn Muhammad ibn al-Karīm al-Kātib al-Baghdādī, 1226. Translated from the Arabic as *A Baghdad Cookery Book* by A. J. Arberry, 1939. (Material in brackets added by K. H.)

Yoo-ke-Omo (from Ga, Ghana)
1 cup cooked black-eyed peas
1 teaspoon ginger
Same ingredients as for *Plain Rice*

Use stock from cooked beans and some water. Stir in ginger powder and beans when butter is added. Excellent with meat or fish dishes.

Omo (Plain Rice—"The Perfect Recipe")

4 cups water	1 teaspoon butter or
1 level teaspoon salt	margarine, or ¼
3 cups uncooked long-grain rice	cup cooking oil

Bring salted water to boil.

Wash rice three times in cold water and then add to boiling water. Add butter. Bring to boil again immediately. Stir once, then cover with a tight-fitting lid. Reduce heat to very low and allow to cook slowly, undisturbed, for 20 minutes. Turn heat off. Remove from burner.

Without lifting the lid, allow rice to steam dry for another 10 minutes. Serve while rice is still hot.

—Dinah Ameley Ayensu (Ghanaian diplomat), in *The Art of West African Cooking*, 1972.

Hopping John

One pint of red peas, one pint of rice, one pound of bacon—let the bacon come to a boil in two quarts of water—skim it—add the peas: boil slowly. When tender, add the rice: let it boil until the rice is well swollen and soft.—Season with red pepper and salt. If liked perfectly dry, it can be steamed, as in boiling rice plain. Serve it with the bacon on top. Salt must be added when nearly done.

—Theresa Brown, in *Modern Domestic Cookery*, Charleston, 1871.

Hopping John

Take a handful of cow peas (small black peas) that have been soaked over night, one onion, parsley and a laurel leaf. Let them boil in a quart and a pint of water for an hour, or until soft. Add two cupfuls well washed raw rice. The rice must cook fifteen or twenty minutes. Then add a quarter of a pound of well-fried sausages, a slice of ham and a small piece of bacon, both cut in pieces and fried. Put your saucepan aside to soak, or dry. Cover closely, Be careful it does not burn at the bottom. If the rice has to be stirred use a fork, as it turns easily, and still can not be stirred too much, or it becomes soggy. Those old-fashioned black pots are the best to use.

—"Uncle John," S[outh] C[arolina]. [Elsewhere described as "the best chef in South Carolina, Mr. Le Garee's and Mrs. Phoenix's cook"], as cited in *Cooking in Old Créole Days* by Célestine Eustis, 1904.

Hoppin' John

On New Year's Day all will have to have green collards for
dinner and "Hoppin John." Tradition says collards will bring you
green-backs and "Hoppin' John" small change the year round—if
they are eaten on New Year's Day. Mrs. M. B. Hutchinson,
Abbeville County uses the recipe given by her kinsman Irvin S.
Cobb in 1900:

"To make 'Hoppin' John,' you take some leftover cold boiled
rice that has been boiled in an iron pot and every grain standing
out like popcorn. Mix your rice with cold boiled Crowder peas—
only upcountry about fifty miles they'd be called black-eyed peas
or in some sections whippoorwill peas. Stir these together and fry
with sweet butter in a hot skillet. And don't bet you won't pass
your plate back for a second helping!"

    —*The South Carolina Cook Book*, South Carolina
    Extension Home-Makers Council, 1984.

At Mars Bluff [South Carolina], Hoppin' John was rice, field
peas (cowpeas), and salt pork cooked together. Everyone at Mars
Bluff had to eat Hoppin' John and hog jowl for dinner on New
Year's Day. Whoever did not eat both would have bad luck all
year.—Have you noticed that Webster's Dictionary calls Hoppin'
John "a stew?" I hope you set them straight.

    —Amelia Wallace Vernon, 1990. Mars Bluff is in the Pine
    Belt, six miles east of Florence, she says.[1]

IN THE UNITED STATES, particularly outside of the South,
dishes featuring rice and beans are largely considered to be lowly fare, all
very well as ethnic manifestations, which have lately taken on an inverse
sort of chic, but hardly cuisine. This is not true in the highly sophisticated
cuisines of Asia. Persian receipts for *pollo* and related rice dishes feature
lentils, fava beans, red kidney beans, yellow split peas, lima beans, and
black-eye peas, just to name examples from a single Persian cookbook.
Rice eaters of antiquity did not need nutritionists to tell them that beans
and rice constituted sound nutrition; such dishes are not only cheap and
nourishing but also delicious, and they have been treasured by rich and
poor alike in those lands, probably for millennia.

In the Americas rice-and-bean dishes are associated primarily with
peoples of African ancestry, and with justice. First, there is reason to believe that in the rice lands of Africa such dishes had long existed, as they
exist in all rice lands. And considering the long cultivation of indigenous
strains of rice and of beans (*Vigna unguiculata* L., variously known as

cowpeas, black-eye peas, etc., and *Cajanus cajan,* variously known as *Angola* or *Congo peas, pigeon peas,* etc.), along with the considerable Muslim presence in Africa, it would be surprising had rice and beans not been combined in dishes using the technique of pilau.

In this regard, I remind the reader that I earlier (p. 12) cited Littlefield concerning Arab "travelers...[who] made numerous references to the presence and use of rice in the Sudan." Perhaps the extent of Arab penetration into Africa can be further highlighted by the role of African armies as recounted in *The Song of Roland,* the poetic account of the battle at Roncesvals in 778. Fighting under the command of the Arabs was "an African called Malquiant, the son of King Malcus. His arms and armor, all of gold inlay, above all others' flash against the sky." The troops, which "number more than fifty thousand," are described as being "blacker than ink and have no white about them, save their teeth," as well as having broad noses. (I cite from Robert Harrison's translation.) In other words, they were definitely African, not simply swarthy Arabs. Even assuming that the number of African troops grew in the telling, they constituted an entire "battle corps," always according to this account. More important than numbers is the fact that the ancient *chanson* depicts an African contingent, the mustering of which bespeaks considerable Arab activity in Africa, which must have antedated the battle of Roncesvals in 778.[2] In France, there are scattered proper nouns as far north as Tours on the Loire evoking *tête-de-nègre* [head of a Negro], as well as *tête-de-maure* [head of a Moor], names generally thought to go back to the Arab invasions early in that century.

In addition to the receipt *"Shūrbā,"* a classic bean pilau using chickpeas (above) from the Baghdad manuscript of 1226, there are others; *"Mulabbaqa"* calls for "half rice, and half lentils, pulse and skinned chick-peas," for example. The meat is mutton, the beans are not the same, but the *structure* is that of hoppin' John. By itself, given the vexing problem of "return influence," the present existence of dishes like hoppin' John in West Africa is not necessarily conclusive. (Regarding the problem of return influence, three of Africa's staples are from the New World: maize, peanuts, and cassava or manioc, this in addition to such products as tomatoes and various *Capsicum* peppers. This happened so soon after the voyages of discovery had started that there was long confusion on their origin, particularly with regard to peanuts, for example, which were brought to North America by way of Africa, where they had been brought by Portuguese slave traders from Brazil.)

But more compelling is the fact that every area in the New World that historically has had a large African presence—Cuba, Brazil, and

South Carolina, for instance—has its particular version of rice and bean dishes, some simple mixtures of rice and beans, but many of them cooked in the manner of a pilau. In the beginning, the choice of bean may have been more or less serendipitous in some cases; in others, it may have reflected the cultural preferences of the African slaves, insofar as they had a choice. It is beyond the scope of this work to detail these dishes, but to name even a few will illustrate this point: "Rice and Peas" [pigeon peas] of Jamaica; "*Pois et Riz Collés*" [red beans and rice together] of Haiti; "*Moros y Cristianos*" [black beans] of western Cuba; "*Congris*" [red beans] of eastern Cuba; "*Jambalaya au Congris*" [cowpeas] of New Orleans; and the "*Feijoada*" [the gargantuan festival dish featuring black beans, many meats, and rice] of Brazil.[3] The *feijoda* apart, these rice and bean dishes are made pretty much the same way as is a pilau, yet each has a distinctive note, with the division of Cuba into black and red bean areas being perhaps the most intriguing.

And from the slave owners' point of view, rice and beans provided cheap, filling, nutritious food, food for which the supplies could be grown by the slaves on a sustenance basis. The pigeon pea of Africa became "so well naturalized [in the Antilles] that it passes for being native," according to the French botanist F. R. Tussac (1808–1827). Writing of black-eye peas in 1756, P. Browne said: "The seeds serve to feed the negros; and are frequently used by the poorer sort of white people; they are observed to be a hearty wholesome food." And J. Lunan, writing of American kidney beans (*Phaeseolus vulgaris* L.) in 1814, reported: "The pods of which, in their young state, are served up by way of greens, under the name of French beans. When dry the seeds are an excellent food for negros." A nice distinction. M. Catesby in 1754 speaks of several varieties of kidney beans in Carolina, noting that "they are also of great use for feeding Negroes, being strong hearty food."

As for the rice, its story must be somewhat different in different places. But I suspect that there was a good deal more cultivation of rice for the farmers themselves to eat than has generally been realized. We know that this took place in South Carolina on an individual basis. Eliza B. K. Dooley says in her *Puerto Rican Cookbook* (1950) that "the rice grown in Puerto Rico is an upland rice," meaning rice that is grown more or less as are other grains.[4] Such rice is particularly amenable to subsistence farming methods. We shall return to this question.

The African-American rice and bean dish of South Carolina is hoppin' John. It features what are variously called cowpeas, red peas, small black peas, field peas, and black-eye peas in receipts of Carolina provenance, not to forget the Crowder peas and whippoorwill peas noted by Cobb.

WHAT ABOUT ALL THOSE NAMES?

Popular nomenclature for legumes or pulse is hopelessly confused; the same plant may be known by several different names and, conversely, the same name may designate different plants in different areas. Not even the terms *pea* and *bean* are well differentiated, as illustrated by black-eye peas, which are more like beans, although not related either to *Phaeseolus vulgaris* of the New World or to *Vicia faba*, the broad bean of the Old World (which originated in the Mediterranean but spread widely very early). That said, it is always *peas* that are used for hoppin' John (not garden peas *[Pisum sativum]*, however).

Nor are the botanists in agreement. In the authoritative *Dictionary of Plants Used by Man* (1974), George Usher places catjang, black-eye pea, and Hindu cowpea under *Vigna catjang* Walp., noting Old World tropics as place of origin, which is not very specific. Under *V. unguiculata* (previously *V. sinensis*) he places the cowpea, horse gram, and cherry bean, with Central Africa given as place of origin. William Ed Grimé, in *Ethno-Botany of the Black Americans* (1979), places black-eye peas, red peas, cowpeas, and calavances under *V. unguiculata*. And he cites R. W. Schery (1952) thus: "Peas in the Deep South of the United States invariably means cowpeas or black-eyed peas *Vigna sinensis*. Actually, this species is more related to beans than to peas. It was introduced into the West Indies from central Africa, and thence into the Carolinas before the early 1700's." And in the late nineteenth century E. Lewis Sturtevant wrote of *V. catjang*: "In the southern states, this species has many permanent varieties, as Red Cowpea, Black-eye pea, and so on. *So conspicuous is this species that in some localities it is made to carry the name of all others, all being referred to as the cowpea* [emphasis added]."

With the botanists in such disarray, it is small wonder that there is no agreement on the popular level, particularly when dealing with historical receipts. But there are occasional clues. Under *V. unguiculata* Grimé cites Lunan (1814) thus: "Calavances, or red bean, and black-betty...the bean of the former is red, that of the latter is black. They are both wholesome food, of which the negroes in general are very fond." So the "cow peas (small black peas)" specified by "Uncle John" in his receipt (above) must be Lunan's "black-betty." And in a letter dated 1796 Thomas Jefferson asks Edward Rutledge, a signer of the Declaration of Independence and father of our Sarah Rutledge, to obtain for him "a red field pea commonly cultivated with you, and a principal article for the subsistence of your farms, which we have not yet introduced...."[5] So these must be the "red peas" called for in *The Carolina Housewife* receipt for "Hopping John" (F 60–61). Mrs. Blake also calls for "cow (or red) peas" in her receipt (F 61).

In any specific district the inhabitants will insist that there is only one proper pea for hoppin' John, the one that is used there, with its own name. But there must have been a number of varieties of *V. unguiculata* in use in the Low Country, although it does seem that the red or black peas were traditionally favored. While closely related, all those peas are surprisingly different in flavor and other characteristics. In practice people in any given corner of the South *know* which pea to use, and as far as the rest of the country is concerned, black-eye peas are generally the most easily available.

Now for the name *hoppin' John*. Most of the proposed origins are demeaning to African-Americans, representing pop etymology of a low order. Even a serious one from *Webster's Ninth New Collegiate Dictionary* (1983) suggesting that it comes by way of "folk etymology" from French *pois de pigeon* [pigeon peas] leaves too many questions unanswered. But in the course of my work with the historical roots of the dish, I believe that I have found the answer. Because this is an original thesis, it is only proper that I defend it in some detail. And because it further illuminates the history of the dish, it should be of some interest.

First, let us take *John*. The ultimate source is Malay *kāchang*, perhaps by way of Malagasy, the Malay-based language of Madagascar, crossing the mainland to the rice fields of West Africa, most likely by way of the Arabs, whence to the rice lands of South Carolina by way of African slaves, where it was assimilated as part of *hoppin' John*, either by the slaves during the evolution of Gullah as the memory of African words began to dim or by the white inhabitants of South Carolina when they became aware of the dish. We now know the points of departure and arrival of the crucial part of the name, in that it refers to the characterizing aspect of the dish: the presence of peas of a type loosely referred to as *kāchang*; the precise itinerary remains somewhat speculative only because there are so many possible routes.

Under *cajan*, the Anglicized form of *kāchang*, the *Oxford English Dictionary* says that it is "applied to various leguminous plants (*Cajanus Lablab, Dolichos, Phaseolus, Soja*, etc.) [parentheses original]." In short, pulse. The Arab form is *kusna* (pronounced somewhat like *kootchna* or *katchna*, with *a* as in father, according to Rudolf Grewe). *A Dictionary of Modern Written Arabic* by Hans Wehr, edited by J. Milton Cowan (1979) defines it as "lentil tare, slender vetch." As with all popular names, it is difficult to pin this down; it is, apparently, not a true lentil but a member of *Vicia*, which includes a number of tares and vetches (the terms are poorly differentiated), some of which are cultivated in North Africa and used as lentils.

Evidently, by extension, *kāchang* in its many forms came to include pulse of all kinds, but I believe that originally it referred only to those peas belonging to *Vigna* and *Cajanus*. (The scientific names of *V. catchang* and *C. cajan* clearly derive from *kātchang*.) *Vigna*, to which cowpeas and black-eye peas belong, is a group whose definition has undergone frequent revision, which accounts in part for the hopeless confusion which characterizes its nomenclature. (Both the *OED* and Sturtevant, for example, rely on nineteenth-century sources, but different ones.) In addition to all the varieties already mentioned, *Vigna* also includes: marble pea, Jerusalem pea, chowlee, chowlu, Chinese dolichos, Tonkin pea, koondii, and surely many others. The name *Tonkin pea* would seem to suggest that it has long been known there, and why not? A mixture of black-eye peas and rice, for all the world a hoppin' John, if a bit on the soupy side—that is, not a proper pilau—seasoned with lemon grass, is sold as street food, piping hot, in Saigon. I believe that this dish is the prototypical beans-and-rice dish of primeval rice lands, including those of Africa; seasoning varies, and cooking the dish as a pilau was a later development that did not take place everywhere. (My daughter took a photograph of this dish, with black-eye peas showing pristine.)[6]

The derivation of *hoppin'* may appear at first glance to be less certain, but I believe that it comes by a circuitous route from Hindi *bhāt*, meaning "cooked rice." One of the pilau receipts in the Baghdad manuscript is named *"Bahaṭṭa"* which Arberry says is a "Persian loan-word" from the Hindi. In Arabic it seems to have disappeared from use, but it was recorded in 1226, thus illustrating once again that words are not constant but often are replaced by others. Curiously, I do not find the word *bhat* in Indian cookbooks published in the United States, at least not in those I own, not even those that have an extensive glossary. I do find it, however, in works published in India and Nepal: *Indian Cookery* by E. P. Veeraswamy (Bombay, 1956), and *Joys of Nepalese Cooking* by Indra Majurpuria of Kathmandu (Kirtipur, 1983–84), in both cases referring to cooked rice. In the latter work, *bhat* is given as the Nepali word; the receipt "Dal bhat," for example, is for a dish with rice and pulse.

The process by which, I suggest, that *bahaṭṭa kāchang* became assimilated to *hoppin' John* is a common phenomenon, one that occurs when people are faced with a strange or unpronounceable word whose meaning they have forgotten or never known: they substitute a known word of similar sound, employing metathesis (transposition of consonants or entire syllables) and elision to make it fit. A classic example in English is the substitution of *sparrow-grass* in the seventeenth century for the earlier *sparagus*, already an aphetic form of Latin *asparagus*. An entire folk etymology sprang up around the term, including the claim that the vegetable was so named because sparrows loved to nest in asparagus beds. From the same period we have English *kickshaws* from French *quelque chose*, referring to a frivolous little dish. The assimilation may be intentionally humorous, as when an acquaintance from Blue Ridge Mountain country, on being exposed to *pirozhkis*, by way of marriage to a Russian, dubbed them *pirjokes*. (Also, see the section below on johnny cake for the story of another such assimilation.)

Keeping in mind the historical consonant shift and the predilection for methathesis and elision, I reconstruct the word as follows: The *b* of *bahaṭṭa* is pronounced like *p* (the ancient Jordanian city of *Bitrā* or *Batrā—a* always sounding as in *father*—becomes *Petra* to Europeans, for example),[7] the *p* and *h* are transposed, and the sound of *t* is dropped, giving us *hop*. *John* is, of course, the final syllable of a softened *kāchang*, as in *cajan*; *ka-* is dropped in favor of an interjected syllable to rhyme with *John*, or perhaps to make sense of the phrase and add a comic note. This would make *hopping* a genteel back-formation from *hoppin'*, which better accords with the structure of Gullah. (The Hindi word for chick-pea is *channa*, so that *ka-* could already have been dropped. In my kitchen, a pilau made with chick-peas is, I regret to say, called *hoppin' Janna*. It is very good.)

My construction is logical: *bahaṭṭa kāchang* and *hoppin' John* both designate rice and peas, products indigenous to Asian and African tropics. And, it stands up under historical scrutiny, while the construction involving *pois de pigeon* does not. The French-speaking slaves of South Carolina played no role in the development of Gullah, nor were pigeon peas (*Cajanus cajan*) ever a crop of any importance whatsoever in the United States, not even in South Carolina. But the plant, a perennial tropical shrub, did flourish in the Caribbean (note the citation of Tussac, above, p. 96], and it is possible that there was some sort of assimilation of *kāchang* to *pigeon* in the French West Indies. If so, it would tend to show that a softened form of *kāchang* was used by Africans in the New World to designate pulse, making the use of *John* all but inevitable in any English assimilation.

CULINARY ASPECTS OF HOPPIN' JOHN

It may come as a surprise to find hoppin' John classified as a pilau, but a little reflection will show that this is precisely what it is, particularly when one finds Persian and Baghdadi receipts involving rice and beans made in the very same way, albeit with different seasonings. I have seen instances of the rice and beans of hoppin' John being served on the same plate but not cooked together, but that is not South Carolina practice.

The Caribbean dishes listed above—that is, all but the *feijoada*—are also pilaus, further emphasizing the kinship of these African-American dishes and further supporting my thesis that pilaus, at least bean pilaus, have long been part of the culinary repertory in the rice lands of Africa. For example, the receipt *"Moros y Cristianos"* is for a pilau; raw rice and sufficient water are added to already-cooked, aromatic black beans, then steamed until "all the water [is] absorbed." (The name, literally *Moors and Christians*, is a wry and irreverent Afro-Cuban allusion to the mixing of the races.) But when rice and beans are cooked separately and served side by side on the plate, the receipt used is *"Frijoles Negros"* (black beans), even though the total ingredients may be identical, thus highlighting the importance accorded the difference in structure. (Caribbean dishes bearing the name of *pilau*, or variants thereof, are the legacy of relatively recent immigrants from India, and while the receipts have undergone a certain amount of naturalization, they are recognizably Indian in composition, with little relationship to the African-American rice-and-bean dishes except in the broadest historical sense.)

Receipts for hoppin' John have remained remarkably traditional for as long as they have been printed. The archetypical ones call for a pint of cowpeas or black-eye peas cooked with a pound of bacon, to which is added a pint of raw rice; the whole is then cooked and "soaked" as usual. Going by the cookbooks, seasonings are spartan: salt and pepper. Some add an onion, some red pepper (cayenne); Miss Rutledge allows fresh mint; "Uncle John" fancied up his version with fried sausages, ham, and bacon; to be sure, he was cooking for the gentry, but it is to be noted that "cabobs of minced meat (mutton)" were an alternative topping in the receipt *"Shūrbā"* from Baghdad (above), and the custom could have been carried over in Africa for more lavish presentations. On occasion other cuts of cured pork were used, say pork jowls or a ham hock. And while contemporary receipts may suggest frozen black-eye peas, the essential composition is respected. That is, in South Carolina. Even the somewhat unorthodox receipt by Cobb (above), included here because of its folkloric allusions and alternative names of peas, differs in composition from the classic versions only in that butter is used instead of bacon. (Be it noted that Cobb was a Kentuckian.)

If the basic structure of hoppin' John is from Africa, or by way of Africa, the characterizing use of cured pork is not. Jessica Harris, in an interview with Nancy Harmon Jenkins in the *New York Times*, describes a dish from the Senegal thus: "Essentially *chiebou niebe* is hoppin' john without the pork. Because the people are Muslims, they use beef." In a telephone conversation, Dr. Harris explained to me that this was a Wolof dish, composed of black-eye peas, rice, and fresh beef, cooked using the method for hoppin' John. Similarly, the Bahian receipt *"Arroz-de-Hauça,"* a pilau not involving peas, calls for *carne sêca* (jerked beef), a reflection of the Muslim presence among the Hausa from Nigeria. The Mandingo, Fulani, and Yoruba groups were also Muslim, at least intermittently, some since the early part of the fourteenth century. This infiltration of Africa by Islam must have had considerable influence on African cookery, as discussed earlier. There were slaves in South Carolina representative of these groups in sufficient numbers to warrant the issuance of beef rations rather than pork, as noted earlier (p. 13). This practice may have diminished somewhat with time. In any event, by the time hoppin' John showed up in the literature in 1838, it was characterized by the presence of pork, probably cured pork, just as other Carolina pilaus tended to be.[8]

HOPPIN' JOHN AS FOLK COOKERY

Hoppin' John is one African-American dish that made it to the Big House. The inclusion of a receipt in *The Carolina Housewife* (1847) by Sarah Rutledge would seem to indicate that the old slave dish had been accepted by some of the most aristocratic elements of the Low Country. And her receipt, the earliest I know of, seems to be prototypical. Obviously, the dish long antedated 1847 in South Carolina, surely going back to the beginnings of cultivation of rice by African slaves; for a receipt to be included in such a work, it must have long before begun to appear on the white plantation owner's table.

The very presence of such a receipt in *The Carolina Housewife* invalidates the entire premise of the work of certain folklorists with regard to the importance of such regional works, including *The Virginia House-Wife* (1824) by Mary Randolph. They complain that such works "are generally treated as though they represent the cookery of the state mentioned in their titles," with the implication that such is not the case, because "these authors were all women of means—well-educated members of upper-class society—and they had their own social prejudices about folk culture and the working man."

But *The Carolina Housewife* is a paradigm of a regional cookbook, most of the receipts having been dutifully copied from "family receipt books of friends and acquaintances." She pointedly omits receipts for general cooking, as mentioned earlier, and includes "Ground Nut Soup" [peanuts], "Benne Soup" [sesame, brought from Africa, or rather by way of Africa], "Red Pea Soup" [the lowly cowpea], and "Seminole Soup" [squirrel, hickory nuts, and "the tender top of a pine tree, which gives a very aromatic flavor to the soup"]. (It is to be noted that there were connections between the African-Americans and the Seminoles formed down through the years as runaway slaves made their way to the then wilderness areas of Florida and lived among the Native Americans.) She also gives nearly a hundred specifically Carolina receipts using rice or maize—or a mixture of the two, a practice very nearly peculiar to the Low Country—and receipts for several types of pilau, a dish all but unique to South Carolina and the adjoining rice lands as they spread, unique at least in American cookery. And, of course, the receipt "Hopping John."

The line between folk cookery and that of the upper classes is not always as clear as the folklorists would have it. The burgeoning merchant classes have always emulated the cookery of the aristocracy as best they were able, and so it has always been, all the way down the line. At various levels of society, costly ingredients or highly labor-intensive dishes posed nearly insurmountable obstacles; even so, such dishes might be indulged in on rare and festive occasions, again as best they were able.

In the other direction, earthier dishes of the rural poor—or of fishermen in coastal areas—would occasionally be adopted by the local aristocracy and become a genuine regional dish, transcending lines of class, and even race, to a point where it came to typify the region in a way that its more elegant dishes could not. In France, such dishes are legion: the *cassoulets* [beans and various meats, including cured meats, cooked in a *cassolo*] of the South-West, the *tripes à la mode de Caen* of Normandy, and the *bouillabaisse* of Marseilles; each is a dish of humble origin which became the very symbol of its home territory and a source of pride to all classes.

We have fewer examples in this country, but Boston baked beans, the New England chowders, and hoppin' John are such dishes. They may not have been served on highly formal occasions, but once accepted, in no way were they relegated to the poor. On the contrary, it has generally been precisely the "well-educated members of upper-class society" who led the way in this process; the middle classes have historically been far more chary of adopting what they feared to be lower-class foods and customs. That is, it is not until the Cabots of Massachusetts and the Rutledges of South Carolina set a low-down bean dish on their table that social climbers in those states dare to follow suit. With trepidation. Meanwhile, the so-called lower classes who developed the dish continue to enjoy it, thankful that something so cheap is so delicious and so satisfying. Nowadays class is in a state of flux, and such changes are more likely to be accomplished quickly and efficiently by means of the hype of food writers, always appealing to the same base characteristic of snobbery among food writers who are more concerned with the status of food than its quality, or to put it in today's terms, with what is "in" and what is "out."

It is difficult to know just when the plantation owners of South Carolina Low Country began to accept hoppin' John as their own, but it must have happened by the time Miss Rutledge gave a receipt for it in 1847. There may have been some lingering ambivalence concerning the old slave dish at some levels of society, namely the middle levels. What can be said, is that she did not include it for the edification of African-Americans. Not in 1847. Nor had they any need of a receipt from Sarah Rutledge to make their own ancestral dish.

Hoppin' John is the signature dish of South Carolina, black and white. As Helen Woodward wrote in her receipt for it in *Two Hundred Years of Charleston Cooking* (1976): "South Carolinians, like my husband, who have been away from home a long time, if they feel a culinary homesickness, always long for something called Hoppin' John, with the accent on John." Yankee though I be, I too get yearnings for it because it is such a satisfying dish; if, in addition, it had associations with home and the days of my youth, those feelings would be even more intense, I'm sure. Fortunately, although it seems so rooted in its home territory, it is a dish that travels well, always supposing that one can find the proper peas—and black-eye peas are everywhere available in the United States—and the *proper receipt, which must be a home grown South Carolina receipt.* I have a collection of receipts from elsewhere, all purporting to be for hoppin' John, one worse than the other. The prize for ludicrousness must go to one from a Pennsylvanian that includes molasses and bread crumbs and dear knows what else, and is so soupy that it is "thickened" with *filé* powder.[9] But proper receipts are not difficult to come by, beginning with *The Carolina Housewife* or other receipts to be found in this work. It is not that they do not vary a bit in detail, as discussed elsewhere, but there are certain parameters which must be respected. That is, if you would call it *hoppin' John.* One thing it is not, and that is a *slabby* stew that has to be thickened with *filé* powder. I am trying to "set them straight," as Mrs. Vernon requested (above).

The early spread of hoppin' John in the United States is difficult to ascertain, but it seems not to have wandered far from the Low Country rice lands. Mrs. Brown of Anderson, well inland, gave a proper receipt in 1871. Mrs. Hill of Georgia gave a classic receipt in 1872, albeit with optional fancy variations. Its early history in Georgia must be roughly parallel to that in South Carolina.

In New Orleans there are two receipts entitled "Hopping John" included in *Cooking in Old Créole Days* by Célestine Eustis (1904), one attributed to our "Uncle John" of South Carolina, the other to a resident of Washington, D.C. There is also a receipt in *The Picayune's Creole Cook Book* (1901), "*Jambalaya au Congri,*" which calls for cowpeas, rice, onion, salt meat [understood to be salt pork], and a square of ham. It is a classic—well, nearly classic—hoppin' John parading under a Creole name formed from Provençal *jambalaia*, meaning effectively pilau, and *congri*, translated in the text as *cowpeas*. I do not find *congri* in standard references; in her receipt from Cuba entitled *"Congris,"* Elizabeth Ortiz calls for "California pink beans (frijoles colorados) or red kidney beans," neither of which are cowpeas, however broad the definition. I propose that *congri* is one more popular name for *Cajanus cajan*, adding it to the list of Congo pea, Angola pea, catjang, grandue, and pigeon pea. The plant has been cultivated in Africa for millennia and came to the West Indies, as I earlier noted (p. 96). As with *cowpea*, the name very likely came to serve for whatever peas were to hand, much as the English term *corn* refers to the dominant grain, be it wheat, oats, or in the New World, maize. That said, I have the impression that in New Orleans the reference is to the small red peas called *cowpeas* in various Carolina receipts, as discussed earlier (p. 97). The term *congri* shows up in Cuba and New Orleans, possibly because a number of slaves came to those places from the same point in Africa; relations between Cuba and New Orleans in this regard are not to be ruled out, but the dish would have long antedated the brief Spanish period in New Orleans, even if only among the African-Americans. In any event, I think that this New Orleans version was an independent—or rather, parallel—manifestation of the African Diaspora rather than a borrowing from Carolina, or Cuba, for that matter.

Outside of rice country, hoppin' John is perhaps less likely to have flourished. Suitable peas or beans were everywhere available to African-Americans, most often being raised on a subsistence level, but outside of the rice lands of Carolina and Georgia, rice was not handed out as slave rations, and slaves would not have had the means to buy it. This is amply documented, as is the reason. Ulrich B. Phillips, in *American Negro Slavery* (1966), cites the case of the Charles Manigault rice plantation, where "In reward for good service, however, Manigault usually issued broken rice worth $2.50 per bushel, instead of corn worth $1." This in rice country. Small wonder that slaves took to growing their own rice in their allotted patches of land, when allowed.

However, there is reason to believe that subsistence rice farming by African-Americans on small patches of land was far more widespread than has generally been realized. For successful commercial production of rice, certain optimal conditions are necessary, one of them being the means of flooding and draining the rice fields as efficiently as possible. (Also, with the advent of labor-saving machinery, it became necessary that the soil be able to support the heavy machines.) But for family use, normal rainfall patterns or arduous but makeshift systems supply sufficient water. And, as noted earlier, rice—at least certain strains—can be grown pretty much as are other grains, variously called *dry rice, upland rice,* or *mountain rice.*

Thomas Jefferson was a great champion of the cultivation of "dry" rice, as opposed to "swamp rice...[which], requiring the whole country to be laid under water during a certain season of the year, sweeps off numbers of the inhabitants annually with pestilential fevers." Apparently nothing came of his efforts to interest the proprietors in South Carolina, but some of the seed rice, "being carried into the upper hilly parts of Georgia, it succeeded there perfectly, has spread over the country, and is now commonly cultivated; still however, *for family use chiefly*, as they cannot make it for sale in competition with the rice of the swamps.... It has got from Georgia into Kentucky, where it is cultivated by many individuals for family use. I cultivated it two or three years as Monticello, and had good crops, as did my neighbors, *but not having conveniences for husking it, we declined it* [emphasis added]." (He gave seed to William Bartram of Philadelphia, where it "produced luxuriant plants...but no seed." One might almost say that the Mason-Dixon line was also the rice line.) This was written in 1808, but the new rice may simply have replaced less successful strains in some areas, as had earlier occurred in West Africa. The "dry rice" referred to by Jefferson in the above passage had been picked up "along the coast of Africa," but had originally been brought there from "Cochin-China" [Vietnam], according to him. (Apropos, the Rice Council informs me that Laotians are raising rice for themselves in the Blue Ridge Mountains.)

There are those who believe that certain rices indigenous to West Africa were at one time so cultivated by slaves in parts of the South. So far, according to Amelia Wallace Vernon, no hard evidence has been found of those African strains, so that if they were cultivated here, they must have been abandoned. Some support for this view can be gleaned from an excerpt of a letter addressed to Mrs. Vernon by Elaine Nowick at the Louisiana State University Rice Research Station in Crowley, Louisiana: "I do not know if *Oryza glaberrima* [the principal African strain] was ever grown in South Carolina but it was collected in El Salvador.... I understand that it was brought from Africa by slaves and has since disappeared from this area." This was accompanied by a photocopy of grains of *O. glaberrima*, a copy of which Mrs. Vernon sent on to me.

For our purposes it is not so important whether the rice grown by African-Americans was *O. glabberima*, Carolina Gold, or rice from Vietnam. The point is that *they were growing rice outside the rice lands.* Mrs. Vernon interviewed in Mars Bluff alone twenty-two people who remembered so growing rice. She says that she "could find no record of Afro-

Americans at Mars Bluff planting their own rice patches prior to 1865," but she supposes that they may have. She "did find evidence that Afro-Americans were cultivating subsistence rice for the Euro-American land-owners in the Pine Belt during the period 1772 to 1865." This is of importance to us, in that it relates to the works of Phineas Thornton and Theresa C. Brown, as is the success of rice in upland Georgia, referred to by Jefferson, in explaining the rice kitchen of Pearlie Walker.

I think it safe to say that most, if not all, of the small growers of rice were African-Americans. First, they knew how to raise it, and a good deal of the cultivation of rice in West Africa must have been on a small scale. But as important, perhaps, is the fact that as eaters of rice, they would have wanted it badly enough to cope with the trouble of husking it, a cruelly arduous task when done by hand, that is, using a mortar and pestle, traditionally women's work everywhere rice has been cultivated. Maize was ever so much less trouble to grow and ever so much less trouble to husk, so that only peoples who felt deeply about rice were likely to have made the effort; this is emphasized by Jefferson's abandoning rice culture and the reason he gives.[10]

In Louisiana large-scale commercial rice production was not intro-duced until 1884, according to figures from the Rice Council. When I ex-pressed surprise at the lateness of the date during a telephone conversation, the spokesperson volunteered that there may have been small-scale cultivation before then, but they do not have statistics. (Such unrecorded rice farming could have started quite early.) Early Louisiana cuisine is also poorly documented; Creole cookbooks did not appear un-til 1885. (A French cookbook, in French, appeared in 1840, but it had first been published in Paris beginning 1814, according to Lowenstein, drawing on Vicaire.) In neither of them do I find any dish remotely re-sembling hoppin' John. In itself this would not be conclusive, but it does suggest that the dish was not known in the white kitchens of New Or-leans. What is more significant is that in *La Cuisine Creole* by Lafcadio Hearn (1885, both editions) a receipt calls for "Patna rice," rice from In-dia; this at a time when European cookbooks were often specifying Caro-lina rice. He does give a receipt with a most intriguing title: "Cedar, or Carolina Rice Birds." It is hardly likely that birds were shipped from Carolina—although perhaps not materially impossible—but it does show that they were associated with Carolina rice, wherever they would have been snared. (Equally telling is the fact that in *Creole Cookery*, issued by the Christian Woman's Exchange of New Orleans (1885), there is a receipt *"Carolina Boiled Rice"* and several rice receipts taken verbatim from *The Carolina Housewife*, as discussed elsewhere [p. 137]). If the only rice raised in Louisiana *prior* to the 1880s had been farmed by African-

Americans on small plots, it would go far to illuminate this little mystery. But by the turn of the century, even the white kitchens of New Orleans had become aware of this dish, at least to the extent that receipts appear in the Eustis work—suspect, because of her Carolina connections—and in the *Picayune* work under a Creole name.

In Virginia, for example, where rice had been cultivated commercially during the last half of the seventeenth century, small-scale cultivation could well have continued. We know that it was feasible even in the uplands, because of Jefferson's success at Monticello. If so, and if African-American slaves in Virginia or elsewhere in what came to be the United States made hoppin' John, it did not come to the attention of the white women who wrote the cookbooks. Such dishes would not necessarily have been called *hoppin' John*, a name which I believe to have been a Gullah assimilation, but I do not find receipts for similar dishes in other likely sources. According to Jefferson, for example, family production of rice spread into Kentucky; since surely it was African-Americans who were growing it, they may also have been making hoppin' John, but I find no such receipt in *The Kentucky Housewife* by Lettice Bryan (copyright 1839).[11]

As I have written so often, the cookery of the poor has ever been ill recorded, and this was particularly true of African-American cookery, so that it is not surprising that I do not find receipts. In the case of South Carolina, I believe that Sarah Rutledge, as a member of the rice aristocracy of the Low Country, would have been more sensitive and more responsive than were writers elsewhere to fine ways of cooking rice, even those practiced by slaves among themselves. In this regard—quite aside from its other virtues as a lovely cookbook—*The Carolina Housewife* is one of our two most important historical cookbooks, the other being *The Virginia House-Wife* by Mary Randolph (1824). Certainly there are other important works, but they tend to be more encyclopedic and less faithful to dishes uniquely of their time and region. For all their aristocratic airs, those two ladies included a lot of peculiarly regional low-down dishes in their works. And that is their glory.

In some areas, however, African-American rice traditions did not flourish, either because most of the slaves in those areas had not come from African rice lands or because they had lost touch with those traditions under slavery. When asked about his memories of rice in his Mississippi boyhood, for example, Thomas Hill indicated that rice had not been "all that important." Yes, he remembered eating rice sometimes, and he remembered eating beans, "but never cooked together," for example. More tellingly, he related how his brother had married a "Geechee girl" from near Charleston, and how this brother "had trouble getting used to having rice at every meal." Not only that, but the rice was "cooked funny," so that "it would go skating around the plate" when you tried to pick it up with a fork. Cooked perfectly, he might have said, authentically "Geechee" style.

Among those who managed to maintain their traditions, all make hoppin' John as if from one master receipt. When asked how her grandmother in Georgia made it, Veronica Walker explained that first a ham hock was "boiled till real tender," then black-eye peas were added, and finally, "when it was time," the rice. For seasoning, it was salt and pepper. "No, nothing else," she said when asked. "The ham hock seasons it." Needless to say, Nell Hill, the "Geechee girl," makes hoppin' John. When I spoke to her on the telephone, she was at first shy, worried that I might want "exact amounts." When I assured her that no cook needed to measure amounts for a dish she had made since childhood, she became more animated. She liked to use pork jowl or ham hock, she said, but actually she mostly used whatever she "had around," meaning in the way of cured pork. She spoke almost as if this constituted a departure from the receipt. And of course, in a way it is.

I report these conversations in some detail to show how traditional those who are raised on hoppin' John are about what goes into it. All of this is in sharp contrast to what certain white writers maintain when they say that African-American receipts can be distinguished from those of white sources by the presence of many and varied seasonings. My own findings are quite the contrary. African-American receipts, ranging from those of Jessica Harris to those of Pearlie Walker and Nell Hill, differ remarkably little in seasoning one from the other. That is, they are often characterized by a *single* personal or cultural note, such as the use of cayenne pepper in place of black pepper, or the sprig of thyme of Dr. Harris, or even the extra meats of "Uncle John," or, for that matter, the ginger of the Ghanaian diplomat. This practice is also followed by those white South Carolinians who have the courtesy and good taste to defer to African-American usage in this regard, so I include the charming sprig of mint suggested by Sarah Rutledge. They all have too much respect for the dish to muddy it up with extraneous and discordant seasonings. I should perhaps correct my statement regarding the replacement of black pepper by cayenne in that the use of cayenne, most often called *red pepper* is more authentically African-American than that of black pepper. Amelia Vernon tells me that African-Americans at Mars Bluff used "red pepper," and that there were those who "had never seen black pepper," this "as recently as the memory of a man born in 1914." Well, of course, and I should have thought of it earlier. Black pepper is imported and has to be bought at considerable expense; cayenne peppers can be grown in a tiny corner of the garden. The use of cayenne has been so associated with

African-Americans that some have claimed it came from Africa; like all *Capsicums*, cayenne is of New World origin, but its use in our South may well have come by way of African slaves, either from Africa, where it took hold very early, or by way of the West Indies. (Being able to cultivate *Capsicum* peppers on a subsistence level at next to no cost must have been a factor in their whirlwind dispersion over so much of the Old World, tropical and semitropical areas in particular, even in India, for example; *Piper nigrum*, that is, black pepper, was a cash crop of great value.)

Outside of the Low Country and those few areas where hoppin' John flourished, it has begun to be known only relatively recently. Even those African-Americans not raised in the tradition have come to reclaim their birthright in this regard, and it is today an honored dish in the soul food repertory. It even became something of an ethnic manifestation for many white yuppies in the North, at least for a day, when the *New York Times* gave its imprimatur to a receipt for it in time to celebrate New Year's Day, 1989, in the traditional South Carolina way. The receipt was given by South Carolina's own John Martin Taylor and was, as is to be expected, perfectly traditional, calling for cowpeas *or* black-eye peas, ham hock, chopped onion, and a dried hot [cayenne] pepper in addition to the rice, all cooked in the classic way, the way of a pilau.[12]

CHAPTER 6

Rice Soups

A Pepper Pot
To three quarts of water, put such vegetables as you choose;
in summer, peas, lettuce, spinach, and two or three onions: in
winter, carrot, turnip, onions, and celery. Cut them very small,
and stew them with two pounds of neck of mutton, and a pound
of pickled pork, till quite tender. Half an hour before serving,
clear a lobster or crab from the shell, and put it into the stew.
Some people choose very small suet dumplings boiled in the
above. Season with salt and Cayenne.
Instead of mutton, you may put a fowl. Pepper pot may be
made of various things, and is understood to be a mixture of fish,
flesh, fowl, vegetables, and pulse. A small quantity of rice should
be boiled with the whole.
—Mrs. Rundell, in *A New System of Domestic Cookery*,
New York, 1817.[1]

WITH ONLY A FEW EXCEPTIONS, the soup receipts in our
work are of no great historical interest. That is, most are perfectly standard receipts to which rice has been added or are simply thin rice gruels
seasoned in various ways.

The fact that six of these receipts feature okra (*Hibiscus esculentus*
L.) is, however, of considerable importance; in addition, there are other
okra receipts. Okra is native to Central Africa and was brought to the
New World by way of the slave trade. *Okra* is derived from *nkru-ma*, its
name in the Twi language of Ghana, according to Jessica B. Harris.
Gumbo, its other name in English, comes from *kingombo* from Angola,
with *kin-* being the "usual Bantu prefix," according to the *Oxford English
Dictionary*. In *Ethno-Botany of the Black Americans* (1979), William Ed
Grimé gives *guiábo* and *guimgombó*, as well, and says that it came here in
the seventeenth century. Dr. Harris says that she has found *quiabo* and
quingombo "currently in use in Brazil and Puerto Rico, respectively."
Wherever there have historically been large concentrations of African-
Americans, one can be certain that okra lends its distinctive mucilaginous
note to the local cookery. I have not seen it remarked on, but surely in any
given area of the African Diaspora the choice of name between *nkru-ma*
and *kingombo* must reflect to some extent the origins of the early African

arrivals. That is, in Carolina, the usual word is *okra*, while in New Orleans *gumbo* is favored, for example. *Gumbo*, or *Gombo*, also refers to the patois of French-speaking Africans of the Diaspora, particularly in Louisiana and the French West Indies, but it might derive from Kongo *nkombo*, referring to a runaway slave.

What is certain is that various African okra stews characterize the cuisines of South Carolina and New Orleans, *with rice the obligatory accompaniment*, although not always explicitly so directed. (Okra has a special affinity for rice; it has long been used in Indian and Persian rice cookery, for example, and Mrs. Blake gives a receipt entitled "Okra Pilau" [F 56].)

The pertinent soup receipts are "Okra Soup [1]" and "Okra Soup [2]" (F 40) from *The Carolina Housewife*; "Okra Soup" from *The Virginia House-Wife*, Maum Sarah's "Okra Soup," and "Faber's Okra Soup" (all F 41); and "Southern Gumbo" (F 46), unattributed. Maum Sarah also gives a receipt entitled "Okra Daube" (F 57), really a gumbo, which is further thickened with rice water, a very ancient stunt. In fact, all these okra soups are gumbos, reflecting the choice of name I mentioned above. The "New Orleans Gumbo" (F 44) from the *The Carolina Housewife* (1847) is made mucilaginous with sassafras (called *filé* in New Orleans), not okra, showing that by that time *gumbo* had already come to be applied to a dish of that texture but no longer necessarily calling for the vegetable that gave it its name, that is, in New Orleans.

Another interesting soup is Miss Rutledge's "Pepper Pot" (F 43–44), in that it seems to come directly from the British West Indies, complete with several meats, yams, plantains, spinach, potatoes, optional seafood, dumplings, and the obligatory characterizing "long red peppers [cayenne]," only lacking the *cassareep*, a cassava preparation, for total authenticity. (On F 44, lines 2 and 3, it should read in reference to the crabs or lobsters: "...picked fine....") This authenticity is not surprising, given the strong South Carolina connections with Barbados and the Bahamas, mentioned in an earlier chapter (p. 6). It is interesting to compare it to the spartan version that came to be considered classic in the United States, consisting of tripe, veal bone, suet dumplings, and the characterizing "pod of pepper"; this version is always claimed by Philadelphia, although the earliest receipt I know for it is given by Mary Randolph in 1824, entitled simply "Pepper Pot." But it was originally an infinitely varied festival dish; Mrs. Rundell actually understood it very well.

"Mulligatawny Soup" (F 44–45) is, of course, from India. The name is from Tamil *milagu-tannir*, meaning "pepper water," so that it can be said to be a dish parallel to pepper pot. Because they do share certain characteristics, it is tempting to suggest a connection, especially since

"Pepper Pot" is specific to another British colony in the West Indies. However, I have not done any research on that question. There are myriad versions of both dishes. (I should note that descriptions of pepper pot (1704),[2] and even receipts for it, antedate the arrival of large numbers of Indians brought to the West Indies by the British in the nineteenth century, so that if there is a connection, it is not that simple.)

That oddity, "Pillau—The Turkish Soup," is dealt with in chapter 3, "Pilau."

CHAPTER 7

The Rice Breads of
South Carolina

Rice Bread—Annual Register
Page 54
Boil a quarter of a pound of rice 'till it is soft and well
seethed. When it is cold knead it up well with ³/₄ lb. of wheat
flour, a tea cup full of yeast and a tea cup full of milk and a small
tablespoon full of salt, let it stand 3 hours then knead it once and
role it up in a hand full of flour so as to make it dry enough to
put into the Oven. When baked it will produce 2 lb. of excellent
white Bread.

> —As recorded in *The Receipt Book of Harriott Pinckney
> Horry, 1770.* Transcribed by Richard J. Hooker, 1984.

Rice Bread
Take 4 quarts of rice beat it into flour, sift it, take one quart
of the [*one word illegible* (coarser?)] siftings and boil it soft,
spread it in your tray and while just warm put in your leaven or
yeast and mix by degrees all the flour in, put it to rise and when
risen which will be seen by its cracking put it into your pans and
bake it. NB. it will be so soft when put in the pans that you may
dip it up.

> —Mrs. Mcpherson in *The Receipt Book of Harriott
> Pinckney Horry, 1770.* Transcribed by Richard J. Hooker,
> 1984. (Editorial "[*one word illegible*]" inserted by
> Hooker; conjectural missing word supplied by K. H.)

Carolina Rice-and-Wheat Bread
Simmer a pound of rice in two quarts of water till it becomes
perfectly soft; when it is of a proper warmth, mix it extremely well
with four pounds of flour, and yeast and salt as for other bread;
of yeast about four large spoonfuls, knead it extremely well: then
set it to rise before the fire. Some of the flour should be reserved
to make up the loaves. Eight pounds and a half of exceeding good
bread will be produced. If the rice should require more water, it
must be added, as some rice swells more than others.

The Rice Breads of South Carolina   115

—Mrs. Rundell, in *A New System of Domestic Cookery*,
New York, 1817.

Carolina Rice and Wheat Bread

Simmer one pound of rice in two quarts of water until it is
quite soft; when it is cool enough, mix it well with four pounds of
flour, yeast and salt as for other bread; of yeast, four large
spoonfuls. Let it rise before the fire. Some of the flour should be
reserved to make the loaves. If the rice swell greatly, and requires
more water, add as much as you think proper.
    —Sarah Rutledge, in *The Carolina Housewife*,
    Charleston, 1847.

Rice Family Bread

One quart of rice flour made into a stiff pap by wetting it
with warm water, not so hot as to make it lump; when well wet,
add boiling water as much as two or three quarts; stir it
continually until it boils, then add one pint of milk; when cool
enough to avoid scalding, add half a pint of good yeast, and as
much wheat flour as will make it of the proper consistency of
bread; put it to rise: when sufficiently risen, it will be necessary to
add a little more wheat flour. If baked too soft the loaves will be
hollow.
    —Phineas Thornton, of Camden, South Carolina, in
    The Southern Gardener and Receipt Book, 1845
    (copyright 1839).

Rice Loaf Bread

Boil one pint of rice soft, add one pint of leaven, three quarts
of rice flour, put it to rise in tin or earthen vessels, dividing into
three parts, when well risen bake.
    —[Miss Mary Joseph Waring], in *The Centennial Receipt
    Book*, [Charleston?], 1876.

Wheat and Rice Bread

1. Boil half a pound of rice in three pints of water till the
whole becomes thick and pulpy. With this, yeast, six pounds of
[wheat] flour and salt to taste, make your dough. It is an excellent
summer bread.
    —Mrs. M. E. Porter, of Price George Court-House,
    Virginia, in *Mrs. Porter's New Southern Cookery
    Book*, 1871.[1]

VARIOUS BREADS MADE OF RICE have surely been made for millennia. Even the ancient Greeks made a rice bread called *orinde*, "which was highly thought of," according to Elizabeth David, and the Greeks did not have rice until around 300 B.C., when Alexander the Great is said to have brought it from Persia. There is reason to believe that all those breads were either flat breads or wafers, usually made of rice flour, although boiled rice, pounded in the mortar and worked, may also have been used. Countless varieties exist in many lands, even lands where rice is not a staple. Wafers made of rice flour have always been prized for their delicacy, and I suspect if for no other reason than that rice flour was often called for in medieval court manuscripts, that such wafers were made in both France and England. I cannot document this suspicion; for one thing, baking was a separate craft from cooking, which accounts for the fact that bread and cake receipts generally are scantily recorded in such manuscripts as have survived. Scattered examples of thin, sweet cakes appear in later works, however, and some of the more traditional receipts for shortbread, for example, call for a proportion of rice flour because it enhances delicacy of texture.

But *raised* breads with rice I believe for a number of reasons to have been a late development in the history of rice: in lands where rice was the only staple, people boiled it; auxiliary foods were eaten *with* boiled rice, much less frequently combined with rice in the more sophisticated manner of a pilau, for example. I believe that the making of breads and wafers is more likely to have developed in areas where rice was very important, was perhaps the principal staple, but where other grain was present as well, as in Persia and northern India, for example, where wheat has historically been grown. And when baking is discussed, there is the question of fuel to be considered, boiling being a more efficient way of preparing rice than baking.

Special techniques are required for the making of raised bread with rice because it is deficient in gluten, the magical protein found in wheat that enables wheat breads to rise in such a spectacular manner. The use of various leavens—yeast and later the alkalis—changes the texture of bread made only with rice flour but produces little appreciable increase in volume; fermentation does take place, but the walls of the air bubbles (formed by living yeasts or chemical interaction between alkali and acid), unlike those formed in good wheat dough, tend to collapse. Yeasted dough made of rice flour does not behave like proper bread dough in other ways; it cannot be shaped, for instance, as is noted in the recipe of Mrs. McPherson, given above. Straight rice bread will always be rather dense, and while this may be considered a virtue in some instances, it does not satisfy the innermost longings for bread among peoples who are historically eaters of wheat.

I do not know how old or how prevalent the practice was in France that Mrs. Stoney cites (F 11) from Bouillet's *Dictionnaire Universel* (1854) concerning the addition of rice flour in the making of bread. I find no mention of rice in *Le Parfait Boulanger* by Antoine A. Parmentier (1778), although he discusses the addition of potatoes, for example, as well as the use of maize. Raymond Calvel, in *La Boulangerie Moderne* (1972), speaks of the addition of rice flour as adulteration, a practice resorted to during famine or siege, a way of eking out scarce supplies of wheat. And it is true that even in small amounts, rice flour would completely alter the characterizing qualities of French bread.

Mrs. David writes: "In times of famine during the sixteenth, seventeenth and eighteenth centuries rice flour was used in Europe to mix with other flours for bread." Such practice must have been limited to the making of white bread, a luxury, because rice was imported into northern Europe. For the coarser breads of the poor, we know that far cheaper peas and beans, for example, were commonly added during times of want, that is, when the poor were lucky enough to have bread at all when famine was raging.

Mrs. David writes that nineteenth-century English writers gave bread receipts calling for the addition of boiled rice "in varying proportions, to add bulk to scarce and expensive wheat flour." As she perceptively notes: "Cooked rice is more effective, makes more bulk, and a much moister loaf than the grain in flour form." Eliza Acton and Lady Llanover, she reports, "considered rice bread one of the best, and best-keeping of all breads."[2] Indeed it is, and in spite of the exotic rice, it improbably seems one of the most English of breads; it makes fine sandwiches and makes wonderful toast, two prime requisites of an English loaf.

The addition of boiled rice, as distinguished from rice flour, in making bread produces a superior loaf, certainly one with superior handling qualities, because it does not dilute the gluten content of wheat flour to anything like the same extent, so that the dough behaves more like straight wheat dough. Since both English and early American flours were "soft," that is, low in gluten, this was clearly a development of some importance.

It was this use of boiled whole rice that was new about the rice bread that became popular in nineteenth-century England. But I am convinced that it was not English in origin. Such practice had long antedated the receipts of Miss Acton (1857) and Lady Llanover (1867), as can be seen by the receipts of Carolina provenance from the *Annual Register*, Mrs.

Rundell (1817), Miss Rutledge (1847), as well as the *Charleston Gazette* of 1830 (F 13, but also see Appendixes to the present work). (Hooker reports that a search for the receipt in the files of the *Annual Register* was fruitless, but he dates the section of the manuscript in which it was entered to the last two decades of the eighteenth century.) Mrs. Rundell was English, to be sure, but she went to some pain to indicate that it was a *Carolina* receipt for rice-and-wheat bread, not one simply calling for Carolina rice. Her receipt and that of Miss Rutledge are identical, the only differences being editorial, that is, of the sort that occur in individual recopying for publication; entire phrases are verbatim. Together, the two receipts give a good lesson in historical method as applied to culinary history: the first appearance of a receipt does not necessarily indicate the original. In this instance the situation is relatively uncomplicated; it was Mrs. Rundell who copied from Miss Rutledge's receipt; or rather, given the lapse in time, perhaps from that of her mother or some other Low Country matron. Miss Rutledge charmingly acknowledges that except for "a few translated from the French and German" her "receipts," which she believed to be original, are "a selection from the family receipt books of friends and acquaintances, who kindly placed their manuscripts at the disposal of the editor," meaning herself.[3]

The rice-and-wheat bread of South Carolina had to have been developed in precisely such a cultural environment, one where the inhabitants of English and French origin historically had been eaters of wheat and, of course, where rice was plentiful. It was a case of eating one's cake and having it too, in a manner of speaking. They had, against all cultural odds, become eaters of rice; they loved their rice and ate it at every meal. *But they also wanted their bread.* That is, *wheat* bread.

Wheat was surely more costly than rice in the Low Country; some wheat was raised in South Carolina, but apparently not enough for people's needs, so that they imported additional supplies from other Colonies. Given the enormous wealth of the rice aristocracy, I doubt that the price of wheat was the determining factor in this development, but wheat's relative scarcity could well have been. (Since rice had at one time been grown commercially in Virginia, the development could perhaps have taken place there, but it did not, primarily because rice never became a way of life in Virginia. In addition, a great deal of wheat of excellent quality was raised there. Mary Randolph gave a highly detailed receipt for bread, wheat bread, in 1824, but not until the third edition, 1828, did she give a receipt for rice-and-wheat bread (F 16). Miss Rutledge, on the other hand, did not give a receipt for yeasted *wheat* bread until her second edition, 1851.) The high price of wheat in South Carolina did make the consumption of it a mark of class. There is noth-

ing new about this; wheat has ever been the noble grain in Europe, for example, with rye, oats, barley, millet, and later maize, depending on
circumstances, the usual grain of the poor. What was different in South
Carolina was the fact that the wealthy enjoyed three staple grains, rice,
maize, and wheat, and loved them all. African-Americans subsisted on
rice and maize; the middle classes presumably added wheat as they could
afford it. (Rye and buckwheat do appear in a couple of receipts in *The
Carolina Housewife* but clearly are of less importance in the Low Country
than elsewhere.)[4]

As we have seen, most of the peculiarly South Carolina culinary
splendors were Asian and African in origin, and African-American in ex-
ecution. The rice-and-wheat bread was perhaps the most original culinary development of the European minority, and certainly the most
important. As I noted earlier, the making of bread, or its supervision, has
historically been the province of the lady of the house, whatever her station, at least in England. The very word *lady* developed from elements
meaning *kneader* and *loaf*, and while this responsibility had lessened with
time, it was still sufficiently traditional in the early days of the Colony to
have weight. Working with wheat and yeast is an art, an art not likely to
have been previously practiced by slaves who came from the rice lands of
West Africa. Certainly the mistress did not engage in the arduous work of
kneading the dough and firing the ovens, but somebody had to supervise
the entire operation from the making and keeping of yeast to the drawing
of loaves from the oven, at least in the beginning.

At the time these rice breads were being developed in South Carolina, baking was done in wood-fired brick ovens, and this was to continue
until nearly mid-nineteenth century, later in many instances, as use of the
monster iron range gradually replaced cooking at the open fireplace. I
have discussed elsewhere the baleful effect this change was to have on the
quality of bread. Suffice it to say here that the art of baking historically
evolved around the use of the brick oven: the superheated dome with its
unique convection patterns; casting the loaf directly on the highly heated
brick oven floor; the initial steaminess generated by the dough itself,
gradually giving way to searing dryness, the principle responsible for the
incomparable crust; and the principle of the "falling" oven, gradually
lowering temperatures—all these characteristics combine to produce a
loaf of quality against which all other loaves must be measured. Bread
does not bake properly in the iron box; the convection patterns are
wrong, steaminess is insufficient early on but somehow persists to the
end, and the loaf cannot be cast on the oven floor but must be baked in
clammy pans—all of which does not permit the formation of the ideal
crust. And while this baking in pans is more forgiving in that it allows the

baking of "slack" doughs—overly soft doughs, especially defective doughs—it even encourages the making of slack doughs, which produce bread with a spongy texture that does not satisfy those aficionados who want their bread to have a good "bite," that is, a springy crumb and a crackling crust.[5]

The receipt from the *Annual Register* (above) shows that the women of South Carolina had solved before the end of the eighteenth century the peculiar problems of working with dough to which boiled rice had been added. The loaf was cast, not baked in pans, as shown by the instruction to dust the loaf with flour "so as to make it dry enough to put into the Oven," which would be quite unnecessary if one were baking in pans. And this was something of an accomplishment, because the proportion of rice, dry weight, was one part to three of wheat, a proportion that was changed in later receipts to one part to four of wheat, giving much better handling properties. The ideal dusting flour for shaping loaves is rice flour, because of its drying qualities, a fact well known in the trade, but I find no hint of this in these household receipts. John Taylor, however, believes that the use of *rice* flour is always implied in historical receipts unless otherwise specified.

It will be noted that Miss Rutledge's receipt "Rice Oven Bread" (F 23) is all but identical to the one from the *Annual Register* (above), except that she bakes it in a pan; certainly it is more prudent to do so. It is also of interest to note that the receipt from *The Centennial Receipt Book* of 1876 is essentially the same as that attributed to Mrs. Mcpherson by Harriott Horry (both given above).

These yeasted rice-and-wheat breads had more success in England than in the United States outside of South Carolina, indeed outside the Low Country, judging by the cookbooks; the only receipt for any sort of rice bread given by Theresa Brown of Anderson, South Carolina, well inland, is entitled "Rice Muffins," but she gives a loving and detailed receipt for wheat bread, as well as "wholewheat" bread, something of a rarity in Southern cookbooks. Phineas Thornton of Camden, South Carolina, does give a receipt for rice-and-wheat bread (above), a rather indifferent one; his receipt for wheat bread is given with much more élan and informative detail. It would seem that wheat was more important than rice in the uplands of Carolina.

Mrs. Hill of Georgia gives a goodly number of receipts for rice bread, but they are all batter breads leavened with cream of tartar and soda, on the order of the myriad receipts in Mrs. Stoney's work, that is, not the classic rice-and-wheat bread. In New Orleans I find a single instance of such a receipt in *Creole Cookery* (1885) straight out of Mary

Randolph's *Virginia House-Wife* (1828); it seems not to have been picked up by succeeding works, at least not in the more popular ones, not even the encyclopedic *Picayune* work, which includes myriad rice breads, among them the legendary *calas*, but bread in New Orleans remained essentially French in character.

Mary Randolph's receipt (F 16), just referred to, calls for an appreciably lower proportion of rice than that given by Miss Rutledge (F 18); even so, she calls for baking the bread in "moulds," emphasizing once again the inherent problem of slack dough. She may have adapted her receipt directly from South Carolina sources—Harriott Horry stayed at Mrs. Randolph's home for a certain time in 1815, for example—but she could equally well have based it on the one given earlier by Mrs. Rundell. (Certainly the receipt given by "A Boston Housekeeper" in 1832 was based on Mrs. Rundell's, of which it is but a slightly paraphrased version.) And in 1871 Mrs. Porter of Virginia gave a receipt (see above, p. 115), showing that apparently the tradition of rice bread introduced by Mrs. Randolph then still lingered. There was also an undated fourth edition of *The Carolina Housewife* (1870s?), so that with the publication of Mrs. Stoney's work in 1902 receipts for this remarkable rice-and-wheat bread had been in print for about a century.

But after Mrs. Stoney's work I find no further published receipts for this bread, not even in South Carolina. I hasten to add that several works listed by Anna Wells Rutledge are unavailable to me, but such as I do have access to give no receipt, and this includes some of the popular works such as *Two Hundred Years of Charleston Cooking* (first published in 1930) and *The South Carolina Cook Book* (revised in 1954). Some do carry receipts for rice bread, but they turn out to be batter breads leavened with baking powder. Elsewhere pickings are even slimmer. I have been unable to comb every work, but I have conscientiously scanned a large number of the most likely ones, including works on bread. While some of the well-intentioned writers of the counterculture gave receipts for yeasted rice bread, they called for rice flour—brown rice flour—and were remarkably poor, totally innocent of the most elementary notions of working with rice—or wheat, for the most part. Truly, they baked the bread of affliction.

The decline in popularity of the rice-and-wheat bread in South Carolina roughly parallels the long decline in the cultivation of rice in that state. Carolinians continued to love their rice, but other factors began to play a role with regard to bread. For one thing, relative prices of rice and wheat were reversed as rice production fell and as new wheat lands were being opened up in the prairies of the Middle West, essentially made possible by expanding rail systems; at the same time, industrialized milling methods made wheat flour cheaper. In addition, home baking declined in favor of industrialized baking.

Insofar as I can ascertain, not until 1979, when *The Carolina House-wife* (1847) was reissued in facsimile, was this receipt again in print. (However, there had been a facsimile (no date, by 1974) of the 1860 edition of *The Virginia House-Wife* with its similar receipt. I have been unable to trace rumors of a facsimile edition of *The Carolina Housewife* earlier in the century.) And in 1980 Elizabeth David's definitive work *English Bread and Yeast Cookery* appeared in an American edition with a receipt essentially adapted from nineteenth-century English receipts, which were in turn based on Mrs. Rundell's "Carolina Rice-and-Wheat Bread." Mrs. David's receipt calls for a proportion of one part rice, dry weight, to six of wheat flour, giving good handling qualities. And in South Carolina there has been a revival of interest in the loaf due to the enthusiasm of John Martin Taylor, a native son who is including a receipt for it in his forthcoming work in Low Country cookery.[6]

RICE JOURNEY, OR JOHNNY CAKES

> Notwithstanding it [rice] is...only fit for puddings...or to make the wafer-like bread called journey cakes in Carolina.
> —Bernard Romans, in *A Concise Natural History of East and West Florida*, 1775.

Journey Cake

Take a pint of Hominy cold mash it and mix well with a gill fine flower then mix 6 Spoonsfull of milk and spread it on your board and spread a little milk over it as you put it down to bake. This quantity for 2 middlesized Journey cakes. When rice is used it should be boild very soft and let stand to cool and mix as above.
> —*The Receipt Book of Harriott Pinckney Horry*, 1770. Transcribed by Richard J. Hooker, 1984.

Johny Cake, or Hoe Cake

Scald 1 pint of milk put to 3 pints of indian meal, and half pint of flower—bake before the fire. Or scald with milk two thirds of the indian meal, or wet two thirds with boiling water, add salt, molasses and shortening, work up with cold water pretty stiff, and bake as above.
> —Amelia Simmons, in *American Cookery*, Hartford, Connecticut, 1796.

To Make Rice Johnny Cakes
To three spoonsful of soft boiled rice add a small teacup of
water or milk, then add six spoonsful of rice flour, which will
make a large johnny cake, or six waffles.
ANOTHER.—Take one quart of milk, three eggs, one
teaspoonful of saleratus [a precursor of baking soda], one
teacupful of wheat flour, and Indian meal sufficient to make a
batter of the consistency of pancakes. Bake quick in pan
previously buttered, and eat warm with butter or milk. The
addition of the wheat flour is found to be a great improvement in
the art of making these cakes.
—Phineas Thornton, Camden, South Carolina
The Southern Gardener and Receipt Book, 1845
(copyright 1839).

Hoe Cake
Three spoonfuls of hommony, two of rice flour, a little butter,
and milk sufficient to make it soft. Bake on a griddle.
—Sarah Rutledge, in *The Carolina Housewife*, 1847.

Rice Journey Cake
Boil a pint of rice soft with salt, mix with it while hot a large
spoonful of butter; when cold add a pint of rice flour and half
pint of milk, beat all together, have ready a smooth board, wet it
and put on it the mixture about an inch thick, baste it with milk,
set the board before some clear oak coals. When brown slip a
thread under the cake and turn it, baste and bake in the same way,
split and butter when hot.
—[Miss Mary Joseph Waring], in *The Centennial Receipt
Book*, [Charleston?], 1876.[7]

Hearth cakes have existed since time immemorial and are well nigh
universal. Patting dough into flat cakes and baking them on a hot rock is
an elementary gesture in cookery: wheat chapatis in India, oatcakes in
Britain, and tortillas of maize in Mexico all have been baked on a bakestone for untold centuries, a striking case of parallel development. The
various grains in these unleavened cakes behave somewhat differently in
baking, but the essential procedure is the same. This is *baking*, or rather,
protobaking; the frying of cakes is altogether something else and a later
development. Bakestones came to vary with local materials and technol-
ogy. If there was no bakestone, not even a flat rock, cakes were baked in
the ashes.
Although hearth cakes had been made in Britain for so long, receipts
did not appear until very late. One reason is that the cookery of the poor

has ever been ill recorded. The poor had no ovens, so the cottager clung to hearth cakes in order to avoid paying the tithe on the manor oven. An equally compelling reason is their utter simplicity. Rich or poor, who needs a receipt for hearth cakes? By the time receipts started to appear, they were precisely for variously enriched or leavened versions, such as muffins in England and in the United States the johnny cake of Amelia Simmons and of Harriott Pinckney Horry.

The English colonists brought johnny cake with them. I make a point of it because students all too often assume that maize, the usual grain used for these cakes in the northern Colonies, bespeaks a Native-American origin. But receipts for breads, pancakes, puddings, porridges, etc., were brought to the New World, with maize then often being substituted for oats, both being fatty grains with no gluten. The Colonists' name for maize was *Indian corn*, *corn* being the proper English term for the prevailing grain, whether it be wheat, oats, or other grain. Their name for cornmeal was *Indian meal*, usually simply *indian*. We thus have Indian pudding, Indian batter cakes, even Indian pound cake, but nobody back then imagined that they were Indian dishes.

This historical tendency for peoples to cling to their traditional recipes when confronted with different grain is illustrated by *polenta* in Italy, *mamaliga* in Romania, and *la mique* and *le millas* in the South-West of France, with maize replacing chestnuts, rye, millet, etc. And the Celts who fled Cornwall in England so many centuries ago brought to France not only their language and names for themselves and for their new land— *Bretons, Cornouaille* (pronounced like *Cornwall,* or nearly), and *Bretagne*, as transcribed in French—but also their bakestones and hearth cake receipts, which they adapted to *galettes* made of buckwheat instead of oats. And in the English colonies of North America, while these same oaten hearth cakes were most often adapted to maize, in South Carolina, Georgia, and Virginia they were also adapted to rice, occasionally a mixture of rice and hominy. (In South Carolina, *hominy* is cooked grits, and *grits* is coarsely milled dried maize, according to John Taylor. Elsewhere in the South it is otherwise, but we are in South Carolina. He also tells me that "most Sandlappers call whole-grain, natural grits 'country grits' to distinguish them from the grocery store product.")[8]

JOHNNY CAKE, THE NAME

The name also comes from England. I have written elsewhere that *journey cake* or *johnny cake*, alternative forms, I took to refer to the ease with which a handful of meal could be mixed with water and baked under primitive conditions, noting that popular forms, such as *johnny cake* for *journey cake*, are notoriously ill recorded. However, I was wrong to accept the popular wisdom; I now believe that *johnny cake* is the earlier form and I thus see *journey cake* as an affected back-formation. *Johnny* had popular associations as a term, "humourously or contemptuously applied to various classes of men," to cite one definition in the *Oxford English Dictionary*. (One nineteenth-century author cited wrote: "'the journey cake,' vulgarly called Johnny-cake," for example. And *johnny cake* was described by an English traveler in 1805 as being made by "The lower class of people.") This interpretation is supported by the fact that *journey cake* was the preferred form in South Carolina and Virginia, for example, two colonies where English settlers came largely from aristocratic families or at least gave themselves aristocratic airs, while in the northern Colonies, where the settlers were often dissidents who tended to be more egalitarian in their beliefs, the usual term was *johnny cake* or *jonny cake*. Further supporting the English source, either directly or by parallel assimilation as discussed below, is its presence in Australia, where it designates a cake of wheatmeal baked in the ashes or in a pan.[9]

And there is etymological evidence; *A Dictionary of American English* cites the presence of *Jonakin* in a New England source of 1675 and of *Jonikin* in 1850, describing it as "thin wafer-like sheets, toasted on a board." The *DAE* cautiously speculates that it is "possibly the original form of *Johnny cake*," a derivation which had already come to me independently in the course of my work on the historical origins of the bread itself. What is incomprehensible is that it lists *Jonikin* as "of obscure origin." That is, the editors seem not to have taken notice of *jannock*, a word from northern England, especially Lancashire, with a citation from the 1500 in the *OED*, referring to "oaten bread made into hard and coarse large loaves," according to Halliwell. (Lexicographers tend to be very weak in culinary lore.) This relationship becomes even clearer when it is remembered that, although now very nearly archaic, *-en* was once a common termination in English, variously indicating the diminutive form, as in *kitten*; the feminine form, as in *vixen*; the plural form, as *oxen*; and other uses such as meaning "made of," as *oaten*, and "likened to," as *ashen*. I suggest that the diminutive form is perhaps most likely for *jonikin* considering that the word clearly referred to smaller, thinner cakes than the "coarse large loaves" referred to as *jannock*. The assimilation of the Lancashire word *jannocken* or *jonikin*—spell it as you will—to *johnny cake* or *jonny cake* among the increasingly Americanized English settlers in the Colonies followed the usual process of substituting a familiar word of similar sound for an incomprehensible one, as I discussed in Chapter 5, "*Hoppin' John*." (The pop historians' suggestion of *Shawnee cake* as the source may be dismissed as pop etymology; it has neither historical nor culinary justification.)

It should be noted that *bannock* also denoted an oaten loaf in Britain. The word entered Gaelic and is indeed claimed by the Scots, but it is derived from Latin *panicium* [bread]. Curiously, the *OED* does not make the connection between *bannock* and *jannock*, but they are manifestly different forms of the same word, with *bannock* apparently being the older and more established form. (Being regional terms, they referred to regional breads which were not necessarily identical.) I find that Noah Webster's first dictionary in 1806, for example, supports this construction in this entry: "Bannoc or Jannoc, n., a loaf made of oatmeal." In fact, as noted elsewhere, oats generally had been replaced by maize in the Colonies, but the two words were recognized as being essentially the same. In 1983 *Webster's Ninth New Collegiate Dictionary* gives the definition of *bannock* in American usage thus: "New Eng[land]: CORN BREAD; *esp*: a thin cake baked on a griddle." (I note that while I leaned on these dictionaries in my research, my conclusions are my own.)[10]

THE STRUCTURE OF JOHNNY CAKES

It must be understood that among the many American hearth cakes—johnny cakes, hoe cake, ash cake, bannock, pone, etc.—differentiation was not rigorous. The composition and baking method of cakes of the same name might vary markedly from one region to another, particularly as they came to be enriched in various ways, just as the same cake might go by other names in other places. Ash cake was wrapped in a leaf and baked in the ashes, but composition varied; *pone* was always of maize, which is proper since it is a Native-American word for bread. What can be said is that all early receipts for *johnny cake*, North and South, explicitly or implicitly, call for placing the dough on a board and propping it up before the fire, as described by Mary Randolph in 1824 (F 34) and Miss Waring in 1876 (above, p. 123). In that sense, *hoe cakes* were *johnny cakes*. Miss Rutledge's receipt for "Hoe Cake" (above, p. 123) was an adaptation to the range, as are the *jonny cakes* of Rhode Island, an adaptation that still survives so vigorously that Rhode Islanders will tell you that their corn griddle cakes—because that is what they are—are the original and only true jonny cakes. The very fact that they insist on spelling the word without the usual *h* shows that it is a vestige of *jannocken*, the little oatcakes of Lancashire.

The adaptation to the iron range of most interest to us nationwide is that described by Thornton in 1845 in his second receipt entitled "Johnny Cakes" (above, p. 123), the earliest such receipt I know of. Miss Rutledge gives a receipt entitled "Pan Journey Cake" (F 34) in the second edition of *The Carolina Housewife* (1851); it differs from her traditional "Rice Journey or Johnny Cake" (F 35) primarily in being slightly enriched in composition rather than being basted during baking, an important point, but the dough does remain a dough. With Thornton's receipt we have what is a typical modern johnny cake; it is made with cornmeal and wheat flour, the dough has become a batter, and it is leavened with alkali. I rather suspect Yankee influence there, remembering that Thornton's wife was from Massachusetts.

(I should note that since I speak of these various hearth cakes in a historical sense, I use the historical terms—or their variants—that is, *johnny cake* rather than the modern *johnny cake*, for example.)

Now for the composition of these cakes. Throughout the Colonies generally—and pretty much nationwide today—the use of maize was so prevalent that dictionaries define *johnny cake* as made of cornmeal. But a 1775 citation in the *OED* (above, p. 122) indicates that rice was used for journey cake in the Carolinas and probably long had been in the Low Country. In the 1780s or so Harriott Pinckney Horry of South Carolina mentioned "rice flour (such as for Journey cake)," and a somewhat later entry is "Journey Cake" (above, p. 122), based on either hominy (boiled grits) or rice. Mary Randolph's only entry in this category is "Rice Journey, or Johnny Cake" (F 34), calling for boiled rice and rice flour; she allows hominy and rice flour as a variation, which she claims "is nearly as good as cassada bread," a tantalizing allusion which suggests that cassava may have been an ingredient of johnny cake in Virginia. For a few decades most Southern writers gave separate receipts for both rice and maize johnny cakes, the latter normally based on hominy and cornmeal just as the former were normally based on boiled rice and rice flour, although, as we have seen, sometimes it was hominy and rice flour. But wherever rice journey cakes existed, both rice and maize johnny cakes had the same structure, that of a precooked grain bound with rice flour or fine cornmeal. (Mrs. Hill of Georgia called for "sifted corn meal" in her "Corn Meal Johnny Cakes" (1872), and Thornton of Camden departed entirely from South Carolina practice in his receipt for cornmeal johnny cakes (above, p. 123). But these were exceptions.) The difference in texture is of more importance than might be suspected.

The rice johnny cake did not exist everywhere in the South: *The Kentucky Housewife* (copyright 1839) gives only one version, a receipt entitled "Johnny Cakes," and it could well have appeared in a Northern cookbook, calling for "sifted Indian meal." Somewhat more surprising at first glance is the absence of *rice* johnny cakes in Louisiana, but it must be remembered that neither the culinary nor linguistic heritage of Louisiana was English. There is a receipt entitled "Johnny Cake" (with no French translation) in *The Picayune's Creole Cook Book* (1901), but it is made with "Indian meal," enriched, and baked in a pan. That is, however, various cakes of maize or rice had previously been made, it is highly unlikely that they would have been called *johnny cakes* until after the Louisiana Purchase in 1803. There were cakes of maize and of rice galore, but they went by other names. While it is dangerous to generalize on the basis of spotty evidence, the rice journey, or johnny cake does seem to have been very nearly peculiar to Carolina, Georgia, Virginia, and perhaps Maryland, at least insofar as I can determine. Considering the wide influence of *The Virginia House-Wife* (1824), this is surprising. It would seem to be further evidence that rice receipts, other than porridgy ones, most easily take root where rice is a respected grain.

Some time in this century rice journey cakes seem to have gone out of style in South Carolina. It is true that with the passing of the kitchen fireplace, the principal characteristic differentiating them from other rice cakes, that of baking them on a board in front of the fire, also passed. (Nationwide, johnny cakes made of cornmeal survived, at least in name, although they are indistinguishable from various other cornbreads or, in the case of Rhode Island, from cornmeal pancakes.) But even receipts for other rice cakes rarified. In *Charleston Receipts* (1950) there is one entitled "Philpy" (based essentially on that of Miss Rutledge [F 20]), as well as a couple for rice muffins, but none for johnny cakes of any kind, although there are various cornbreads. In *The South Carolina Cook Book* (revised 1954), I find no rice cakes whatsoever. I do find receipts entitled "Corn Pone," "Corn Meal Hoe Cake," and other cornbreads, which is all very well, but it is sad that not one rice bread remains in this popular work.[11]

OTHER RICE BREADS AND CAKES

Savannah Rice Cakes

Mix ten ounces of ground rice, three ounces of flour, eight ounces of pounded sugar; then sift by degrees into eight yolks and six whites of eggs, and the peel of a lemon shred so fine that it is quite mashed; mix the whole well in a tin stew-pan over a very slow fire with a whisk, then put it immediately into the oven in the same, and bake forty minutes.

Another.—Beat twelve yolks and six whites of eggs with the peels of two lemons grated. Mix one pound of flour of rice, eight ounces of flour, and one pound of sugar pounded and sifted; then beat it well with the eggs by degrees, for an hour, with a wooden spoon. Butter a pan well, and put it at the oven mouth.

A gentle oven will bake it in a hour and a half.
  —Mrs. Rundell, in *A New System of Domestic Cookery*,
  New York, 1817.[12]

I am not about to detail all the other receipts for various rice breads
and cakes; there are some ninety-eight in all, including those for croquettes. While there are certain nuances of texture in the endless variations within certain categories, the receipts do tend to be repetitive.

Historically they also tend to be less interesting than receipts for rice-
and-wheat bread or rice johnny cakes, for example, in that origins are
more diffuse, and similar cakes have existed in many lands. That is, there
are fewer mysteries and less that is peculiar to Carolina. Rice cakes leavened with "yeast powder," that is, baking powder, are perhaps an exception in that they were almost surely developed in Carolina; baking
powder came late on the world culinary scene. Various alkalis had entered
bread making as an additive and as early as the eighteenth century were
typically used in certain spiced cakes in various parts of northern Europe.
In the United States its use in baking is documented by 1796, and in 1801
there appeared a receipt entitled "Handy-Cake or Bread" calling for leavening with potash and sour milk, bespeaking long acquaintance with the
principles of chemical leavening. During the nineteenth century, the wan-
ton use of alkali came to characterize American baking, threatening to
drive out older and more delicious—as well as more healthful—forms of
leavening such as eggs and yeast.[13] As explained earlier, rice lacks gluten,
so that while either yeast or baking powder does change the texture of
rice cakes, making them more porous, there is no great increase in volume. Eggs, in addition to their innate leavening power, enhance that of
other leaveners as well as improving flavor, and it will be noted that such
receipts in this work almost invariably include eggs.

Receipts for pancakes, waffles, and muffins require no comment except to note that outside the rice lands in this country, they were the rice
breads most widely accepted, largely, I suspect, because they did not require special techniques; leftover rice could be dumped into the batter
and baked without further ado.

RICE CROQUETTES, OR FRITTERS
(*Beignets de Riz*)

Calas
Bel Calas tout chauds! (Beautiful *calas*, piping hot!) is the cry
of the black woman who sells them in the street, from wooden
bowls wrapped in a spanking clean napkin which she carried on

her head. *Calas* are eaten with coffee at the morning market; they're delicious!

A cup of rice boiled soft in water and allowed to cool; add a big spoonful of yeast and half a cup of water, then beat it well together; the following morning add an egg, a bit of salt, a small spoonful of sugar, a big spoonful of ordinary flour—rice flour is preferable, but difficult to obtain—beat it all well together; then drop this mixture by spoonfuls, one at a time, into lots of very hot lard, turning them until they are nice and brown...and place them close to the fire on a plate covered with a warm napkin. They are eaten with *café au lait*.

> —Célestine Eustis, in *La Cuisine Créole À L'Usage Des Petits Ménages*. New Orleans, 1904. (Ellipses original).

Callers

Take about 5 cents worth of rice, soak and pound it in a mortar; let it stand over night, then add the yolks of 3 eggs, put in a dessertspoonful of yeast powder [baking powder], enough flour to make a light batter, add the whites of the eggs well beaten; have a pot of boiling lard, and cook as for fritters.

> —*Creole Cookery*, Christian Woman's Exchange of New Orleans, 1885.[14]

There is one category of Carolina rice cake that deserves closer examination, that of croquettes, not only because of their own interest, but because of their historical kinship with the *calas* of New Orleans. There are eleven receipts—well, actually twelve—of this type in our collection, none identical to those for *calas*, but with receipts in either group differing as much among themselves as each group from the other, with a number of closely parallel ones. They are: "Rice Croquettes [1]" and "Rice Croquettes [2]" (F 65); "Rice Croquettes [3]" and "Rice Croquettes [4]" (F 86); Miss Rutledge's "Rice Cookies," Maum Peggy's "Breakfast Fry Breads," and Mrs. Dill's "Rice Flour and Hominy Fritters" (F 25); Miss Rutledge's "Rice Flour Balls" (F 24) and "Rice Flour Puffs" (F 81), the puffs receipt, unlike the balls receipt, calling for both yolk and white of egg an important point, as we shall see; "Rice Croquettes," from [*Fifty Years in a*] *Maryland Kitchen* (F 81); Mrs. Huger's "Pan Cakes" (F 31); and "To Make Wafers" (F 13), a muddled receipt of which a more accurate version is given in the appendixes to the present work under its proper title, "To Make Rice Puffs," different enough from that by Miss Rutledge not to have been copied by her from the earlier work. Most are not sweetened, although several are sugared after frying. Several use rice flour, an occasional characteristic of *calas*.

Before we proceed, a bit of technical information: *fritter* (from French *friture*, a generic term applied to any food fried in *deep* fat) may designate any of several types, from the simplest, a pancakelike batter dribbled into boiling fat—or food dipped in such a batter before frying—through elaborate shaped doughs, and extending to include those composed of various chopped foods incorporated into enough batter to bind. And, of course, to produce a crust. As Brillat-Savarin put it, "The entire merit of a good *friture* is due to *la surprise*," That is, the crust must form instantaneously on immersion into the boiling fat, or it becomes soggy and greasy. Historically batters for fritters and pancakes have not always been well differentiated, with old receipts often stating that they could be used for either, although fritter batters do tend to be richer in eggs. It is primarily the *depth* of the cooking fat that determines the difference in texture in the final product; anything deeper than a film of fat to obviate sticking to the pan progressively increases the crispness and delicacy of the crust, due to the fact that large quantities of boiling fat hold heat better when lumps of dough are dropped in it, thus assuring *la surprise*. Clearly, fritters require rather more flair in frying than do ordinary pancakes, which process is not so much frying as protobaking. I make a point of this because, clearly, Mrs. Huger's "Pan Cakes" are actually fritters, as are Miss Rutledge's "Rice Cookies," whatever their names.

It is significant that Sarah Rutledge avoids using the English term *fritter* for any such concoction calling for rice; it is used but once in Mrs. Stoney's collection. The usual name in Carolina is *rice croquette*, which is telling; in New Orleans it is *calas*. But when all is said and done, they are rice fritters or, more appropriately, *beignets de riz*, and if they were called that there would be no mystery whatsoever about their origin. (In French cuisine *croquette* normally designates the type of fritter represented by Mrs. Huger's "Shrimp Croquettes and Rice" and Mrs. Hill's "Rice Croquettes" (F 66–67), usually bound with heavy white sauce.) We shall return to this French connection.

The lengthy receipt entitled *"Calas"* in *The Picayune's Creole Cook Book* (1901), "From one of the last of the olden Calas women, one who has walked the streets of the French Quarter for fifty years and more... [crying] *'Belle Cala! Tout Chaud!*,'" differs from that of Mrs. Eustis (above) primarily in specifically calling for "a little [wheat] flour to bind," as well as a higher proportion of eggs. (Actually, the presence of even a little wheat flour results in an airier product because of the gluten in wheat, as explained earlier (p. 116.) The *Picayune* editor notes that they may also be made of rice flour, explaining that "in olden days the Cala women used to pound the rice themselves in a mortar till they reduced it to a fine powder of flour," explaining the complaint of Mrs. Eustis in this regard. That is, there were no longer slaves to toil in the kitchen. The editor also notes with contempt the practice in some households of mixing leftover rice with "self-raising flour" (flour mixed with premeasured baking soda and cream of tartar).

As can be seen, *calas* are emphatically identified with African-American women. Certainly it was they who made and sold them. And I believe the name to be African. All over the African Diaspora, particularly in the Caribbean but also Brazil, for example, various forms of *akkra* are applied to all manner of fritters, *akkra* being a term with the same meaning from West Africa, specifically the Yorubas, according to Jessica Harris. (Actually, I believe the term, as *akkra*, to derive from Arabic. In *A Baghdad Cookery-Book* [1226] I find a receipt entitled *"Aqrās Mukarrara,"* manifestly the same word, particularly in light of the fact that the receipt concerns little round cakes of fermented dough stuffed with marzipan [the translation says "dressed"], fried in sesame oil, and finally strewn with scented sugar. What are they but doughnuts? I point out that they also were originally round lumps of dough. I have discussed Arab culinary influences in Africa in Chapter 3, "Pilau." I am told that *aqrās* designates a rounded cake, which is also the essential meaning of *beignet* [from *buyne*, Old French for rounded lump]. But from Africa comes a receipt entitled *"Akla,"* fritters of ground black-eye peas, given by Dinah Ameley Ayensu in *The Art of West African Cooking* (1972). I point out that *akla* is a simple alteration of *akkra*, one involving confusion between the consonants *l* and *r*, a common one, particularly when words cross linguistic borders. I note also that *cala* is a metathetic form of *akla*, an even more common alteration involving transposition, and I propose this derivation for *cala*. To show that my proposal rests on solid ground, I note that black-eye pea fritters are known in Curaçao as *calas*, rather than the more usual *akkras*.[15] In the receipt entitled "Callers" (above) we find yet another type of alteration, that of substituting a word of similar sound for an unknown one, as I discussed in Chapter 5, "Hoppin' John." As is so often the case, there is a bit of seeming reasonableness in the substitution, here involving the fact that the *calas* were indeed "called" on the streets of the French Quarter. I suggest that *callers* was an Anglo form; the Christian Woman's Exchange was not French. (Note also the use of the term *fritter*.) I have not seen the word *callers* so used elsewhere, much less an explanation.

Actually, fritters are among the most universal of foods. Bertrand Guégan, citing Cato the Elder (234–149 B.C.), describes *beignets* that were made by allowing batter to drip through a hole pierced in the bottom of a cup directly into a pot of boiling oil, producing "unexpected shapes," a system that is still practiced today in many parts of the world.

When they had cooked to a golden brown, they were drained and served with honey. And again in the Baghdad manuscript there is a receipt entitled *"Luqam al-qādī"* [literally "judge's mouthful," according to Arberry] which calls for pinching off pieces of fermented dough the size of hazelnuts, then frying them in oil, dipping them in syrup and sprinkling them with sugar. I note the presence in modern Greek cookery of *loukoumades*, virtually identical fritters dipped in honey, which Theresa Karas Yianilos claims go back to classical times—and why not?—but their present name would seem to derive from *luqam al-qādī* (as is evident when *al-q-* is elided), a name very likely acquired during the long Turkish occupation.

Medieval manuscripts of Europe give numerous receipts for all sorts of fritters, as do cookbooks down the centuries. Many kinds of fritters are made for sale in outdoor *souks* [markets] all over the Middle East and North Africa. Nice is the home of *li panissa* [*panisses* in French], fritters made of chick-pea flour and thus related to various pulse fritters round the world. They were sold on the streets of Nice by vendors crying: *"Li panissa! Tout caud! Tout caud!* [*Tout chaud*, piping hot]," precisely as *calas* used to be in New Orleans. *Li panissa* are still cried in the streets of Nice. It is not that they much resemble rice fritters, but the practice demonstrates a continuity of certain customs.

Fritters came to the American Colonies. In the North they were usually called *doughnuts* or *crullers*, both specifically associated with Dutch settlers, although English and German settlers also made various fritters. In the South, generally the picture was not that different with respect to fritters: Mary Randolph of Virginia (1824), for example, gave five receipts in all, one entitled "Dough Nuts—A Yankee Cake," and Mrs. Bryan of Kentucky (1839) gave *"Oley-Koeks"* [an old Dutch word for doughnuts], "Dough Nuts," and "Crullers."[16]

But in South Carolina and New Orleans, we find rice croquettes or *calas*—call them what you will but they are *beignets de riz.*

    Another Kind of Beignets Which Are Called Tourrons
      Cook some rice with milk...it must be quite stiff, and when it has cooled, pound it in the mortar, adding sweet almonds if desired, which must also be pounded. Put the mixture in a pan, add about half as much (wheat) flour, several raw eggs, a little salt, and white wine or milk as you see fit: mix it all well together, and cook it to a paste...that is neither too firm nor too soft....
      When you have sufficiently heated lard in a pot,...take a middling spoonful of paste, and drop it into the pot.

> Cook the *beignets* on both sides...and when they are cooked,
> you must lift them out as dry as possible, and allow them to
> drain; then arrange them on a platter, and sprinkle them with
> sugar before eating them.
>
> —*Le Patissier François, Quatriesme Edition,*
>   *à Troyes,* [1690(?)].[17] First edition 1653, in which
>   this receipt also appears.

The receipt above establishes an early presence of the concept of rice *beignets* in France. These Troyes editions are remarkable in that they were issued by *"La Bibliothèque bleue"* in a very cheap format to be sold far and wide by *colporteurs*, itinerant peddlers who sold door to door and hawked at fairs, a popular phenomenon that is credited with having distributed "tens of millions" of books over a period of three centuries, from about 1600 on. Very few cookbooks were on their list, but any work issued in that series cannot be dismissed as having had limited influence because it was available only to the aristocracy or the very wealthy. (The most important cookbook in this series was *Le Cuisinier François* by La Varenne, first published in 1651.) They were more successful in those parts of France where proper French was spoken, but they reached into homes of great diversity, from thatched cottage to *château* and presbytery, but above all, homes of *la petite bourgeoisie* of the provinces of old France—all according to Daniel Roche, who has studied the phenomenon.

Actually, it was not this work from Troyes that first introduced the concept of *beignets de riz* to France; that had occurred by 1505, as I shall later explain. But the wide dispersion of these *livrets bleus* [blue paperbacks, if you will] must have greatly facilitated and accelerated the process by which professional cuisine for the aristocracy seeped down to the popular level. Eighteenth-century works picked up on rice *beignets*; even *La Cuisinière Bourgeoise* (1753) gives a receipt entitled *"Beignets de blancmangé"* calling for rice flour. The base is indeed *blanc manger*, as it is also for the *tourrons* of the previous century, in that either rice flour or pounded boiled rice is used in the same way as in the ancient receipts given earlier (p. 28); in both cases, rice and eggs are then cooked together to a suitable paste. These two receipts are the forerunners of "Rice Flour Puffs" (F81) given by Sarah Rutledge in 1847. Hers are finer, because the eggs are not cooked in *blanc manger* but are mixed in raw, in the manner of *pâte à chou*, which is used to make *beignets soufflés*, otherwise indelicately known as *pets de nonne* (nun's farts), a receipt for which, under an earlier name, *"Pets de Putain"* (whore's farts), may be found in the 1654 edition of La Varenne's *Le Cuisinier François*; raw eggs were added, as they still are, or the *beignets* would not have puffed so spectacularly and the naughty names would not have occurred to anyone. (It is the raw whites which are crucial.) A better receipt, mentioning its use for *petits choux*, appears in *La Cuisinière Bourgeoise* (1753). So structurally Miss Rutledge's "Rice Flour Puffs" is an adaptation of old receipts for *pets de putain*, substituting rice flour for wheat, an adaptation recorded by Carême in *Le Cuisinier Parisien* (1828), giving a receipt entitled *"Grand Beignet Soufflé et Seringué"* (that is, shaped using a pastry bag). Actually the concept is much older than that, at least as it involves cooked rice, as we shall see, although it does not carry the name of *"Beignet Soufflé."*

In *Les Soupers de la Cour* (1755) Menon gives a receipt for *"Baignets Italiens"* calling for cooking a quarter of a pound of rice in milk until it is "very thick," to which he adds, "a small handful of [wheat] flour [and] three eggs, white and yolk," as well as flavorings, including sugar; "small mounds" of the dough are formed to be fried in deep fat, and when they are of a "fine color," they are placed on a screen to drain and sprinkled with sugar to be eaten hot. This is essentially the classic rice fritter of Carolina, identical in concept to that of "Rice Croquettes [3]" (F 86), differing only in flavoring, an extraneous detail, and is not that different from several other receipts, especially "Croquettes [2]" (F 65) and Maum Peggy's "Breakfast Fry Breads" (F 25). Note particularly the presence of a small amount of wheat flour, a characteristic of this type, a factor which increases airiness, as discussed earlier. For that matter, it also differs little from the *Picayune* receipt for *calas* except that the latter calls for yeast and fermentation, an important point, but one to be explained in terms of evolutionary development; by the early nineteenth century, at least, receipts for *beignets* in French works were routinely calling for allowing the batter to "rise" for several hours before frying, specifically to make them more airy. (Also, one is a soft dough, the other a heavy batter; while important, it is a detail.) I note that Mrs. Huger's "Pan Cakes" (F 31)—actually fritters—calls for leavening with yeast.

I am not unduly concerned about the fact that these receipts appeared in France mostly after the Huguenots had fled from there. They clung tenaciously to their language and culture, and I suspect that a number of French cookbooks found their way into Huguenot households, including possibly *Le Patissier François*, *Le Cuisinier François* (both in editions from the mid-seventeenth century into the eighteenth, including the popular blue paperbacks), *Les Soupers de la Cour*, and almost surely *La Cuisinière Bourgeoise* (1746), which was as popular in France as was *The Art of Cookery* by Hannah Glasse (1747) in England and the Colonies, each going through innumerable editions into the nineteenth century. And there were other cookbooks in which similar receipts might well have appeared, as happened with *Dictionnaire Portatif de Cuisine* (1772), for example.[18]

The same situation concerning French cookbooks obtained in New Orleans, only more so. In 1840 *La Petite Cuisinière Habile*, first published in Paris early in the century, appeared in New Orleans in French; in 1859, an edition of *The Modern Cook* by Francatelli, a pupil of Carême, was published; and in 1904 *La Cuisine Créole À L'Usage Des Petits Ménages* by Célestine Eustis appeared in French.

I propose that it was primarily this French connection that accounts for the historical presence of rice fritters in Carolina and New Orleans but hardly anywhere else in the United States; and when they did appear, as with "Rice Croquettes" from *Maryland Kitchen* (F 81), it was by borrowing. I propose that the receipts came to Carolina and New Orleans from France or, more accurately perhaps, by way of France. I find a receipt for "*Frictelli de riso*" given by Maestro Martino in *Libro de Arte Coquinaria* (in manuscript, last half of fifteenth century) not so different from that given in *Les Soupers de la Cour*, as well as one entitled "*Altre frittelle di riso.*" The Martino work was lifted virtually in its entirety by Platina for his famed work *De Honesta Voluptate* (1475, the earliest extant printed cookbook), where these receipts appear as "*Fritella Ex Riso*" and "*Frictellae ex Riso,*" so that when *Platine en françoys* was published in Lyons (1505), receipts for *buignets de ris* began to appear in print, going through many editions into the seventeenth century. And from Spain in *Arte de Cozina* (1611), Francisco Martinez Montiño gave two receipts entitled "*Buñelos de Manjar blanco,*" one of which is the prototype of that for *tourrons* in *Le Patissier François* (above), with whole phrases having simply been translated from the Spanish. (I am grateful to Rudolf Grewe, who brought this work to my attention and pointed out the similarities.) So one can say that *beignets de riz* had long been known in France, as had been—based on much earlier documentation—all sorts of other *buignets*, *roysolles*, *crespes*, etc., which are in varying degree parallel dishes in that they are all fritters. But they also seem to have been associated with the French in England, for example, as shown by a delightful receipt entitled "A French Dish" from *Elinor Fettiplace's Receipt Book*, a family manuscript collection dated 1604, which involves boiled rice, pounded almonds, and rosewater, all beaten together and fried as cakes.[19] I think that a direct Spanish connection with New Orleans in this regard is far less likely than a French one; the Spanish were there for only about four decades, and the overwhelming presence was French.

I wrote earlier of the African connection in regard to *beignets de riz*. Certainly this was a factor, one of sufficient importance to permit African-American women to have imposed their own name for the dish in New Orleans. But if rice fritters had been brought from Africa, one could reasonably expect them to show up all over the African Diaspora—as with the rice and bean pilaus, for example—and this is not the case. I find *accras* galore in the various Caribbean and South American cuisines, based on perhaps a score or more different products—some over and again, as salt cod, black-eye peas, etc.—but nothing in the way of rice, at least as recorded in the cookbooks. In *Les Antilles À Travers Leur Cuisine* (1967), for example, Dr. Nègre gives eleven receipts for *acras*, not even counting a number of additional suggestions; none is for rice, and this pattern is fairly typical. It may be that it is ill recorded, but I think it fair to say that the rice fritter does not characterize those cuisines in the way that it does that of New Orleans and Carolina. To be sure, *calas* have all but faded into folklore, and that may be part of the story elsewhere as well. That said, I believe that it was the important French presence in those two areas that accounts for the specific receipts for what are *beignets de riz*—and their transmission—that is, the important presence of French women, *les ménagères*, who were comparatively rare in the French West Indies. (A parallel situation may have obtained in the Spanish West Indies.)

I have not mentioned the presence of rice as a factor in these *beignets de riz*. In Carolina it may have been a determining one, in that plantation owners would have been avid for rice receipts. But rice came late to Louisiana; the Rice Council says 1884, and while there may long have been sustenance rice farming previously, rice did not dominate New Orleans society in anything remotely the way it did Charleston society. Nor did it dominate New Orleans cuisine in the same way. While rice was the obligatory accompaniment for various African stews known as *gumbo*, and there was *jambalaya*, this does not quite constitute a rice kitchen, not even when you add *calas*. In *Creole Cookery* (1885) there is a receipt with the title "Carolina Boiled Rice" in addition to at least four other rice receipts. "To Prepare and Boil Rice" and "To Make a French Pilau" among them, taken verbatim from *The Carolina Housewife*. As I noted earlier, Lafcadio Hearn specified "Patna rice" in 1885. And as late as 1904 Mrs. Eustis called for *"riz Caroline première qualitép"* in *La Cuisine Créole À L'Usage Des Petits Ménages.*[20]

I suggest that rice and rice cookery were associated with African-Americans in New Orleans, so much so that when they learned to make *beignets de riz* by following the dictation of the French mistress—surely succeeding beyond the skills of the mistress—they appropriated them, seeing an opportunity of eking out a precarious living by making and selling them, crying them on the streets in the manner of vendors down through the centuries. All of this is consistent with the supposition that African-Americans had long carried on subsistence farming of rice, primarily for their own use, and that commercial rice production did not come on the scene until after the end of slavery, so that the *white kitchen* of New Orleans never quite became a rice kitchen in the way it had long since in the rice lands of South Carolina. Not until the turn of the century, when there was a flurry of cookbooks published in New Orleans, was there what can be described as a rice kitchen; its beginnings are well documented in *Creole Cookery* (1885) with its "borrowing" of Carolina receipts for boiling rice and "French Pilau," among others.

This scenario is somewhat speculative, to be sure, but given the fact that parallel receipts for what are *beignets de riz* characterize the cookery of New Orleans and South Carolina Low Country, places where there was an important French presence, I propose it as a possible explanation of the puzzle, indeed, the only one that accounts for the known factors.

PRACTICAL NOTES ON BREAD

It is beyond the scope of this work to discuss in any detail the art of making bread. Entire books are written about it, the best of which among those addressed to home bakers is Elizabeth David's *English Bread and Yeast Cookery*. As with so much of our cookery, the quintessential American loaf came from England. The American edition (1980) provides American equivalents for her English weights and measures and discusses methods whereby baking in a brick oven may be approximated but does not alter her admirable text and traditional measures. (I make a point of this because such is not always the case.) As noted earlier, she also includes a receipt for rice-and-wheat bread.

In addition, John Martin Taylor includes a traditional Carolina receipt entitled "Rice and Wheat Bread" in his forthcoming work on South Carolina Low Country cookery, enhanced by helpful instructions for the modern baker.

However, I do specifically point out that one ounce of fresh, compressed yeast is ample to raise a dough based on one pound of dry rice and four pounds of wheat flour, as in Miss Rutledge's receipt. (*In extremis*, two scant teaspoons of dry granulated yeast may be substituted.) In our fevered search for speed in all things, Americans have come to use far too much yeast, forgetting that yeasts are living plants and should not be forced. In my own baking, I use minuscule amounts of yeast—even less than here suggested—and my bread is the better for having undergone the traditional long, unhurried fermentation which is necessary to develop fine flavor. Using too much *dried* yeast is especially pernicious; it is of a different strain than other yeasts and desiccated to the point of imparting the flavor of sere, dusty leaves. Less is better. The worst that can happen is that rising may take rather longer than planned. The optimal *proportion* of yeast, any yeast, is dependent on many factors, but it may be said that it *declines* with a rise in ambient temperatures (including that of the flour and water), with the size of the batch, time allowed for rising, etc. There is also the quality and age of the yeast to consider; the fresher the yeast the better the bread, which is why I prefer to use less and grow my own perky yeasts. In short, there are no absolute measures of yeast; it is largely a matter of attitude.

As noted, "yeast powder" is effectively baking powder, actually a mixture normally composed of two parts of cream of tartar to one of baking soda, and sometimes spelled out in the receipts, although proportions are not consistent. Amounts, when specified, are wildly erratic, even among similar receipts. As I discussed earlier, breads made of straight rice flour do not increase in volume to any great extent; increasing the proportion of baking powder, in my experience, only increases the horrid chemical aftertaste that alkalis always leave, so that I suggest using the lowest proportions suggested, those given in "Pooshee Rice Bread" (F 21), for example, of one teaspoon of "yeast powder" to a pint of flour. (Also, see *Yeast powder* in Glossary.) This formula is more authentic than modern double-acting baking powders. It is also better.

Even more so than with yeast, Americans have always been prone to use far too much baking powder. In recognition of this, Mary Stuart Smith, in the *Virginia Cookery-Book* (1885), discusses how "even soda biscuits may be rendered palatable.... The first rule is to use the baking powder *sparingly*. A teaspoonful, in conjunction with some acid, is enough to lighten a gallon of flour, instead of a quart, as ordinary cooks imagine [emphasis original]." (In context, it is clear that she means a teaspoon of baking *soda*, along with the requisite acid, making it equivalent to a tablespoon of baking powder.) The point is highly perceptive, and while rice flour may require a bit more than does wheat flour, it is well to remember that less is better.

Please note that the amount of baking powder in Mrs. Parker's receipt for "Rice Griddle Cakes" (F 31–32) is a scribal error; the original calls for two *teaspoons*.[21]

As noted earlier, the receipt from the *Charleston Gazette*, "To Make Wafers," is a hopeless muddle, the scribe having leapt from a receipt of that title to the next, actually "Rice Puffs," without having finished that for wafers. For a more accurate version of the *Gazette* receipts, none of which I have tried, see the Appendixes.

Also, I have not tried Miss Rutledge's receipt for "Loaf Rice Bread" (F 15), but I question the amount of liquid; a similar receipt, "Ashley Rice Bread" (F 14), calls for close to a pint more, and this turned out fine. However, "Loaf Rice Bread" was copied correctly.

Indian shops carry rice flour, as do stores catering to Hispanic peoples, particularly those from the Caribbean; health food stores carry brown rice flour, which is not authentic in Carolina receipts but works fine. If like Mrs. Eustis you cannot find rice flour, it can be made with the authentic mortar and pestle, or a food processor, or a grain mill, should you have one. Sift out any coarse particles and use them for something else—boiling up for use in rice bread, for example. Note Miss Rutledge's perceptive remarks on the differences among rice flours (F 17–18).

A special note on baking traditional journey cakes, that is following the old receipts calling for dough, not batter: I find that results approximating the old way of baking them in front of the fire can be obtained by baking them under a broiler. They must be placed at some distance from the source of heat, or they will char before they are baked. Proceed as directed in the receipts, spreading the dough no more than an inch thick on an oiled baking sheet, turning the cake over when crusty on top with the help of an outsized spatula so that the bottom can bake the same way. Some old receipts say to baste the cakes with cream or melted butter, an excellent procedure.

CHAPTER 8

Sweet Rice Dishes of
South Carolina

La Terrinée ou Bourgoule
This is a sort of rustic flan, popular at all village festivals in
Lower Normandy. Mix 125 grams of Carolina rice, 85 grams of
fine sugar, half a teaspoon of pounded cinnamon, a pinch of salt,
and two liters of rich milk. Pour into an earthenware dish, place
in a *bain-marie* [larger pan of hot water], and bake in the oven for
three hours. Serve hot or cold.
　　　—Austin de Croze, in *Les Plats Régionaux de France*,
　　　　　Paris, 1928.

Le Riz à la Brehatine
[as made in Saint-Brieuc, Brittany]
In a large, flared earthenware basin, place eight liters of fresh
milk, 500 grams of good rice, 500 grams of sugar, one teaspoon of
salt. Carry the dish to the *boulangerie* [bakery] so that it may be
put into the oven as soon as the bread is drawn, and leave in the
oven five or six hours, that is, until the oven is cool.
　　This is a comfortable dessert for some thirty people, very
much appreciated at wedding parties and other village events. . . .
　　It is served cold or lukewarm, as desired, in the dish in which
it was cooked.
　　　—Austin de Croze, in *Les Plats Régionaux de France*,
　　　　　Paris, 1928.

Poor Man's Rice Pudding
Sweeten a quart of milk to your taste; stir into it a small tea-
cup of washed rice, and put a spoonful of butter in the middle of
the dish; put it into the oven, and bake an hour.
　　　—Sarah Rutledge, in *The Carolina Housewife*,
　　　　　Charleston, 1847.[1]

IN HER FOREWORD to the 1976 edition of *Two Hundred Years of
Charleston Cooking*, Elizabeth Hamilton writes: "But don't look for rice
pudding. The very idea of sweets with rice upsets Charlestonians who
take rice very seriously." *Pace* Mrs. Hamilton, there is a receipt entitled

"Rice Pudding" in that very book, and there are some fifty-five sweet rice receipts in Mrs. Stoney's collection, most of which are of impeccable Low Country provenance, leading off with fourteen from Sarah Rutledge of Charleston. (It is not that Mrs. Hamilton was altogether wrong. It is true that the very idea of sweet pilaus with fruit seems to have been held in horror in Charleston, although they were honored in Persia, their land of origin. I have found only one such receipt of Carolina provenance, as noted in Chapter 3, "Pilau," and that was in the same work for which she wrote the foreword.)

More than forty of these sweet recipes may be classified as puddings, all of them evolved from English and French recipes for *blanc manger*, following various lines of development that differed somewhat in the two cuisines. (It will be remembered that the earliest receipts were borrowings from the Saracens, as discussed in Chapter 3, "Pilau.") Thirteen of these receipts, five of which are called "Rice Blanc Mange" (F 82, 83), descended fairly directly from those early ones. Others in this subcategory are: "Snow Ice Cream" (F 81), which is not frozen; two receipts entitled "Rice Jelly" (F 89, 90); two receipts called "Rice Flummery" (F 83, 84); and a number of others, such as "Rice Milk," without eggs (F 89). These last dishes also hark back to the seventeenth-century flummery, a sort of jellied dish originally made with oats. But the name early came to refer as well to other jellied dishes, as did the name *blanc mange*, so that their histories are tangled and, as can be seen here, ill differentiated. In addition to her "Rice Blancmange," for example, Miss Rutledge gave "Arrow-Root Blancmange," "Gelatine Blancmange," and "Isinglass Blancmange" (1855). Because of their blandness, all of these dishes were also associated with invalid cookery.[2]

Twenty-four of the rice puddings are of a conventional type using a custard base, varying considerably in richness and in certain structural details. Some call for rice flour, for example, using essentially pastry cream technique. Four are baked in a crust, staring with Miss Rutledge's "Rice Flour Pudding" (F 77) and Mary Randolph's "Rice Pudding" (F 72) following an earlier nomenclature that so classified custardy mixtures baked in an open crust. (Early American receipts for pumpkin pie were called "Pumpkin Pudding," for example. That is, the designation of *pie* was reserved for dishes encased in pastry, as meat or apple pies—or in rice, as the Carolina *rice pies*.) This differentiation was becoming archaic elsewhere, as shown by Mrs. Parker's "Rice Pie" (F 80), also a custardy rice pudding baked in a crust, but seems to have lingered in the Low Country. Miss Rutledge's "Rice Cheese Cakes" (F 79–80) are handled precisely as is the "Rise Florentine" found in the early seventeenth-century manuscript transcribed as *Martha Washington's Booke of Cookery*, although the richness of the custard is reminiscent of even earlier cheesecakes "made without cheese curd," for which there are also receipts therein. Flavorings are different, but the lineage is direct.

In stressing the English provenance of these custardy rice puddings, I do not mean to imply that they were not made elsewhere. But English custard techniques were admired even by the French, and a majority of the early settlers in Carolina were English, so there is little mystery. The rice pudding of French cuisine, *gâteau de riz*, is as often called *pouding au riz*, even *pouding au riz à l'anglaise*, especially in its simpler versions; even so, it is often baked in a caramel-lined mold or glazed. Other sweet rice dishes in French cuisine tend to be showpieces, a rather different affair from the homey rice puddings of England and of Carolina. I do not propose to detail all the other puddings. Some are baked in a dish, some are boiled; a few are garnished with meringue, although none of Carolina provenance, I might note.

Perhaps the most interesting from a historical point of view and the most associated with Carolina is the category represented by Miss Rutledge's "Poor Man's Pudding" (given above, p. 141), Miss Porcher's "Poor Buckra Pudding" (F 72), Mrs. Burckmyer's "Poor Man's Pudding" (F 77), Maum Maria's "Woodlawn Rice Pudding" (F 76), Mrs. Kollock's "Rice Pudding" (F 91), and "Belvidere Rice Pudding" (F 72), attributed to Mrs. Howard of Maryland. (According to Jan Longone, Mrs. Howard's estate was named Belvidere, so I must suppose that the dish was named for that rather than for Belvidere Plantation of Carolina Low Country. She included a number of rice receipts clearly of Carolina provenance.) This dish comes straight from French country cooking, as illustrated by the receipt from Saint-Brieuc calling for taking it to the village bakery. Both Normandy and Brittany claim the dish; it did not enter French national cuisine, not even French home cooking outside those two provinces, at least insofar as I have been able to ascertain. The procedure outlined in the "Belvidere Rice Pudding" is precisely that given to me by Norman friends, always with the explanation that it was not to be found in the cookbooks, and except for the most meticulous regional works from those adjoining French provinces, it is so. Some of the Huguenot settlers must have brought the receipt with them. The dish remained remarkably classic in Carolina; two receipts call for a spoonful of butter, but this is the only deviation in composition, with only the replacement of cinnamon by nutmeg in one receipt and by vanilla in another. (According to Jean Seguin, cinnamon is invariable in Lower Normandy.) There is a change of method to be noted in Mrs. Burckmyer's receipt; I cannot

imagine why, because the oven method is every so much simpler and assures a better texture. The brown skin that forms is an integral part of the
dish, as noted in the Belvidere receipt. It is amusing to think of members
of the rice aristocracy calling the dish "Poor Buckra Pudding" [poor
white man's pudding]. It is true that Curnonsky and de Croze describe
the dish as *"un flan populaire au riz,"* which in French refers not so much
to its being popular as to its being lower-class. This is further emphasized
by its popular names in Norman patois, such as *Teuregoule* [*tord-gueule*,
literally "twist-gullet"], and *Bourgoule* [literally "stuff-gullet"], both referring to the filling qualities of this relatively cheap dish.

I note that the basic structure of this dish is essentially that of Indian
pudding of New England, indicating that there must have been unrecorded receipts for somewhat similar spartan puddings made of other
grains, oat grits in particular. (Sir Kenelme Digbie [1669] does give a receipt called *"Rice & Orge mondé"* [pearl barley]—actually too separate
parallel ones—which is not too different except that the grain is to be
soaked "in the Chimney-corner" several hours before being cooked for
some additional hours; it is not done in the oven, however, at least not in
his receipts, but the proportions are comparable.)[3]

Carolina Snow Balls
(*americane*)
Take four good siz'd apples. Scoope out the cores. Put in
them a little lemon peel shred fine or grated—just to season them.
Have ready 4 pieces of thin cloth—divide half a pound of rice into
4 parts—which lay in the cloths and set an apple in each. Tye
them up tight, put them into cold water and boil them two hours.
Turn them carefully out, that they may be smooth & eat them
with melted butter—sugar and wine if agreeable.
   —*The Lucayos Cook Book. (The Bahamas, so named by
   Columbus.)...Kept...from AD 1660 to 1690, by a Noble
   Family of Elizabethan England*, Nassau, Bahamas, 1959.

To make Carolina Snow Balls
Take half a pound of rice, wash it clean, divide it into six
parts; take six apples, pare them and scoop out the cores, in which
place put a little lemon-peel shred very fine; then have ready some
thin cloths to tie the balls in; put the rice in the cloth, and lay the
apple on it; tie them up close, put them into cold water, and when
the water boils they will take an hour and a quarter boiling: be
very careful how you turn them into the dish that you do not
break the rice, and they will look as white as snow, and make a
very pretty dish. The sauce is, to this quantity, a quarter of a

pound of fresh butter melted thick, a glass of white wine, a little
nutmeg, and beaten cinnamon, made very sweet with sugar; boil
all up together, and pour it into a bason, and send it to table.
—Hannah Glasse, in *The Art of Cookery*, London, 1796.[4]

We now come to something of a curiosity, "Carolina Snow Balls."
And the earliest receipt I have found for them is even more of a curiosity.
It is found in a work for which there is scanty documentation, which is a
polite way of saying virtually none at all, only a poor photograph of the
purported volume, "Bound in full ancient Sheep-Skin," as if the photograph could not be of any old bound book. I make a point of this because
it bears on the authenticity of the receipt. I cannot vouch for it, not having seen the work, nor so much as a photograph of a single manuscript
page. However, the transcribed text of some 260 receipts "feels" right.
The capricious spelling is typical of the period; there are no striking
anomalies, that is, no more than one so often discovers in any hitherto
unfamiliar work, in the sense that every manuscript is idiosyncratic, at
least a little. There is the seeming anachronism of a receipt "Carolina
Snow Balls" by 1690, an early date but not a materially impossible one.
That is, if the cultivation of rice had indeed become firmly established by
1690, as some sources indicate, such a receipt could have been developed
very early. And since some of the original Lord Proprietors came from
the Bahamas, and even more significantly, since the islands were given to
the Carolina Colony by the Crown in 1670, such a receipt could have been
swiftly transmitted.

I believe that the document is authentic but amateurishly edited and
published. Indeed, its very amateurishness can be said to be a sign of its
authenticity, in that the skill and knowledge necessary to have fabricated
such a convincing text would surely have also produced some semblance
of documentation. The financial rewards would not have been sufficient
to warrant such labor; the owner of the manuscript, who did what "editing" was done, is not named, so that there is not even the reward of public recognition, nor does the text contain any material suggesting the
possibility of a hoax with the idea of discomfiting scholars or playing a
joke on them. As to the earliness of the date, I think that the owner did
not realize that in family manuscripts of this nature, unless unequivocally
dated at the end as well as at the beginning, entries often continued to be
added for a surprisingly long period. In other words, if the entry date for
"Carolina Snow Balls" is understood to be more like 1700, it would not
seem in the least anachronistic. Even so, 1690 is not impossibly early.

With this lengthy proviso, I suggest that the Lucayos receipt may be
a very early one; the next in date that I find is given by Hannah Glasse in

1796 (it may have appeared in somewhat earlier editions). It resembles the Lucayos receipt, which should not be too surprising, considering that by whatever route, they both came from South Carolina sources. Mrs. Rundell gave a receipt "Snowball" (1808) nowhere near as detailed.

The dish is not unique to Carolina in this country; a similar receipt called *"Echaudés de Riz,"* or "Rice Dumplings," is given in *The Picayune's Creole Cook Book* (1901), with this introduction: "It was the old Creole negro cooks who first evolved that famous Creole dessert Rice Dumplings." Actually, I believe they came straight from Carolina and were originally an adaptation of any of several apple dumpling receipts from Europe, such as *"Bourdelot"* of Normandy, consisting of an entire cored apple individually wrapped in pastry before cooking. Nowadays they are usually baked, but Norman friends tell me that in the days before most people had home ovens, they were more often boiled. It is considered a country dish and specifically Norman in France. But in England Mrs. Beeton (1861) gave otherwise identical receipts for boiled and baked apple dumplings, which shows that the concept was familiar there as well and very likely had long been. (She also gives a receipt for "Apple Snowballs" encased in rice, but that I suspect came from Mrs. Rundell's receipt.) The *Picayune* work and Mrs. Hill of Georgia also each give otherwise identical receipts for boiled and baked apple dumplings individually wrapped in pastry.[5]

As I noted earlier, desserts were traditionally the domain of the mistress of the house, something in which she took personal pride, often actually going so far as to make then herself, which accounts for the continuing European character of most of them. Nothing is more natural in rice country than to substitute rice for pastry in such a dish, and this is what happened, whether it was the idea of the mistress or of the African-American cook.

The receipts for this dish included by Mrs. Stoney are Mrs. Blake's "Rice Dumplings" (F 79), very detailed and of Low Country provenance, and Mrs. Hill's "Snow Balls" (F 80). Curiously, I find no receipt from Miss Rutledge. They finally became old-fashioned; I find no receipt for them in any of the popular Carolina works of this century, for example.

It should be noted that a number of dishes discussed under other categories, notably the sweet or sugared rice croquettes (see the section on these; pp. 129–138) as well as the sweetened rice cakes (see Chapter 7, "Breads") could be classified as desserts; I have chosen to discuss them according to their construction.

CHAPTER 9

Rice in Invalid Cookery

Rice

[Rice is]: Astringent, Repercussive, and Spermatogenetick....

The Broth. It is made either with simple Water, or with Mutton Broth. It nourishes much, restores a weakned and decayed Body, but binds not the Body as that made with Milk.

The Milk. It is an excellent thing for stopping all sorts of Fluxes of the Belly, and restoring such as are labouring under a Consumption, especially where there is an Ulcer of the Lungs....

The Pudding [rice boiled with milk "till dissolved," after which are added eggs, sugar, raisins, and nutmeg]. *This* as also the *Broth* and *Milk,* nourish much, strengthen such as are weak, restore such as are Consumptive, encrease Seed, and makes the feeble Vigorous.

　　　—William Salmon, in *Botanologia,* London, 1710.

Racahout (Cuisine Arabe)

A powdered mixture which serves to prepare an analeptic [restorative, stimulating] gruel; it is composed thus. Use:

White sugar	550 grams*
Vanilla sugar	5 grams
Cocoa	60 grams
Sweet Acorns	60 grams
Rice flour	60 grams
Potato starch	45 grams
Salep	15 grams

It is mixed to a paste in cold water, then cooked in water, milk, or bouillon.

　　　—Joseph Favre, in *Dictionnaire Universel de Cuisine,*
　　　Paris (1894).

---

*Judging by other formulas, this is surely a misprint for 250 grams (just over a cupful), which is more than sufficient.

Racahout des Arabes (Mrs. Devereux.)

$^1/_2$ pound best French chocolate. $^1/_4$ pound arrowroot.*
1 pound rice flour. $^1/_2$ pound loaf sugar, sifted.

These materials are to be thoroughly mixed and rubbed
together. A *dessert spoonful* of this mixture should be slightly wet
with *milk* or *water*, then stirred into *one pint* of *boiling milk*, and
boiled five minutes. This is excellent food for invalids or
convalescents. Serve hot, as a beverage; or make much thicker, to
be eaten cold as a delicate pudding.
        —Mary Johnson Lincoln, in *Mrs. Lincoln's Boston Cook-
        Book*, Boston, 1883[1]

AS A LOYAL DAUGHTER of the land of Carolina Gold rice, Mrs.
Stoney may be forgiven for being perhaps a bit overenthusiastic in extol-
ling the strengthening qualities of rice (F 5–9), but it is true that wherever
rice has been known, its use as appropriate and comforting food for invalids has been particularly appreciated. It is soothing, nourishing, easy
to digest, and is specific for cases of diarrhea. Most of the receipts in this
section are self-explanatory in this regard.

    But Mrs. Blake's *"Racahaut"* (F 88), more properly *racahout*, de-
serves attention. This stimulating and nourishing concoction for invalids
was popular in France particularly during the nineteenth century; a receipt is still given in *Nouveau Larousse Gastronomique* (1967). Lexicographers say that the word is Arabic, referring it to *rāqaout*, but in his
Dictionnaire Étymologique de la Langue Française (1964), Oscar Bloch,
citing the appearance of *râcahout* in French in 1833, notes that *rāqaout*
"is not assured," meaning that it has not been found in Arabic. This in
itself is not necessarily conclusive; culinary terms are notoriously ill recorded. The word is, however, apparently flawed in form as well, so that
it may have been wrongly transcribed from some other Arab word.

    The receipt as it appears in French sources no longer has much rela-
tionship to what may, or may not, have been an analeptic potion from the
classical period of Arab preeminence in medicine. That is, chocolate is
from the New World, as are vanilla and potatoes, but they are of less consequence here. The other important elements had long been known to the
Arabs; rice was a staple, with its own medicinal virtues. Salep, a tuber of
the *Orchis* family, originally from India, was described in 1694 thus:
"This Root not only prevents the Womans Coming before her time [that
is, spontaneous abortion], but also gives a safe, speedy, and Easy Delivery

---

*This amount is wildly excessive and must be in error; see Mrs. Blake's receipt (F 88).

when Natures Time is accomplisht"; this according to John Peachie in England, who said that salep came from Turkey. (It is in use in the Middle East today, not only medicinally but also as food.) It was administered in caudles, that is, warm sweetened beverages of varying composition. And it was the Arabs who spread the Persian art of working sugar, indeed its very use; specifically, it was they who introduced it into the pharmaco-poeia, not only for its own putative medicinal virtues but also in the form of a syrup as a vehicle for bitter medications—an important development.

But knowledge of the administering of chocolate gruels for medici-nal reasons dates back to the seventeenth century in France. In *De l'Usage du Caphé, du Thé, et du Chocolate* (1671), Philippe Sylvestre Dufour, drawing on a Spanish work translated into french in 1631, discusses this use at some length, nothing that chocolate "fortifies the stomach," is "oppilative [constipating]," and fattening. He plays with certain charac-teristics of chocolate which are opposites: it is both astringent and unctu-ous or buttery, for example, discussing these qualities in the light of the Galenic system of humors, a subject beyond the scope of this work. What is particularly interesting is his account of its preparation in the "Indies," that is, Mexico, in this instance; it is taken hot with *"Atolle,"* which is made by mixing maize flour with water to a paste and then boiling it with more water to "a very thin gruel [*une bouillie fort claire*]." Insofar as structure is concerned, this differs from *racahout* little beyond the choice of grain and the absence of sugar. In a later edition (1688), he says that chocolate is to be given when the stomach is "exhausted and weakened by colic, diarrhea, windiness," and other digestive upsets. He also gives a formula from the "Indies" calling for seven hundred cocoa beans, one and a half pounds of sugar, two ounces of cinnamon, fourteen grains of *Chilé* or Mexican pepper, one-half ounce of cloves, three pods of vanilla or two ounces of aniseeds, and *Achiote* the size of a hazelnut. Nothing is said about preparation, but in context I suppose that this mixture was pounded to a powder and mixed with the *Atolle* referred to earlier. *Atole* is still a popular drink in Mexico today, according to Diana Kennedy, who gives a receipt called *"Champurrado"*, translated as "Chocolate-flavored atole," made with *masa harina* [a specially prepared cornmeal], choco-late, cinnamon, sugar, and water. She says that atole is sometimes made with ground rice nowadays. Of the ingredients listed in these two Mexican receipts, separated by three centuries in time, chocolate, chile pepper, va-nilla, achiote, and maize are from the New World; sugar, cinnamon, cloves, aniseeds, and rice, the Old World.

As noted earlier, there are strong Arab elements in the French re-ceipts for *racahout*, and certainly the French attributed them to the Arabs. But it now seems that there was medical knowledge of a thickened chocolate potion in France that antedated the appearance of *racahout* by more than a century, at least as recorded. To be sure, the Arabs could have independently developed such a beverage based on rice, and this formula would have better pleased the French palate. Chocolate, it should be noted, came to France early, by way of Jews fleeing the Spanish Inquisition, which continued to rage against *conversos* (Jews and Moors who had converted to Catholicism under duress) for centuries; it was not abolished until 1820, although its most virulent period was probably during the sixteenth and seventeenth centuries. I have not done independent research on the introduction of chocolate to France, but the manufacture of chocolate was long associated with the Jewish community of Bayonne; nor do I know when the Arab world learned of chocolate, but I rather suspect that the Arabs—especially the physicians, who were preeminent and historically alert to medicinal uses of new substances—also had had time to learn the secrets of chocolate before they, too, were finally purged from Spain.

Curiously, in the early texts which I have consulted, I found little on the stimulating properties of chocolate. But these qualities, due to the presence of theobromine, a caffeinelike substance, had become known and much appreciated in France at least by the time of Brillat-Savarin, who wrote about chocolate and its invigorating qualities in 1826. He does not mention *racahout* by name but does note that a "most distinguished pharmacist" of Paris sold various medicinal chocolate mixtures: "Thus, for persons who are thin, he offers an analeptic chocolate with salep; for those who have delicate nerves, an antispasmodic chocolate with orange flower water; for those with irritable dispositions, chocolate with almond milk...and so forth.[2] Salep was regarded as an important active ingredient of French formulas for *racahout*, so that it may be that the pharmacist was in effect offering *racahout*, or something very like it, some time before the first citation of the word in 1833.

The American receipts do not greatly resemble the French ones except insofar as the structure of a thickened chocolate beverage is retained, although in different proportions. Mrs. Blake's receipt is so similar to that given by Mrs. Lincoln, differing essentially only in the amount of arrowroot, that the Mrs. Devereux to whom the receipt is attributed must have been from South Carolina, where the name is a prominent one. Judging by the title, "*Racahout des Arabes*," I think it may be assumed that the receipt came from an unknown French source.

I also find a receipt "*Racahaut*" in Mrs. Howard's *Fifty Years in A Maryland Kitchen* (1873) which is identical to that of Mrs. Blake (F 88), including the variant spelling of *racahaut*. As noted elsewhere, (p. 143),

Mrs. Howard seems to have borrowed a number of rice receipts from Carolina sources, and in spite of the chronology of receipts as published, I believe that Mrs. Blake—or her mother perhaps, given the lapse in time—was the source of this receipt.

I find no mention of *racahout* in other historical American cookbooks, not even those with an extensive section on invalid cookery, so that its use cannot have been very widespread in the United States outside of Carolina, even supposing that I have missed an appearance or two, or even more. I do, however, find *rachahout* in a most unlikely source, the *Wise Encyclopedia of Cookery* (1971), defined as "a Turkish dish made from *palamoute*, a compound of dried acorns, sugar, spices, and aromatics," which comprises the entire entry, with no mention of chocolate, perhaps in error; nor is there any suggestion that it had been in use in the United States.[3]

CHAPTER 10

A Few Words on the *Carolina Rice Cook Book* and Its Contributors

THIS CHARMING BOOKLET, containing some 237 receipts for rice, was compiled in 1901 by Louisa Cheves Smythe Stoney, wife of Captain Samuel Gaillard Stoney, a figure in his own right but most pertinently chairman of the Carolina Rice Kitchen Association, seated in Charleston. According to John Martin Taylor, the work was "offered at the South Carolina Interstate and West Indian Exposition as a 25-cent souvenir," adding that "the exposition was a sort of world's fair meant to inject some spark in the moribund Carolina economy." He notes that the historian Walter Fraser described the exposition as "a picturesque disaster."

Worse times were yet to come. As discussed earlier, the cultivation of rice, along with the opulent society it engendered and supported, was doomed by the end of slavery, as the skilled African-American hands gradually left the industry and the proprietors were left to their own devices, muddling along with unskilled immigrants, as movingly recounted by Theodore D. Ravenel (cf. p. 15). The devastating hurricane of 1911 was the deathblow.

But we still have the *Carolina Rice Cook Book*, which has become exceedingly rare. It is not that the work is strikingly original. It was a promotional effort, and most of the receipts are simply gleaned from a number of nineteenth-century works, most notably *The Carolina Housewife*.

But Mrs. Stoney also included receipts obtained from the interested ladies of Low Country society, including some of the proudest names of the old rice aristocracy and their cooks, to be sure, although they are seldom credited and if they are, then by their old slave names. In short, it is a period piece, but this is what is important about the work. That is, it reflects one aspect of the period, the unique rice kitchen of Low Country Carolina, the glory of which was also beginning to fade as the old African-American cooks departed from the scene, one after the other. Here too, industrialization was an important factor in the decline of this kitchen, but more important still was the absence of the skilled black hand in the kitchen, which had passed on those skills to succeeding generations in days gone by. Harriet McDougal, Mrs. Stoney's granddaughter, tells me that when *Charleston Receipts* appeared in 1950, many were shocked for find a receipt entitled "Faber's Pilau" calling for margarine. Margarine! "Faber was a *butter* man. He never would have used margarine," she said. She ought to know; Faber had been the Stoney's cook for decades. We shall return to Faber. Still, I never fail to be impressed as to how classic the cuisine of Low Country Carolina managed to remain through the nineteenth century. I cannot say the same for the twentieth.

Let us turn to the contributors of those 237 receipts. I should note that the number is fairly arbitrary, depending on how you count them; two are inadvertently repeated (one of these is misattributed, as well), and in a number of instances, there are really two receipts under a single title. Where significant, I note these errors as they arise. These and other errors are listed in "Errata in the Text of the *Carolina Rice Cook Book*." I also append a short glossary of unfamiliar terms.

As already noted, Mrs. Stoney's most important source was *The Carolina Housewife*, by A Lady of Charleston, the first edition of which appeared in 1847, at the apogee of Low Country cookery. The "Lady" is, of course, Sarah Rutledge (1782–1855), daughter of Edward Rutledge, a signer of the Declaration of Independence and sometime governor of South Carolina, in short, a member of an aristocratic family. In her milieu, it is said, a lady's name was published only in connection with three events: birth, marriage, and death. She never married.

The first edition exists in facsimile with a perfectly delightful and enlightening introduction by Anna Wells Rutledge, who refers to Miss Rutledge as "Cousin Sally," and from which I have essentially lifted these few biographical details.

Mrs. Stoney seems to have used the third edition of 1855 for the fifty-nine receipts included from *The Carolina Housewife*; that is, forty-six of these appeared originally in 1847, nine more in the second edition of 1851, and four more again in 1855. (I have not thought it necessary to indicate first appearance unless it seemed significant in some way.) All these receipts appear as given in the third edition, with only a few changes of the sort Mrs. Stoney was prone to make. (In *A Preliminary Checklist of South Carolina Cookbooks Published Before 1937*, Anna Wells Rutledge notes a fourth edition with no date, a work which I have not seen.) I also present four additional receipts from 1847 not included by Mrs. Stoney, making a total of sixty-three from Miss Rutledge if I have counted correctly. I have discussed elsewhere the tremendous importance of this work. It is unique.

In terms of frequency, although not in importance, I place next *Mrs. Parker's Complete Housekeeper*, by A Veteran Housekeeper [Mrs. E. C.

Parker], which first appeared in New York in 1888. I find in her 1891 edition, the only one available to me, all the twenty-two receipts that Mrs. Stoney attributed to her. She seems to be something of an interloper in the Stoney collection; I have been unable to find out much of anything about her, but from internal evidence she could hardly have been a South Carolinian, calling a *pillau* a *Turkish soup*, for example (F 46). I even doubt that she was a Southerner, active as she was in the domestic science movement, which was a phenomenon of the North.

The next work is *Fifty Years in A Maryland Kitchen* by Mrs. B. C. Howard (1801–1896), which first appeared in 1873. Mrs. Stoney selected twenty-one receipts from this lovely work, a real period piece, all of which I have found in the first edition. (The "revised" edition is a travesty of modernization.) Mrs. Howard's work shows that, while rice held a position of some importance in Maryland cookery, it was not sufficient to qualify as a rice kitchen; the receipts for rice are all borrowed, for example.

Mrs. Stoney attributes nineteen receipts to *Mrs. Hill's New Cook Book,* by Mrs. A. P. Hill, Widow of Hon. Edward Y. Hill, of Georgia, 1871 (copyright 1870, an edition I do not find in the bibliographies). All of them I have found in this edition. The receipt "A French Pilau" (F 55) is mistakenly attributed to her; it comes from *The Carolina Housewife*, as correctly attributed on F 51. Mrs. Hill's work is more encyclopedic than the Carolina work, but I have the impression that Miss Rutledge had been rather more faithful in recording the cookery of Low Country Carolina than was Mrs. Hill with that in Georgia; her receipts tend to be fussier, suggesting for example in her receipt "Hopping John" that it could be made with chicken and "green English peas," rather than with "pickled pork" and proper dried peas—a perfectly good dish, to be sure, but not a hoppin' John. But perhaps this is one way in which Georgia cookery differed from that of Carolina. It was also written a generation later.

Of previously published sources, at least insofar as I can ascertain, there remain two to mention, one being *The Virginia House-Wife* by Mary Randolph (first edition 1824), from which Mrs. Stoney selected eight receipts, including her excellent "Rice Bread" (F 16); there is also an interesting "Black Puddings", blood puddings (F 69), which did not fit into any of the categories I discussed earlier; they contain rice, which is highly unusual. The receipt "Rice Blanc Mange" (F 82) is misattributed; it comes from *The Virginia House-Wife*. The receipts included by no means exhaust those given for rice by Mrs. Randolph. I cannot say which edition was used except that from internal evidence it could not have been earlier than 1831 (that on which all succeeding editions were based).

The remaining published source is *The Charleston Gazette* (April, 1830), represented by five receipts, all using rice flour, unfortunately riddled with errors in transcription. What appears to be a more complete and accurate version is given in the Appendixes.

The contributed receipts fall into three main categories: those given by the good ladies of Carolina Low Country, always accorded the courtesy of a title, either Mrs. or Miss, as the case may have been, with only rarely mention of a given name; African-American cooks, designated by old slave names, excepting Faber, who was male; and those attributed to plantations. Many are anonymous.

Among the ladies, eighteen receipts are attributed to Mrs. Huger, fifteen to Mrs. Blake, five to Miss Porcher, five to Mrs. S. D. Stoney, and four simply to a Mrs. Stoney. (One can only speculate as to which Mrs. Stoney is being referred to.) Each gave at least two or three receipts that are invaluable in that they shed light on what sort of receipt was deemed worthy of preservation at a time when it was becoming increasingly evident that the old days were forever beyond recall. Many other illustrious names are among the contributors, some with a single receipt. Beyond noting their milieu, it did not seem necessary to undertake the endless and possibly futile research that more specific identification would have entailed.

As I indicated earlier, it is reasonable to suppose that most of these ladies' receipts actually came from their cooks—or cooks of a previous generation—however they were attributed. Only five African-Americans are explicitly credited: Maum Sarah with three, Maum Grace with two, Maum Maria with one, Maum Peggy with one, and Faber with one. In *Charleston Receipts* (1950), a Samuel Faber, described as "a superior cook," is identified by Mrs. Albert Simons (Harriet Stoney) as having "always been with our family," and I wondered whether he might be our Faber. Over the telephone Harriet McDougal, our Mrs. Stoney's granddaughter, said, "Of course he's our Faber." She said that he was an exceptional person, one of those bigger- than-life individuals, who had been a respected figure in Charleston, active in his community and known to the gentry as well, because he always officiated as doorman at the St. Cecilia Ball, largely because of his imposing appearance. He was only a boy when he entered service in Mrs. Stoney's kitchen, according to her granddaughter, and was "a wonderful cook."[1]

There is, in addition, a Mr. Valdez, a gentleman since he is accorded a title, to whom are attributed three receipts (F 70) which are Spanish, or perhaps Spanish Creole, not typical of traditional Carolina practice.

Without further ado let us proceed to the *Carolina Rice Cook Book*.

The Facsimile

Carolina Rice

Cook Book.

COMPILED BY

MRS. SAMUEL G. STONEY.

PUBLISHED BY

CAROLINA RICE KITCHEN ASSOCIATION,

SAMUEL G. STONEY, Chairman.

A. B. MURRAY,   JNO. L. SHEPPARD,
HENRY C. CHEVIS.   HENRY J. O'NEILL,
            Committee.

CHARLESTON, S. C.

Presses The Lucas-Richardson Co.,
Charleston, S. C.

CHARADE.

My First, a grain, in this old town
   We cannot dine without it,
Tho' farther North they really know
   Not very much about it,
My Second is not man nor beast
   And yet, like human kind,
He wears a feather in his cap
   And flaunts it in the wind.
My Whole subsists upon my First,
   (That's why it is delicious)
And to my First the Planter thinks
   This little thief pernicious.
But when he sees the little thief
   Well dressed upon the platter,
A dainty morsel, served in style,
   Oh! that's a different matter.
              —ELIZA PERONNEAU MATHEWES.

For answer see next page.

RICE BIRDS.

"Select the fattest birds, remove the entrails, bake them whole or split them up the back and broil. Permit no sacrilegious hand to remove the head, for the base of the brain of the rice bird is the most succulent portion. Or the birds may be placed in either shape in a round bottom pot with a small lump of butter, pepper and salt, and cook over a quick fire. Use no fork in eating. Take the neck of the bird in the left hand and his little right leg in the right hand. Tear away the right leg and eat all but the extreme end of the bone. Hold the bill of the bird in one hand and crush your teeth through the back of the head, and thank Providence that you are permitted to live. Take the remaining left leg in your right hand and place in your mouth the entire body of the bird, and then munch the sweetest morsel that ever brought gustatory delight. All that remains is the front portion of the head and the tiny bits of bone that formed the ends of the legs. To leave more is to betray your unappreciativeness of the gifts of the gods."

Carolina Rice Cook Book.

RICE.

The most nutritious, the most easily digested, and at the head of fourteen hundred várieties, stands Carolina Rice. Richer in fats, more highly flavoured than any other variety of Rice known, it is to-day the standard of excellence amongst rice consumers, not only in this country, but throughout the rice countries of the world. Carolina Rice Seed has been used in Japan, India, and China, but the peculiar advantages of our soil and climate, which seem to develop the grain to its highest perfection, have enabled us, for over two centuries, to maintain this high standard, and it is still admitted that Carolina Rice is superior to every other variety in the world. According to carefully prepared statistics, rice is the principal food of fifty-four per cent. of the inhabitants of the globe. Rice is more generally and widely used as a food material than any other cereal. A combination of rice and legume is a much cheaper, complete food ration than wheat and meat, and can be produced on a much smaller area.

Amory Austin, B. S., in his admirable treatise on rice, (see Report No. 6. U. S. Department of Agriculture, January, 1893,) says:

"The famous Carolina Rice is esteemed especially among foreign consumers as the best rice in the world." Mr. Austin gives the following results of analysis of rice made by Stow's Experimental Station: "Rice contains a slightly larger amount of total nutritious matter than wheat or rye, the exact proportion being one pound of rice equivalent to 1.043 pound of wheat, or to 1.040 pounds of rye. Maize approaches more nearly, the proportion being 1 to 1.038. Rice is more nutritious than whole oats, one pound of the former being equivalent to 1.163 pound of the latter, while it contains 3.70 times as much nutritious matter as potatoes, 1.87 times as much as fat beef, and 3.21 times as much as lean or good ordinary beef." Quoting from same authority. "It contains a large proportion of carbonhydrates, which are transferred in the animal economy into fats; of these it contains on the average from 70 to 80 per cent, while other cereals contain from 60 to 70 per cent. only.

"Boiled Rice is digestible in one hour, while the same amount of roast beef requires three hours for digestion."

The comparative time of digestion of some of

our leading food products, will emphasize the
superiority of rice.

	Hours.	Minutes.
Rice, boiled	1	0
Wheat bread	3	15
Oat meal	3	0
Irish potatoes, boiled	3	30
Round steak, medium fat	3	0
Loin steak, medium fat	3	0
Oyster stew	2	0
Salmon, fresh	1	45
Apples, uncooked	1	50
Tomatoes, fresh	2	30

As a safe diet for invalids, under almost all
conditions, it is now acknowledged by the best
medical authorities. As a food for Strong Men
the following clipping is a fit illustration:

"RICE AS A STRONG DIET."

"This appears to be the belief of the Japanese,
and there seems to be good evidence for it. A
traveller in that far-off country says:

"The Japanese have made a race of giant men
—a race of wrestlers. These wrestlers often
weigh 200, 300 and 400 pounds. At the Impe-
rial Hotel, in Tokio, they brought their champion wrestler to my room. He was prodigious
in size and as fat and fair as a baby. He was a

Hercules in strength, but looked like an over grown cherub of Correggio.

'What do you eat?' I asked.

'Rice—nothing but rice.'

'Why not eat meat?'

'Meat is weakening. Beef is 70 per cent water. Rice is 80 per cent. food. I ate beefsteak once, and my strength left me. The other man ate rice and threw me down.'

My courier said: 'This wrestler is the Sullivan of Japan. No one can throw him.'

"That Rice, which every chemist knows to be mostly composed of starch, would possess such elements of force appears incredible. If we had been told that these wrestlers had lived on wheat, or corn, or barley, we should be quite ready to accept it. Yet the strong porters of South America are said to live on Rice.

"But if meat is so essential in the generation of strength as is popularly supposed, how shall we account for the extraordinary physical endurance, longevity of the rhinoceros, the hippopotamus, the elephant, and the horse?"—*Hawaiian Commercial Journal.*

As the birth place of Rice in America, as the leading Rice producing State for over two centuries, and as the only section of this great continent where Rice has been appreciated at its true value, and prepared as it should be, it is peculiarly appropriate that the public should be enlightened with our methods of preparation introduced by Carolinians through this medium, to the variety of nutritious and delightful combinations which are given in this book. The majority of these receipts have been in constant use for over a century, passing from generation to generation, precious heirlooms, jealously guarded by the dear old housewives of the past, and many of them now for the first time appearing in print.

MRS. SAMUEL G. STONEY.

Charleston, S. C., Dec 1901.

TO PREPARE AND BOIL RICE.

Wash one pint of Rice; add to it a quart and a pint of water, and a tablespoonful of common salt; boil over a quick fire for ten minutes, stirring occasionally. Then pour off all or nearly all the water; cover the vessel and put on a very slow fire, and allow it to steam for 15 minutes at least, stirring occasionally. The proper washing is very important. The Rice will be soft or grainy, according to the quantity of water left on it when put to steam, and the length of time allowed in the steaming. The larger the quantity of water and the shorter the steaming the softer will be the rice.

CAROLINA HOUSEWIFE.

TO BOIL MIDDLING RICE.

Wash and pick 1 quart rice, put into 2 quarts of boiling water; just before it boils pour off water and steam until done. Salt water to taste.

TO BOIL SMALL RICE.

Wash and pick 1 quart rice, put into 2 quarts of boiling water, just before it boils pour off water and steam till done. Salt water to taste.

ANOTHER WAY OF PREPARING RICE.

Boil your rice in the ordinary way, in a pot lined with china. After being well soaked, dip the pot into cold water, and it will come out into a cake.

CAROLINA HOUSEWIFE.

BREADS.

Of the rice smalls a large portion is ground into flour. It is used by millers and bakers for mixing with wheaten flour, and for dusting purposes.

A mixture of 10 per cent. to 20 per cent. of rice flour to flour ground from wheat containing a good percentage of gluten, improves the color and its keeping qualities, and makes a lighter and better loaf. It quickly absorbs the moisture of the flour of wheat harvested in a damp condition.

The quotation from Bouillet's Dictionary of Sciences given below shows that it is much esteemed in France for mixing into bread:

"Rice is a food easy of digestion; its flour, mixed with that of wheat, when the proportion amounts to no more than a fourth, gives us a bread very agreeable to the taste, and one which keeps fresh longer. When ground into flour (creme de riz), rice cooks much more readily than when it is whole."—*Bouillet's Dictionary des Sciences.*"

Creme de riz is much used in Europe and America as a food for infants nad invalids on account of its digestive properties. Rice flour is also employed in considerable quantities for the sizing of cotton goods.

The smalls should be well ground by rolls or stones, and dressed fine.

RICE FLOUR.

[From the Charleston Gazette, April, 1830.]

"Some notice of the preparation of this article for domestic purposes was made in the daily prints a week or more since. Through the polite and friendly attention of Colonel Vanderhorst we have been favored not only with a specimen of a very superior article prepared under his own direction, but with the proper manner of making use of it. We do not know that we can do a better service to our Southern trade than by giving these various modes of its preparation, in order to overcome difficulty in the use of it arising entirely from a general ignorance of the article in its present form. Our readers will observe that we do not arrogate to ourselves the framing of these valuable prescriptions. We never boiled rice in all our lives, though we have some little credit for ability in encountering it in a different way. But the ladies to whom we are specially indebted on more occasions than one have graciously informed us where we have been in fault. For the making of *rice bread,* then, you are required to—

"Boil a pint of rice soft; add a pint of leaven, then three quarts of flour; put it to rise in a tin or earthen vessel until it has risen sufficiently; divide it into three parts; then bake it as other bread, and you will have three large loaves.

"To Make Journey or Johnny Cake.—To three spoonsful of soft-boiled rice add a small tea-cup of water or milk; then add six spoonfuls of the flour, which will make a large journey cake or six waffles.

"To Make Rice Cakes.—Take a pint of soft-boiled rice, a half-pint of milk or water, to which add twelve spoonsful of the flour, divide it into small cakes and bake them in a brisk oven.

"To Make Wafers.—Take a pint of warm water, a teaspoonful of salt, a pint of boiling water, beat up four eggs, stir them well together, put two to three spoonfuls of fat in a pan, make it boiling hot and drop a spoonful of the mixture into the fat as you do in making common fritters.

"To Make Pap Pudding.—To a quart of milk and a pint of the flour—boil

them to a pap, beat up six eggs, to which
add six teaspoonfuls of Havana sugar and a
spoonful of butter, which, when well beater
together, add to the milk and flour, grease the
pan in which it is to be made, grate nutmeg
over the mixture and bake it.

After all this is done, the sooner they are
eaten the better."

ASHLEY RICE BREAD.

Stir one tablespoonful of butter into a pint
of rice flour, beat light two eggs, two teaspoonful of salt, add them to the flour and butter,
one half of a yeast powder, dissolve the tartaric acid in water, and the soda in a pint of
milk. Stir them quickly together, and bake
the mixture immediately. The lid of the oven
should be heated as well as the bottom.

CAROLINA HOUSEWIFE.

BEAUFORT RICE BREAD.

A pint of boiled rice, half a pint of hominy,
three pints of rice flour, mixed with water
enough to make a thick batter; add a teacup of
yeast and a teaspoonful of pearlash. Put the
mixture into a deep pan, well greased, and let
it rest for eight or ten hours. Bake in rather
a brisk oven.　　Carolina Housewife.

POTATO AND RICE BREAD.

One quart of rice flour, one tablespoonful of mashed sweet potato, one tablespoonful of butter, mixed with half a pint of yeast, and one pint of milk. Bake in a pan, and in a moderate oven.   CAROLINA HOUSEWIFE.

LOAF RICE BREAD.

A pint of rice flour, three eggs, a spoonful of butter, a salt spoonful of salt. Beat the eggs quite light; stir in the butter, flour and salt. Dissolve a yeast powder in a little warm water, mix it well with the other ingredients; pour into the pan and place immediately in the oven. This bread requires nearly an hour's baking in a moderate oven.   CAROLINA HOUSEWIFE.

LOAF RICE BREAD.

Beat 1 quart of rice into flour and boil 1 pint of rice. very soft. Set your leaven over night, allowing 1 pint of wheat flour to one-half pint yeast and one-half pint of water. Stir the leaven, soft rice and flour together and put in a large vessel to rise, and sprinkle with rice flour over the top. When it rises stir it up and put it in a pan to bake. Your boiled rice should be cold.   MRS. CAIN.

A CONVENIENT BREAD FOR TEA.

One half-pint of grist boiled soft, 2 eggs, one half-pint rice flour and a little salt mixed well and baked in plates.   Mrs. S. D. Stoney.

WALWORTH RICE BREAD.

One teacup of warm hominy, with 1 tablespoonful of butter, beaten well into it, 1 tablespoonful of sugar and 1 egg rubbed together; one half-pint of milk, 1 quart rice flour, salted to taste, 1 teaspoonful of soda and 2 of cream of tartar dissolved in 2 cups with a little water and stirred in just before you put the mixture in the pans.   Mrs. S. D. Stoney.

EUTAWVILLE RICE BREAD.

One pint rice flour, 3 gills of milk, 2 eggs, 1 tablespoonful of butter, 1 tablespoonful of yeast powder, salt.   Mrs. S. D. Stoney.

RICE BREAD.

Boil six ounces of rice in a quart of water, till it is dry and soft; put it into two pounds of flour, mix it in well; add two teaspoonfuls of salt, two large tablespoonfuls of yeast, and as much water as will make it the consistence of bread; when well risen, bake it in moulds.
        Virginia Housewife.

RICE BREAD.

Three pints of rice flour, 3 heaping table-spoonfuls of hominy, 5 eggs, 1 tablespoonful of butter, 1 cup of milk, 1 teaspoonful of soda and 1 of cream of tartar. Bake in a quick oven, a little while. Sugar added to this, makes a very nice bread for tea.   MRS. HUGER.

RICE BREAD.

Take a pint of rice left from dinner, cover with water over night. In the morning add 1 pint of wheat flour, 2 eggs and 1 tablespoonful of butter, salt, yeast powder, and milk enough to make it consistency of custard. Bake in patty pans.   MRS. HUGER.

WEENEE RICE BREAD.

A tablespoonful of rice boiled to a pap; while hot stir into it a large tablespoonful of butter; then add a gill and a half of milk or cream, four tablespoonfuls of very light yeast. Stir these ingredients well together, and rub in two quarts of beaten rice flour gradually; salt it to taste. Turn the mixture into a well greased pan and set it to rise. When light bake in a moderate oven until quite brown. About an hour is required for the baking of this bread. If the rice flour manufactured for sale is used, a smaller quantity will be necessary; the mixture must be just so stiff as that a spoon will stand in it. CAROLINA HOUSEWIFE.

CAROLINA RICE AND WHEAT BREAD.

Simmer 1 pound of rice in 2 quarts of water until it is quite soft; when it is cool enough, mix it well with 4 pounds of wheat flour, yeast and salt as if for other bread. Of yeast 4 large spoonfuls. Let it rise before the fire. Some of the flour should be reserved to make the loaves. If the rice swells greatly and requires more water, add as much as you think proper.

CAROLINA HOUSEWIFE.

PINOPOLIS RICE BREAD.

Three gills of rice flour, 2 eggs, 1 spoonful of butter, 1 half-pint of milk, 2 spoonfuls of yeast powder mixed in the flour and baked in small pans. MISS M. E. PORCHER.

GIPPY RICE BREAD.

One pint of rice flour, 1 pint sour milk, 2 eggs, teaspoonful of soda, dissolved in a little water. Bake in a deep pan in a quick oven.

ST. JOHN'S RICE ROUND BREAD.

One half-pint of rice boiled soft, 3 eggs, 1 teaspoonful of butter, 1 teacup of milk, and as

much wheat flour as will make the consistency
of pound cakes. Drop on a hot pan; bake, do
not turn over. MISS M. E. PORCHER.

RICE BREAD.

One half-pint soft boiled rice, 1 half-pint rice
flour, 2 eggs, tablespoonful butter, salt and milk
enough to soften it till it will drop from the
spoon. Bake in small pans.

MISS JANE BROUGHTON.

RICE BREAD.

One pint rice flour, 3 eggs, 1 tablespoonful of
butter, 1 half-pint milk, 1 teaspoonful salt, 1
half teaspoonful soda, 1 half teaspoonful cream
of tartar. Mix flour with cream of tartar and
put soda in just as you are about to bake.
Clabber or buttermilk can be used instead of
cream of tartar. MRS. C. W. KOLLOCK.

RICE BREAD.

One pint of rice flour, 2 eggs beaten light.
Wash and work well into this: One tablespoonful of butter, half a pint of new milk, a
little salt and half a teaspoonful of soda, and a
quarter of a teaspoonful of tartaric acid dissolved in a little milk. When mixed put it into

a tin an inch and a half deep. Have the oven
ready and bake half an hour. A little sugar
makes the rice bread very nice cake.

MARYLAND KITCHEN.

PHILPY.

One gill of rice, boil it, and when cold rub it
smooth with a spoon, moisten with water a
gill of rice flour, mix it into the rice. Beat one
egg very light, and stir it well into the mixture.
If too stiff, add a spoonful or two of milk.
Bake it on a shallow tin plate. Split and butter
it when ready to serve.

CAROLINA HOUSEWIFE.

PANY GETTA.

One pint of rice flour, 1 pint of milk, 4 eggs,
1 tablespoonful of butter, 3 teaspoonfuls yeast
powder, 1 teaspoonful salt. Grease pan; bake
in quick oven. MISS PORCHER.

TO MAKE BREAKFAST BREAD.

Use 2 teacups fresh ground Carolina rice
flour, 1 teacup best wheat flour, 1 teacup of
milk, 2 eggs, 1 dessertspoonful butter, 1 dessertspoonful sugar, 2 heaping teaspoonful baking
powder, salt to taste. To the above mixture
add sufficient water to reduce stiffness. Bake
in large or small tin pans, as desired.

MRS. J. L. SHEPPARD.

RICE CORN BREAD.

One pint of boiled rice, 1 pint corn meal, a dessertspoonful of lard, 1 pint of butter (or sour milk), 2 eggs beaten well; mash the rice smooth, add the lard to it, stir in the last a teaspoonful of soda; bake in shallow pans.

MRS. HILL.

POOSHEE RICE BREAD.

One pint of rice flour, add 1 pint of milk, 3 eggs, 1 spoonful of butter, 1 teaspoonful of yeast powder; put in a deep pan and bake in a quick oven.

OPHIR RICE BREAD.

Four spoonfuls of soft-boiled rice, 1 table-spoonful of butter, 2 eggs, 1 gill of milk; stir in rice flour enough to make it stiff; bake in cups half filled.

RICE BREAD.

One-half pint of grist, 1 gill of cullens,* boil together, then put to cool, salt and a pint of leavens, 3 pints of rice flour put to rise; when it commences to rise, heat your oven and bake.

MRS. HUGER.

*Rice broken coarsely in a mortar.

A RICE CAKE.

One pint of rice flour, 1 egg (the yolk and white beaten separately), a small teacup of milk, a teaspoonful of salt. These ingredients must be well mixed together, and just before baking stir in a teaspoonful of soda dissolved in a half wineglass of milk. Bake in a pan in a hot oven for half an hour.

CAROLINA HOUSEWIFE.

RICE BISCUITS.

Boil soft a half pint of rice, when cold add to it half a pint of rice flour, a spoonful of fresh butter, a half a pint of milk and sufficient salt; mix all well together, and drop it in large spoonfuls on tin sheets in the oven; bake till quite brown. CAROLINA HOUSEWIFE.

RICE BREAD.

One pint of rice flour, one-half pint of clabber, one-half teaspoonful of soda, 3 eggs, the yolks well beaten, and the whites whipped to a froth, a teaspoonful of salt, a dessertspoonful of butter; put the flour, eggs and butter into a bowl, stir well together, adding the clabber gradually, add a little hot water to the soda, when dissolved pour into the pan and bake.

MRS. HUGER.

ALABAMA RICE BREAD.

One pint of rice boiled soft, 6 eggs beaten light, 1 pint of milk, half a pint of corn meal, a dessertspoonful of lard, a dessertspoonful of butter, a teaspoonful of salt. Rub the ingredients well together, and bake in small tins or muffin rings.　　　Carolina Housewife.

RICE BREAD.

One quart of soft boiled rice, 1 quart of leaven, 1 pint of rice flour, 1 teaspoonful of salt; mix well and put into the pan in which it is to be baked; as soon as risen bake.

Mrs. Huger.

RICE OVEN BREAD.

One-fourth of a pound of rice boiled very soft, three-fourths of a pound of wheat flour, 1 gill of yeast, 1 gill of milk and a little salt. Bake in a pan in a moderate oven.

Carolina Housewife.

RICE SPIDER BREAD.

A cup of rice boiled soft, 2 cups of flour, 3 eggs. Let the rice be cold; then beat the flour and rice together, add the eggs, beat the mixture well together, and bake in a hot spider.

Carolina Housewife.

RICE BREAD.

One teaspoonful of butter, 1 teaspoonful of
salt, 1 pint of milk, 10 tablespoonfuls of rice
flour, 1 even salt spoonful of soda, 1 even salt
spoonful of tartaric acid dissolved in a tablespoonful of water. Beat white of eggs separately. Rub yolk of eggs, butter and salt together, then add the flour, thinning with milk,
as necessary. Then add the white of egg, and
last the soda and tartaric acid. Mix well and
bake half hour in a regular oven.

MRS. BURCKMYER.

SOUR CREAM RICE BREAD.

Mix 1 pint of sour cream or buttermilk with
2 eggs, 1 pint of rice flour and a tablespoonful
of butter. Add salt and about a teaspoonful of
soda (enough to sweeten cream). Bake in well
buttered china-cups. MRS. HUGHES.

RICE FLOUR BALLS.

A pint of milk to a pint of flour; let the milk
boil, stir in the flour with a little salt, add the
yolk of an egg, roll into balls, and fry them
with butter or lard. CAROLINA HOUSEWIFE.

RICE DROPS.

Half a pint of hominy, half a pint of milk, 1

pint of rice flour, 2 eggs, a large tablespoonful
of butter and a little salt. Beat all well together and drop on a tin sheet.

CAROLINA HOUSEWIFE.

BREAKFAST BREAD.

One pint of hominy, 1 pint of rice flour, 2
eggs, 1 tablespoonful of butter, salt; milk
enough to make a thin batter; drop into a frying pan well greased and fry. MRS. HUGER.

RICE FLOUR AND HOMINY FRITTERS.

Take some cold hominy, with milk and 1 egg,
mix it up into balls with rice flour, not too stiff;
to be fried. MRS. DILL.

RICE COOKIES.

One pint of soft boiled rice; add as much rice
flour as will make a batter stiff enough to be
made into cakes. Fry them in nice lard. Salt
to the taste. CAROLINA HOUSEWIFE.

BREAKFAST FRY BREADS.

One-half pint rice boiled soft, 1 gill of wheat
flour, 1 egg, one-half pint of milk; put a
large spoonful of lard in a round bottom pot,
and when boiling drop in the mixture by the
spoonful, and let it stay until brown.

MAUM PEGGY.

ST. JOHN'S RICE FLOUR MUFFINS.

One gill of rice flour boiled in a cup of milk like pap, when cold add one-half teaspoonful of butter, 2 eggs, one-half pint rice flour, beat lightly and bake in rings.

RICE MUFFINS.

One-half pint of soft-boiled rice, 1 spoonful of butter, 2 eggs, 2 spoonfuls of yeast, salt, 3 pints of wheat flour; mix at night and bake in rings in the morning. Mrs. Huger.

RICE MUFFINS.

To a half pint of rice boiled soft, add a teacup of milk, 3 eggs well beaten, 1 spoonful of butter, and as much wheat flour as will make the thickness of a pound cake. Drop them about the oven. They do not require turning.
Carolina Housewife.

RICE CAKES.

One-half pint of hominy, one-half pint milk, one-half pint rice flour, 2 eggs, 1 spoonful of butter and a little salt; to be dropped on tin sheets. Mrs. Huger.

RICE EGG CAKE.

One-half cup of rice flour boiled stiff, add a large teaspoonful of butter. When cold add 3 eggs, well beaten, and a cup of rice flour. Drop it on a tin sheet and bake quickly.

CAROLINA HOUSEWIFE.

RICE CAKES.

One pint of soft boiled rice, while warm stir in a dessertspoonful of butter, then add half a pint of milk, half a pint of rice flour, 1 egg and a little salt; bake either in patty pans or in a large pan. MRS. HUGER.

SOFT RICE CAKES.

Melt a quarter of a pound of butter or lard in a quart of sweet milk. Beat 2 eggs light, add as much rice flour as will make it into a batter, mix it with half a teacup of yeast and a little salt. When light bake on a griddle, like buckwheat cakes. CAROLINA HOUSEWIFE.

RICE CAKES.

Take 1 pint of soft boiled rice, half a pint of milk or water, and 12 teaspoonfuls of rice flour. Divide into small cakes and bake in quick oven.

CAROLINA HOUSEWIFE.

RICE CAKES.

Three eggs, a tablespoonful of butter and 1
of cream, half a pint of milk, the same of hominy, and 6 or 7 tablespoonfuls of rice flour. All
the ingredients to be well rubbed up in a marble mortar and baked on tin sheets.

CAROLINA HOUSEWIFE.

RICE CAKES.

One pint of soft boiled rice, a teaspoonful of
butter, an egg, half a pint of milk and a half
pint of rice flour; salt to taste. Beat all together and bake in patties.

CAROLINA HOUSEWIFE.

RICE CAKES.

Beat 3 eggs well, add 1 quart of milk, a tablespoonful of wheat flour and a little butter and
salt, then stir in as much rice flour as will make
a thin batter. Add a teacup of yeast; set to
rise, and bake on a griddle when light.

CAROLINA HOUSEWIFE.

RICE CAKES.

Pick and wash one-half pint of rice,, and boil
very soft. Drain it and let it get cold. Sift one
and one-half pints of rice flour over the pan of

rice, and mix in a quarter of a pound of melted
butter, with a salt spoonful of salt. Beat 5
eggs very light, stir them into a quart of milk.
Beat the whole hard, and bake in muffin rings.
Send to table hot; eat with butter, honey or
molasses.   MRS. BLAKE.

RICE BATTER CAKES.

Add to warm hominy milk and 2 eggs, add
rice flour to make it stiff. Batter baked on the
spider as buckwheats.   MRS. DILL.

TO MAKE RICE FLOUR GRIDDLE CAKES.

Use 2 ounces butter or sweet lard, 1 pint milk
near boiling point, 1 or 2 eggs, beaten light, 1
tablespoonful of wheat flour, about 1 pint and
a half fresh ground Carolina rice flour, one-half
teacup good yeast, or half cake compressed
yeast; salt to taste.

To the milk, just before boiling point is
reached, add butter, then pour slowly over rice
flour, stirring constantly from the middle of the
bowl.

Dissolve yeast, to which add wheat flour,
and set to rise, until the rice flour mixture has
cooled.

When the rice flour mixture is about luke-
warm add the yeast mixture. Beat long and
well, then stir in eggs, well beaten, and salt.

Cover batter and set to rise over night in warm place. Before cooking thin to right consistency with luke-warm milk or water. Cook on soapstone griddle or in waffle iron.

Use only luke-warm water to dissolve yeast. Instead of using butter and milk, water and lard can be used, making a very economical dish. Mrs. J. L. Sheppard.

RICE CRUMPETS.

One and one-half pints of beaten rice flour, 1 pint of milk, 1 large dessertspoonful of butter, 4 dessertspoonfuls of yeast; salt to the taste. Stir these ingredients well together, and set the mixture in a covered vessel to rise in a warm place. Just before baking stir in half a teaspoonful of salaratus dissolved in a little water. Bake on a griddle. Two eggs may be used, and 3 are thought an improvement.

Carolina Housewife.

CRUMPETS.

One gill of yeast, 1 tumbler of warm water, 1 egg and a little salt, 4 large spoonfuls of wheat flour, and then stir in ground rice flour until it is stiff; set to rise at night; in the morning, if necessary, thin with a little milk; bake quickly on a griddle; if acid add a little soda.

Mrs. Huger.

RICE SLAP JACKS.

Three eggs, 1 pint of sour milk, 3 tablespoonfuls of soft boiled rice; salt to the taste. Beat the eggs light, add the milk and rice and a sufficient quantity of flour to make it the proper consistence. Stir in a teaspoonful of pearlash dissolved in a little water, and make on a griddle or in rings.   CAROLINA HOUSEWIFE.

RICE GRIDDLES.

Boil soft 1 gill of rice; while hot stir into it a teaspoonful of butter; beat 2 eggs very light and mix them with the rice after it becomes cold; add 1 gill of rice flour, one-half pint of milk. Stir all together before baking. Bake quickly on hot griddle, and the cakes will rise much.
CAROLINA HOUSEWIFE.

PAN CAKES.

Two large spoonfuls of hominy, 3 of brown sugar, 4 of rice flour, one-half pint leaven, 1 tumbler of warm water and a little salt, then stiffen with wheat flour and set to rise; when risen fry in boiling lard.   MRS. HUGER.

RICE GRIDDLE CAKES.

Two cups of cold boiled rice, 1 pint of flour, 2 tablespoonfuls of baking powder half tea-

spoonful of salt, 1 egg and a half pint of milk.
Bake brown and serve with honey.

Mrs. Parker.

RICE GRIDDLE CAKES.

Soak half pound of rice. Boil soft, drain and
mix with it a small cup of butter, let cool and
add a quart of milk, a little salt and 6 eggs.
Sift in a quarter pound of flour with a teaspoonful of baking powder. Bake well on
greased griddle. Mrs. Parker.

RICE GRIDDLE CAKES.

One and one-half pint of cold boiled rice, put
to soak in warm water, enough to cover it.
Mash the rice well and make a batter, just be
fore using, with 1 quart of sour milk, 1 light
quart of flour; salt to taste, and 2 eggs well
beaten. The batter should be moderately
thick. Stir in a teaspoonful of soda just before
frying. Mrs. Hill.

RICE FLOUR BATTER CAKES.

Beat 3 eggs separately; make a batter rather
stiff by stirring into the yolk of the eggs alternately a large teacup of rice flour and milk.
To a tumbler of hot rice, or small hominy well
boiled, add a heaped dessertspoonful of butter
or lard; stir in the white of the egg beaten to a
stiff froth; mix well with the yolk. Fry on the
griddle. Mrs. Hill.

RICE CAKES.

Take a pint of rice that has been boiled soft; add to it a teacup of flour, 2 eggs well beaten, a pinch of salt and enough butter to make a thick batter; throw into the batter a tablespoonful of melted lard, and bake on a hot griddle.

RICE GRIDDLE CAKES.

In the morning put half a pint of rice in soak. After dinner boil it very soft, mash it fine, and add a teaspoonful of butter and set it aside to cool. At tea time add 3 eggs, 1 pint of milk, and a little less than 1 pint of flour and a little salt. Beat all well together and bake in cakes on the griddle.   MARYLAND KITCHEN.

RICE FLANNEL CAKES.

Boil a bowl of rice very soft and let it cool. A pint of flour (or a little more, as your judgment directs), a tablespoonful of butter and half the quantity of lard. Not quite a quart of sour milk and cream mixed, more than half of the latter if you have it, in which case put less lard; 4 eggs beaten light just before mixing. Mix the rice first in the cream and milk, beat in the egg, then the saleratus dissolved in a little milk, and lastly the flour to bind it. Bake as buckwheat or flannel cakes.

MARYLAND KITCHEN.

RICE JOURNEY OR JOHNNY CAKE.

Boil a pint of rice quite soft, with a teaspoonful of salt; mix with it while hot a large spoonful of butter, and spread it on a dish to cool; when perfectly cold, add a pint of rice flour and half pint of milk; beat them all together till well mingled. Take the middle part of the head of a barrel, make it quite clean, wet it and put on the mixture about an inch thick, smooth it with a spoon, and baste it with a little milk; set the board aslant before clear coals; when sufficiently baked slip a thread under the cake and turn it; baste and bake that side in a similar manner; split it and butter while hot. Small hominy boiled and mixed with rice flour is better than all rice; and if baked very thin, and afterwards toasted and buttered, it is nearly as good as cassada bread.

VIRGINIA HOUSEWIFE.

PAN JOURNEY CAKE.

One-half pint of rice, 1 dessertspoonful of butter, 2 tablespoonfuls of milk, 2 tablespoonfuls of fine rice flour; boil the rice quite soft and stir the butter into it while hot. If the bread is wanted for breakfast the rice must be boiled the night before; and if wanted for tea, it must be prepared in time for it to become cold before

the other ingredients are mixed in. When ready
to bake, stir in the milk and rice flour. Spread
the mixture about one-half inch thick in a shallow pan and bake about half hour in a moderate oven. CAROLINA HOUSEWIFE.

ST. JOHN'S JOHNNY CAKES.

One pint of soft rice, one-half pint rice flour,
1 tablespoonful of butter, fresh milk enough to
soften enough for baking; have two oak boards
about 12 inches long and 6 inches wide. Spread
the mixture on one board and lean it up in front
of a good fire till brown, and then pass a cord
between the cake and the board to loosen it.
Place the other board in front of it quite near
and turn the first board over. The cakes will
then be on the second board; lean it up in front
of the fire and bake until brown. This requires
an open fire.

RICE JOURNEY OR JOHNNY CAKE.

One-half pint of soft boiled rice, with just
flour enough to make the batter stick on the
board; salt to taste; spread it on the board
thin or thick as it is wanted. Baste it with
cream, milk or butter; cream is best. Set it
before a hot fire and let it bake until nicely
browned; slip a thread under it to disengage it

from the board, and bake the other side in the
same manner, basting all the time it is baking.
CAROLINA HOUSEWIFE.

RICE JOURNEY OR JOHNNY CAKE.

For two cakes: Twelve tablespoonsful of
cold hominy well boiled; half a pint of rice
flour. Mix it with cream and milk.
MARYLAND KITCHEN.

WHITE HALL RICE WAFFLES.

One pint of soft rice, one-half pint rice flour,
1 teasponful of butter, a little milk to make
them brown.

RICE AND WHEAT FLOUR WAFFLES.

Waffles are very good when made of thin batter composed of soft boiled rice and a small
portion of either rice or wheat flour, with a
spoonful of butter.   CAROLINA HOUSEWIFE.

RICE WAFFLES.

One quart of flour, 1 cup of boiled rice, 5 eggs,
1 teaspoonful of salt, 2 teaspoonsful of baking
powder; add milk to make it thin. Bake quickly
in well greased waffle irons.   MRS. PARKER.

One pint of boiled rice mixed with half a tea-

cup of butter, 1 pint of flour, teaspoonful of
baking powder, half a teaspoonful of salt, 6 eggs
and cream to make batter thin. Beat very light.

MRS. PARKER.

RICE WAFFLES.

Boil a small teacup full of coarse rice flour
(or rice) to a pap, and to it put a pint of fine
rice flour, one-half pint of milk, one-half of
water, a little salt. Heat your irons and grease
them with a little lard; then pour in the batter,
and bake the waffles to a light brown.

CAROLINA HOUSEWIFE.

RICE WAFFLES.

A teacup of rice flour, 2 large teaspoonsful of
beaten rice boiled to a pap, a small teacup of
milk and 1 egg. This will bake four waffles.

CAROLINA HOUSEWIFE.

WAFFLES.

A teacup of cold hominy, half a spoonful of
lard, the same of butter, 2 tablespoonsful of
wheat flour, 12 of rice flour; salt to the taste.
Rub the butter and lard in the hominy; add the
flour and a sufficient quantity of water to make
a paste; rub it until very light, and then add
milk enough to make the batter so thin as that
it may be poured in the iron.

CAROLINA HOUSEWIFE.

RICE WAFFLES.

One pint of soft boiled rice; half a pint of wheat flour; 3 well beaten eggs, 1 teaspoonful of butter, 1 pint of milk.

MARYLAND KITCHEN.

RICE WAFFLES.

To a half a pint of rice boiled soft and mashed very fine, a tablespoonful of butter. Set it to cool, and just before baking add 1 egg and a half pint of flour, and 1 pint of new milk, or half a pint of cream and same of milk. This is better than all milk. MARYLAND KITCHEN.

RICE WAFFLES.

Make a half tumbler of nice corn meal mush. While it is warm stir to it a teaspoonful of butter. Make a smooth batter by beating in well 2 eggs, 1 pint of rice flour 1 even teaspoonful of soda, sifted in with the flour. and sweet milk to make a thin batter; salt to taste. Just before baking stir in 2 tablespoonsful of cream of tartar, previously dissolved in warm water. This is an excellent receipt for batter-bread. Bake in a quick oven in a pan 2 or 3 inches deep. Eat hot. MRS. HILL.

RICE WAFFLES.

Two teacups of hominy, 1 dessertspoonful of butter. 1 egg, 2 large spoonsful of wheat flour, 1 pint of rice flour, a little salt and one-half pint of milk and 1 quart of water.

MRS. HUGER.

RICE WAFFLES.

Boil 2 gills of rice quite soft, mix with it 3 gills of flour, a little salt, 2 ounces of melted butter, 2 eggs beaten well, and as much milk as will make it a thick batter. Beat it very light and bake in waffle irons.

VIRGINIA HOUSEWIFE.

RICE WAFFLES.

Put 1 pint of sweet milk in a stew pan; a teacup of boiled rice; add to it a tablespoonful of boiled butter; as soon as the butter melts take the pan from the fire; beat 4 eggs well, and stir them alternately, making a smooth batter, the milk and 1 quart of sifted flour; salt to taste. Bake and serve hot, with rice.

MRS. HILL.

SOUPS.

OKRA SOUP.

Cut up in small pieces one-quarter peck of okra, skin one-half peck of tomatoes, and put them, with a shin or leg of beef, into 10 quarts of cold water. Boil it gently for seven hours, skimming it well. Season with cayenne or black pepper and salt. A ham bone boiled with the other ingredients is thought an improvement by some persons. Serve with rice.

Carolina Housewife.

OKRA SOUP.

Cut up in fine slices 2 soup plates of okra and put it into a digester with 5 quarts of water and a little salt at 10 o'clock. At 11 o'clock put meat into the digester; at 12 o'clock peel one and one-half soup plates of tomatoes, and after straining them through a colander throw them into the digester; then season with salt and pepper. Allow all the ingredients to boil until 3 o'clock, when it is fit to be served up.

N. B. If you dine at 2 begin at an hour earlier with each ingredient.

Carolina Housewife.

OKRA SOUP.

Get two double handsful of young okra, wash
and slice it thin; add 2 onions chopped fine;
put it into a gallon of water at a very early
hour in an earthen pipkin, or a very nice iron
pot; must be kept ·steadily simmering, but not
boiling; put in pepper and salt. At 12 o'clock
put in a handful of lima beans; 1.30 add 3
young cimlins, cleaned and cut in small pieces,
a fowl, or knuckle of veal, a bit of bacon or
pork that has been boiled; add 6 tomatoes with
the skins taken off; when nearly done, thicken
with a spoonful of butter, mixed with 1 of flour.
Have rice boiled to eat with it.

VIRGINIA HOUSEWIFE.

OKRA SOUP.

Fry in the soup pot about 1 pound of lean
bacon; add at once 2 quarts of okra sliced, and
fry; then add 3 quarts of tomatoes peeled and
sliced, and put back on the stove to simmer.
Thicken with the gruel from the boiling rice
and serve with rice.   MAUM SARAH.

FABER'S OKRA SOUP.

Put on to boil early a shin of beef; after it
boils put in 4 quarts of okra cut up, one 3-pound
can of tomatotes. Boil for hours.

TOMATO SOUP.

To a gallon of broth made of any kind of fresh meat liked (veal is best) or poultry, add 6 dozen medium sized tomatoes, which have been cut up, but not skinned; stir to the tomatoes a good tablespoonful of brown sugar to soften their extreme acid taste. Put them to stew gently and steadily in a well covered soupkettle. Salt to taste. Boil 2 hours, then strain the soup through a colander; return it to the kettle. To a large teaspoonful of nice, sweet butter rub in a tablespoonful of flour. Put this to the soup; let it simmer for 10 or 15 minutes. When the flavor of onions is not disliked 1 or 2 may be used, shred fine, or a few heads of eshalots, and put to boil the same time the tomatoes are. The flavor of onions must be so delicate as to be scarcely recognized. The cook must ascertain of those to be served, and add or diminish as may be proper. Serve with rice.   MRS. HILL.

CHICKEN SOUP

Cut up the chicken and break all the bones; put into a gallon of water and let it simmer for 5 hours, skimming it well; the last hour add, to cook with the soup, a cup full of rice and sprig of parsley; when done let kettle remain stand ing on the table for a few minutes, when skim off

every particle of fat, then pour all on a sieve
placed over a deep dish; remove bones, pieces
of meat and parsley; press the rice through the
sieve; now mix the rice by stirring it with the
soup until it is smooth; season with pepper
and salt.   MRS. MURRAY.

TOMATO SOUP.

Skim and strain 1 gallon of stock; take
3 quarts of tomatoes, skin and put in the stock.
Make a paste of butter and flour and stir in.
Half an hour before serving add one-half pint of
rice.   MRS. PARKER.

PEPPER POT.

Take one-half peck of spinach, pick and boil
it as for dinner; drain off the water, and chop
it up fine. Put into a soup-kettle 6 quarts of
water, 3 pounds of beef or veal, about 1 pound
of pork, which must be scalded to draw out the
salt, a piece of ham with the ham bone is preferable, and boil about an hour. Then add the
spinach, a dozen potatoes, or 4 pounds of yam,
3 plantains peeled and cut up into pieces about
3 inches long, and small dumplings. Let all
these ingredients boil together slowly for four
or five hours. Just before serving add some
pickled peppers (cut up) and 1 or 2 long red

peppers. If you have crabs or lobsters previously boiled, add a small quantity, pickled fine, about half hour before serving. Serve with rice.   Carolina Housewife.

NEW ORLEANS GUMBO.

Take a turkey or fowl, cut it up with a piece of fresh beef, put them in a pot with a little lard, an onion, and water sufficient to cook the meat. After they have become soft add 100 oysters, with their liquor. Season to your taste, and just before taking up the soup, stir in, until it becomes mucilaginous, 2 spoonsful of pulverized sassafras leaves. Carolina Housewife.

CREME De RIZ.

Three pounds of veal (the leg is best), pulled with forks, 5 pints of water, one-quarter pound of rice. Simmer very gently until reduced to half the quantity; strain through a sieve, and season to your taste. It is very nourishing, and well made is of the thickness of good cream.

MULLIGATAWNY SOUP.

Take a chicken and boil it down to a rich gravy; then take another chicken and cut it up without boiling; place it in a saucepan with the following ingredients, and brown it well: Ginger, chilies (a small red pepper), 1 clove of garlic, one-quarter pound of onions, salt, lime or lemon juice, and melted butter. Add a few coriander and anise seed. Allow this to simmer over the fire until it is a nice brown. Pour over it the gravy already made, and let it remain on the fire for 15 minutes. The soup can be as well made of beef or veal, and some persons prefer it. Rice should always be handed with it.

MARYLAND KITCHEN.

RICE SOUP.

Put 6 ounces of rice in a 2 quart pot of water; boil for 1 hour; thicken with 2, 4 or 6 yolks of eggs, some cream, a little flour, 6 ounces of butter, with salt and nutmeg. Serve Parmesan cheese, grated, to be eaten with it.

CAROLINA HOUSEWIFE.

POT AU FEU.

Take a good size beef bone and extract the marrow and place in a pot; put on a slow fire, after covering with water, and allow it to simmer all day. Next morning remove the grease, add a large onion stuck with cloves, tomatoes. rice and other vegetables which one may fancy. Just before serving burn a little brown sugar and put in. MRS. PARKER.

PILLAU—THE TURKISH SOUP.

Put 3 slices of raw ham in a soup kettle, also a knuckle of veal, a large fat chicken, and such vegetables as are desired. Boil slowly. When the meats are all done, take them up and trim the meat carefully from the bones. Put in a kettle with a little rice and the liquor in which they were boiled; season with cayenne peppers. Boil and add 1 ounce each of raisins, dried currants and stoned cherries. Boil 20 minutes and serve. MRS. PARKER.

SOUTHERN GUMBO.

Slice 2 large onions, fry, have ready a good sized chicken cut up; put in with the onions and fry brown. Have a quart of sliced okra and 4 large tomatoes; put all with the chicken in a stew pan and pour hot water over it. Let boil until thick; season with salt and red pepper pods. It must be dished and eaten with rice boiled.

CORNED BEEF SOUP.

When the liquid in which beef and vegetables have been boiled gets cold, skim off the grease; add tomatoes and a teacup of walnut catsup; boil half an hour; add rice and any other vegetables desired and boil until done.

MRS. PARKER.

KNUCKLE OF VEAL SOUP.

Early in the morning put a knuckle of veal into a small sized pot filled with water, with 3 or 4 large onions chopped fine, a bunch of thyme and celery tied together, a slice of bacon, pepper and salt. Cover it well and boil until 12 o'clock. Then throw in 3 tablespoonsful of rice and boil steadily until dinner time.

MARYLAND KITCHEN.

CHICKEN SOUP.

One very large chicken, or 2, according to the quantity required. Old chickens are best. Put on a large saucepan with about 2 quarts of water to 1 chicken. Throw in 2 onions, a small bunch of parsley, 1 carrot and a small piece of lean bacon. Let them boil for about half an hour; then take it off, and set it on embers at the side, so as to not boil away the first water, which forms the soup; and if it should not be enough a half pint can be added at the last. Let it remain on the embers, simmering slowly, until within half an hour of dinner time, when a small tablespoonful of flour mixed with water is stirred in. Then take off the soup and strain it, and if there is much grease, skim it. Put it back into the saucepan, and keep it hot until ready to serve; when a teacup of new milk or cream can be added, if desired; but the soup must be boiling and the cream just stirred in, and the whole taken off immediately. Time required for making this soup is five hours. Boil rice separately in water, and throw it in a few minutes before serving.

MARYLAND KITCHEN.

SOUP, A La REINE.

Take soup stock, or buy 3 or 4 pounds of beef. Crack all the bones. Put in a pot and cover with water; set over a slow fire, where it will boil. Skim and add a teacup of cold water; let it simmer gently for 4 or 5 hours. An hour before dinner take a quart of fresh or canned peas, some celery, half a chopped onion, 1 large sliced potato and a few sticks of macaroni. Boil until soft, and then force through a sifter into a stew pan with a small portion of liquor in which they were boiled to keep them from burning, and a small lump of butter. Let all stew for a few minutes, then, having removed every particle of fat from the soup, strain it over the vegetables. Let all cook together, and add while boiling a little rice flour, melted in cold water. Some little disks of toasted bread may be put into each plate. When putting in salt and pepper add a teaspoonful of sugar.

MRS. PARKER.

GOOD SOUP.

Cut in pieces 1 pound of meat, cover with cold water and boil for 3 hours; let it stand over night; remove all the fat, bring to a boil; cut 1 cauliflower in slices, the corn from 1 dozen ears; break into small pieces 1 quart of butter beans, slice 1 onion, cut 3 radishes, and add all to the soup with 1 green pepper and a little salt. Cook one hour and add 1 quart of tomatoes. When tender remove. Simmer the rest for 4 hours. When nearly done put in a teacup of rice.   MRS. PARKER.

POTAGE A LA BISQUE.

Take 50 crawfish, or shrimps would be a good substitute. Wash them in eight or ten waters; put them into a saucepan with salt, pepper and a small quarter of a pound of butter. Put it over a warm fire, and stir for 15 minutes. Then drain the water from the crawfish. After washing it in several waters, boil some rice for 15 minutes in broth or water. Drain off the water and put the rice in a mortar with the crawfish. After they are well picked, put them into a saucepan, stir in a little of the broth of the pottage, which you pass through a sieve. When your puree is done, thin it with the broth, which must be neither too thick nor thin. Then take the shells of the crawfish, put with them the butter in which they were first cooked, and pass this puree through a sieve or colander. It should always have a red color. Put it into a saucepan over a slow fire, and be careful that neither of them boil, but both are very hot. Put crust under the bread which you put in the tureen, and pour a little broth over the bread. When serving, pour the first puree over the bread, then that of the shells. This puree of the shells must be put into the soup to give it a fine color. Make this pottage of meat or water, as you please.

MARYLAND KITCHEN.

THICKENING FOR SOUPS AND GRAVIES.

The best thickening for either soup or gravy, of any kind, from cooter soup to turkey gravy, is the water that is poured from the boiling rice before it is set to steam. Rice and rice flour are good, too.   MAUM SARAH.

Meat, Fish and Side Dishes.

CAROLINA PILAU.

Boil 1 and one-half pounds of bacon; when nearly done, throw into the pot a quart of rice, which must be first washed; then put in the fowl (one or two, according to size), and season with pepper and salt. In serving up, which should be done as soon as possible after the fowls are cooked enough, put the rice in a dish, and the bacon and fowl on it.

CAROLINA HOUSEWIFE.

TO MAKE A FRENCH PILAU.

Boil a pair of fowls; when done, take them out and put your rice in the same water, first taking out some of the liquor. When the rice is done, butter it well, cover the bottom of your dish with half of it; then put the fowls on it; and add the remainder of the liquor; cover the fowls with the other half of the rice, make it smooth, and spread over it the yolk of 2 eggs well beaten. Bake in a moderate oven.

CAROLINA HOUSEWIFE.

POULET Au RIZ.

Cut up a chicken; put it in a skillet with an onion cut up in small dice, butter, lard, a small shallot minced up, pepper, salt, 2 cloves and a leaf of bay. Parboil the chicken, and while cooking slowly, take some rice, scald it with boiling water, throw this water off and scald it twice more in the same way. Change the chicken into a saucepan, adding to it the ingredients as above. Put the rice into a skillet in which the chicken has been cooked and cool it. If you like it, you may brown it a little, but each grain must be distinct and whole. Serve in the same dish with the chicken, which must be placed on the bed of rice.

MARYLAND KITCHEN.

RICE AND TOMATOES.

Wash a cup of rice, and put it on the fire with sufficient water to boil it. Add to it a teaspoonful of salt, 7 or 8 large tomatoes cut fine, 2 onions chopped, a tablespoonful of butter and 2 green peppers cut round, the seeds having been first taken out, or it would be too hot.

Boil all together until the rice is well cooked and almost dry.

A spring chicken, cut in small pieces and boiled with the above, is very nice.

MARYLAND KITCHEN.

PILAFF.

Two measures of broth to 1 measure of rice. The broth must be flavored with tomatoes, and boiling, when the rice is thrown in and allowed to boil on a quick fire until it consumes the broth (this takes about 20 minutes). Then a little boiling butter must be stirred in, then let it stand covered on the fire for a few moments before serving. A stew of cold turkey or a fowl can be put in just before the butter. In that case the bones and carcass of the fowl must be boiled in the broth.   Mrs. Huger.

INDIAN PILAU.

Slice a large onion very fine, and divide it into shreds. Then fry it slowly in a quarter pound of butter until it is equally, but not too deeply, browned. Take it out and fry in the butter half a pound of rice.

As the grain easily burns, it should be done over a very slow fire until it becomes a light yellow tint. Then add a sufficient boiling broth to boil the rice soft inthe usual way, each grain remaining separate. Also add a quarter of a ounce each of cloves, peppercorn and allspice, tied in a piece of muslin, 3 onions, if you like their flavor, and salt to the taste. Before serving take out the spices and onions, and serve with the meat the broth was made from. It ought to be a loin of lamb, cut in joints, which after being taken out of the broth should be peppered, salted and fried. Place the meat on a large flat (hot) plate, and pour over it the stewed rice, which ought to be a rich brown color.

Garnish with hard boiled eggs cut into quarters. This dish must be eaten hot. Malaga raisins are often boiled with the rice, and chicken substituted for the lamb.

MARYLAND KITCHEN.

CAROLINA PILAU.

Take a large fowl, dressed, cover the breast with flat slices of bacon, secured by skewers. Put in a stew pan with 1 sliced onion. Season to taste with pepper and a little mace. Have ready 1 pint of rice that has been well picked, washed and soaked. Corn the fowl with it; put in as much water as will cover the whole. Stew for about half an hour, or until the fowl and rice are thoroughly done, keeping the stew pan closely covered. Dish it together, p acing the rice over the whole dish, fowl and bacon arranged on top.

MRS. BLAKE.

TOMATO PILAU.

Cut up the fowl; fry in a large tablespoonful of lard; fry with it an onion. Peel 1 pint of tomatoes, cut them up fine, season with pepper and salt and a teaspoonful of sugar. When the onion and chicken are of a light brown color, take them up and put them in a stew pan; add the tomatoes and pour over boiling water to cover the fowl. Have ready 1 pint of rice well washed. Stir this into the chicken, mix all thoroughly; simmer gently until tender. Add a large teaspoonful of butter. This should not

have gravy. Green corn may be grated and
used. MRS. HILL.

SAUSAGE PILAU.

This is made as the rice pilau, using sausage
that have been stuffed, but not smoked. The
smoked taste is imparted to the rice. Parboil
liver and kidneys, and use them for pilau.

They, as also the sausage, should be cut into
fine pieces. MRS. HILL.

A FRENCH PILAU.

Boil a pair of fowls; when done take them
out, and pour your rice in the same water, first
taking out some of the water. When the rice
is done, butter it well, cover the bottom of your
dish with half of it; then put the fowls on it,
and add the remainder of the liquor; cover the
fowls with the other half of the rice, make it
smooth, and spread over it the yolk of 2 well
beaten eggs. Bake in a moderate oven.

MRS. HILL.

RICE PILAU.

Carve the chicken into joints, as for frying,
put into a stew pan, with a few slices of pickled
pork or fresh pig cut in thin slices. Season
highly with red and black pepper; salt to taste.
Cover the fowl with water. Let it stew gently;
skim until the water looks clear. Have ready
1 pint of rice washed and soaked. Stir this
slowly into the stew; 15 minutes will complete

the cooking after the rice is added. When the rice is nearly done, should there be too much gravy, leave off the cover until sufficiently reduced. This dish should only be moist. No gravy is required; make it rich with butter.

The fowl, if a full grown one, is sometimes left whole. The rice is first put into a dish, and the chicken laid on top. Tongues, both of beef and hog, are good used in this way, before being smoked. Birds are as good in pilau as chickens.

MRS. HILL.

TOMATO PILAU.

To 1 quart of tomatoes, boiled until tender, add one-quarter of a pound of bacon, 2 quarts of rice and 1 quart of boiling water, and let it steam until done, stirring at intervals.

OKRA PILAU.

One quart of okra, 1 pound of bacon, 1 pint of rice. Slice the bacon and cut up the okra, as for soup, fry together until a light brown, then put into a little over 1 quart of water and add the rice. Boil all together until the rice is well done. Serve very hot in covered dish.

MRS. BLAKE.

A FRENCH PILAU.

Boil a pair of fowls; when nearly done add a glass of Madeira wine, some spices and a large teaspoonful of butter; add a large onion chopped fine, stew until done. Boil 1 quart of the rice in the liquor, when done put the rice in a dish and put the fowls on top.

MRS. HUGER.

OKRA DAUBE.

Take one-fourth pound of breakfast bacon and fry in your soup pot; then add 1 quart of okra, slice and fry that; then put in 1 and one-half quarts of tomatoes, peeled and sliced, and put the pot back on the stove, where it will simmer for several hours. Before serving add enough of the gruel from your boiling rice to thin a little.   MAUM SARAH.

RICE PIE.

Boil a pint of rice, mix into it well a large tablespoonful of butter, line a deep dish with this, and have ready a nicely seasoned stew; made of beef or any cold meat; add hard boiled eggs if approved, put them into the dish, and cover over the whole with buttered rice. Brown it in the oven. Some persons mix a raw egg with the butter and rice, which is an improvement.   CAROLINA HOUSEWIFE.

RICE CHICKEN PIE.

Cut up the chicken as for frying. Stew it with the giblets (and a little cold ham cut up fine) until the meat will leave the bones easily.

Pick off the meat in large strips, leaving only
the meat on the small part of the pinions. Season the gravy with cury powder, or highly
with pepper, a large tablespoonful of butter,
an onion and a little parsley, if they are liked.
Boil a pint of rice with a little salt, pour a layer
of this, then all of the chicken; pour in the
gravy and add a thick covering of the rice.
(This may be too much rice, the quantity will
depend upon the size of the fowl.) Bake half
an hour or less time, in a moderate oven, or in
a stove not too hot. For baking this use a deep
earthen dish and send to the table in it.

Mrs. Hill.

WALWORTH CHICKEN AND RICE PIE.

Take one fowl, cut it up as for frying and put
in a tightly covered bucket and place bucket
in a pot of boiling water. Boil until chicken
is tender, then cut the meat from large bones.
Have ready a baking dish and 2 quarts of rice
boiled very dry, 1 dozen sliced hard-boiled eggs.
Place one layer of rice in dish then a layer of
chicken and so on until dish is full, having a
layer of rice on top. Pour over the gravy from
the fowl. If the fowl is thin use butter in addition. Bake until the top is crisp. This may
be varied by adding 1 quart of stewed tomatoes
to the other ingredients. Mrs. S. D. Stoney.

RICE PIE.

Boil a quart of rice rather soft, stir into it a spoonful of butter, little less than a pint of milk and 2 eggs. Lay in the dish nearly half of the mixture, then put in two chickens, cut up and season with pepper and salt; cover it over with the remainer of the mixture and bake it. A nice brown crust will form on top. The rice must be salted when boiling. Any other meat may be substituted for chicken. When chicken or turkey is used, ham or bacon, cut into small pieces, may be strewed through the pie.

CAROLINA HOUSEWIFE.

RICE PIE.

One-half pint of rice boiled soft, one-half pound of butter, 3 eggs, one-half pint of milk and two chickens, pepper and salt to taste, put in a dish and bake.   MRS. DILL.

RICE PIE.

Pick clean a quart of rice, wash well, tie in a cloth, put into a pot of boiling water and boil until perfectly soft. Then drain and press it as dry as possible; mix it with 2 ounces of butter and 2 tablespoonfuls of mild grated cheese. Take a small tin butter kettle, wet the inside, put in the rice and stand in a cool place till quite cold. Then turn it out carefully (it should retain the form of the kettle), rub it over with the beaten yolk of an egg, and set it in an oven till lightly browned. Cut out from the top of the mass of rice an oval lid, about 2 inches from the edge, so as to leave a flat rim or border all around. Then excavate the mould of rice, leaving a standing crust all round and at the bottom about 2 inches thick. Have ready some hot stewed oysters or birds, brown or white fricassee. Fill up the pie with it, adding the gravy. Lay on the lid and decorate it with sprigs of curled parsley stuck in all around the crack where the lid it put on.

MRS. BLAKE.

RICE PIE.

To a pint of rice boiled rather soft add a scant pint of milk, a lump of butter, 2 beaten eggs, pepper and salt. Let these ingredients be well mixed and spread one-half the quantity in a deep baking dish; next lay pieces of raw meat with seasoning (slices of ham an improvement) and butter. Then put remainder of the rice mixture and bake for an hour or more.

MRS. BLAKE.

HOPPING JOHN.

One pound of bacon, 1 pint of red peas, 1 pint of rice. First put on the peas, and when half boiled throw in the rice which must be first washed. When the rice has been boiling half an hour, take the pot off the fire and put it on coals to steam, as in boiling rice alone. Put a quart of water on the peas first, and if it boils away too much add a little more hot water. Season with salt and pepper, and, if liked, a sprig of green mint. In serving up put the rice and peas first on the dish and the bacon on the top. CAROLINA HOUSEWIFE.

HOPPING JOHN.

One pint of cow (or red) peas, 1 pint of rice, 1 pound of bacon. Let the bacon come to a boil in 2 quarts of water, skim it, add the peas, boil slowly. When tender add the rice, let it boil until the rice is well swollen and soft. Season with red pepper and salt. The salt is to be added when nearly done. If liked perfectly dry it can be steamed as in boiling rice plain. Serve with the bacon on the top.

MRS. BLAKE.

BUBBLE AND SQUEAK.

One small or half of a large cabbage, 1 pound of bacon, 1 pint of rice. Let the bacon come to a boil. skim it and add the cabbage. When tender add the rice, boil until rice is swollen and soft. Season with pepper and salt. Take out cabbage, chop fine, return to pot to steam. Mix all well together and serve with bacon on top. MRS. BLAKE.

POULET DE SUISSE.

Boil 1 cupful of rice in 4 cupfuls of water.
Stir gently; when done set in the oven with
doors open half an hour until dry. Cut up
some cold chicken and set it over the fire in a
saucepan with a little strong soup stock, add
salt, pepper, a tablespoonful of walnut catsup
and a teaspoonful of extract of celery, rub a
lump of butter in corn starch to thicken. Let
boil. Put the rice in a ring upon a heated
dish, pour the minced chicken over and lay
upon it lightly half a dozen poached eggs.

Mrs. Parker.

CHICKENS STEWED WITH TOMATOES.

Cut the chicken up and fry it lightly. Then
make a rich brown gravy by dredging a little
flour into the fat that the chicken was fried in.
Put water sufficient to make a bowl of brown
gravy, cut up your tomatoes and put them on
to stew, a quart of tomatoes after they are
skinned, a medium-sized onion, cayenne and
black pepper, salt and parsley. When all are
mixed put in the chickens, pouring in the gravy.
To that put a quarter of a pound of butter and
stew it for two hours. Then put in a pint bowl
of rice and let it stew slowly for an hour longer.
It must be a moist stew.

CALIFORNIA CHICKEN.

Take 2 young chickens, cut up and stew; when done add a little minced parsley and onions. Take 4 large pepper pods, soak in water, strain and pour in the juice, add salt, butter and a little flour to the chicken to thicken. Fill a large dish with boiled rice and pour the chicken and gravy on it.

MRS. PARKER.

CURRIED CHICKEN.

Fry in the pot you make the curry in three slices of bacon, 2 onions; cut up the chicken in small pieces, slice 3 large potatoes, put in with pork and onions, cover with water and cook until done, salt and pepper. Put in 3 table-spoonfuls of curry powder, mix with water, boil and dish over boiled rice. Serve with green peas or young corn. MRS. PARKER.

CASSEREAU.

Take a heaping pint of rice cooked as if for dinner, have a fowl boiled, have a rich tomato sauce. Mix the rice and sauce together, adding a heaping tablespoonful of butter, salt and pepper; put a layer of rice in the bottom of your dish, then add the fowl, cut up, and a few pieces of ham or bacon, and then put the rest of the rice on top; bake until brown.

MRS. HUGER.

COMPOTE OF CHICKEN.

Cut the meat from the bones in large slices, and lay them in a mixture made of 2 eggs, a teaspoonful of mustard, pinch of salt, a teacup of stock and flour to make a thick batter. Fry some scraps of fat bacon and lay them on a piece of chicken well covered with batter and fry them brown. Make a gravy of a little soup stock, flavored with nutmeg, a little pepper and a glass of sherry wine. Thicken with corn starch rubbed into a little butter. Pour a little on a flat dish and lay pieces of chicken on it. Garnish with rice croquettes. MRS. PARKER.

POULET AU RIZ.

Cut up a chicken, put it into a skillet with an onion, cut up into small dice, butter, lard and a small shallot minced up, pepper, salt, 2 cloves and a leaf of bay. Parboil the chicken, and while cooking slowly take some rice, scald it with boiling water, throw this water off and scald it twice more in the same way. Change the chicken into another saucepan, adding to it the ingredients as above. Put the rice in a skillet in which the chicken has been cooked and cook it. If you like it you may brown it a little, but each grain must be distinct and whole. Serve in the small dish with the chicken, which must be placed on the bed of rice, pyramid form. MARYLAND KITCHEN.

RICE CROQUETTES.

One quart of boiled rice mixed with 3 eggs, pepper and salt. Make in the form of a cork, roll them in grated bread or crackers and fry them in sufficient boiling lard to cover them.

RICE CROQUETTES.

To 1 and one-half cups of soft-boiled rice add one-half cup of wheat flour, one-half teaspoon of salt, 2 eggs and a little butter. Mix well and mould into shapes. Fry in boiling lard.

CROQUETTES OF POULTRY.

Take any kind of cold fowl, remove the skin and sinews, chop the meat very fine, pound it in a marble mortar or grind it; soak an equal quantity of stale bread in just sweet milk enough to moisten it (this should be soaking while the meat is being prepared). Press the milk out of the bread, add nearly an equal quantity of butter, work out into the mixture the yolk of 3 eggs boiled hard and grated, seasoned with nutmeg, salt and pepper. Beat the white of 2 eggs to a froth, stir them into the mixture; mould in a wine glass or make in cake or balls and fry in hot lard. If the mixture is too stiff moisten it with a little cream. Take them up clean of grease; a perforated skimmer will do this better than a spoon; lay

a napkin upon a flat dish and lay the croquette
on that. Garnish with lemons cut in rings,
parsley or celery; serve pickle with it in a
separate dish. A handsome way of serving croquettes or meat salads is to form upon a flat
dish, the shape of the dish a wall of 2 inches
high with rice boiled soft; add a little milk to
make it soft enough to be rubbed through. Boil
3 or 4 eggs hard, take the yolks out carefully
and grate fine, cut tne white in rings of uniform
size; put the yolks evenly on the outside of the
wall. Place the rings tastily around the wall
on the outside, sticking a row of cloves upon the
edge to keep them in place. This square inside
may be filled with croquettes, salad, forcemeat
balls or small birds, making a beautiful supper
dish.   MRS. HILL.

RICE CROQUETTES.

Wash and pick well a teacup of rice; boil it
in 3 tumblers full of sweet milk; season it with
salt, pepper and nutmeg if liked. Stir the rice
frequently when nearly done to prevent its
scorching. When thick and dry, spread it upon
a dish to cool. Chop fine and pound in a
marble mortar, oysters and any kind of cold
fowl, fresh meat, liver, kidney or fish, equal
quantities of the meat mixture to nearly fill the
opening; close the whole securely, roll the balls
in the beaten yolk of egg, then in bread crumbs

and fry in boiling lard. This may be varied by seasoning rice with lemon, vanilla, cheese and stuffing the balls with any kind of jelly, jam or dried fruit. These make a nice dessert, with arrowroot or cream sauce.　　　Mrs. Hill.

SHRIMP PIE.

To 2 plates of shrimps add 1 pint of moderate soft-boiled rice, three-quarters of a pound of butter, salt and pepper to taste, and bake it.

Mrs. Huger.

SHRIMP PILAU.

Take 1 pint of rice, boil grainy, while hot add a heaping tablespoonful of butter, 1 pint of milk, mace, pepper and salt to taste; have two plates of picked shrimps; put alternate layers of rice and shrimps, letting the first and last layers be of rice. Beat up the yolk of an egg, put it over the rice and bake.

Mrs. Huger.

SHRIMP CROQUETTES AND RICE.

Boil soft 1 pint of rice with salt, pound a plate of shrimps; when the rice is cold add the shrimps, with a heaping tablespoonful of butter, 1 egg, well beaten, and pepper to taste; fry in boiling lard.　　　Mrs. Huger.

TO HASH FISH.

Take any kind of cooked fish (salt mackerel is very good prepared this way); mince the meat fine and season with pepper; have a third as much Irish potatoes cooked and mashed as there is fish; cut up fine 3 hard-boiled eggs, stir this mixture together; into a stew pan put a tumbler of water, boiling, and a large tablespoonful of butter; stir the fish into the stew pan and allow it to simmer until thoroughly hot, cover dish. This is a nice breakfast dish and should not be prepared until the last moment. Cold fish may be made into a pilau; remove all bones; cook the rice and add the fish pulled into flakes, just long enough to become hot; season high with cayenne pepper. Some persons like mace. This may be used or not, as preferred.   MRS. HILL.

SHRIMP PIE.

Boil 1 quart of rice dry. With this mix well 2 teacups of tomato juice, 1 pound of butter, 3 eggs, pepper to taste, one-half teaspoonful of curry. Sprinkle black pepper over the shrimps. Put layers of mixture and layers of shrimps till the pan is filled. Pour a gill of milk over the top before baking. This is for 6 plates of shrimp.   MISS TAFT.

PEPPERS OR TOMATOES WITH SHRIMPS.

Rub together 1 plate of boiled shrimps and 1 pint of rice, boiled soft, and 1 tablespoonful of butter. Salt and pepper to taste. Stuff tomatoes and bake until tender. Use bell peppers instead of tomatoes, if preferred.

MRS. STONEY.

CASSEREAU.

Boil your rice dry and mix with it a rich tomato sauce. Arrange around the edge of a dish and pour into the middle a good stew of beef. Bake until the edges are crisp.

MRS. C. N. WEST.

BLACK PUDDINGS.

Catch the blood as it runs from the hog, stir it continually till cold to prevent it from co-agulating; when cold thicken it with boiled rice, add leaf fat chopped small, pepper, salt, and any herbs that are liked, fill the skins and smoke them two or three days; they must be boiled before they are hung up, and prick them with a fork to keep them from bursting.

VIRGINIA HOUSEWIFE.

RICE OMELETTE.

One teacup of boiled rice, 1 teacup of sweet milk, 3 eggs well beaten, a level tablespoonful of butter; season with grated ham, a little

minced onion, pepper and salt to taste. Bake
a light brown; much cooking will spoil it.

AROZO AMARILLO.

Soak 4 grains of Spanish saffron in cup of
warm water. When water becomes very yellow
pour into a pot with 2 quarts of boiling rice.
Serve when rice is done.   MR. VALDEZ.

AROZO CON PIMIENTO.

Pick and wash 1 quart of rice and put in
with 4 bell peppers sliced. If seeds are left in
it will be very hot. Boil as in directions for
boiling rice.   MR. VALDEZ.

PIMIENTO RELLENO.

Hollow out 6 bell peppers and stuff with
rice boiled rather soft. Put in pot with a piece
of bacon and water to cover them and boil until
tender.   MR. VALDEZ.

STUFFED TOMATOES.

Boil 1 teacup of rice rather soft. Hollow out
6 ripe tomatoes. Butter your rice well and mix
with 4 hard-boiled eggs, some of the scraps of
tomatoes and a little salt and pepper. Stuff
the tomatoes with the mixture and bake until
tender.   MRS. STONEY.

TOMATOES A LA FROMAGE.

Stuff 6 ripe tomatoes with rice boiled rather
soft and well buttered. Sprinkle on top of rice
a little grated parmesan cheese. Bake until
tender.   MRS. BLAKE.

STUFFED PEPPERS.

Boil rice rather soft, butter well, chop up a few olives and mix. Stuff your peppers and bake. MRS. STONEY.

PEPPERS WITH RICE AND EGGS.

To 1 teacup of rice boiled rather soft add 4 hard-boiled eggs and 2 teaspoonfuls of butter. Salt and pepper to taste. Stuff your peppers and bake. MRS. STONEY.

FRIED RICE.

Take any cold dinner rice and fry in butter until brown; or boil rice soft, pour into a dish to cool, then cut into strips, dip into egg and fry in butter or lard. MAUM GRACE.

CROWDED EGGS.

Mash fine 1 dozen hard-boiled eggs, season to taste. Mix with soft-boiled rice, not as much rice as egg. Bake in a pan. MRS. THOMAS.

DESSERTS.

BELVIDERE RICE PUDDING.

Two quarts of new milk, one gill of rice, one teacupful of brown sugar, one stick of cinnamon about three inches in length. Wash the rice to remove the floury particles and put into an oven in the dish in which it is to be served, with the sugar, cinnamon and half of the milk; reserve the other half to add, a little at a time, as the first stews away. It requires to stew slowly, not boil, from three and a half hours to four, and, when finished, should be rather thick and look like rich yellow cream. No milk must be added the last half hour, as it should be covered with brown skin when sent to table. It should not be stirred or disturbed except by the addition of the milk, whi'e in the oven.

MARYLAND KITCHEN.

POOR BUCKRA PUDDING.

Wash 1 tablespoonful of rice, put in 1 quart of milk sweeten to taste, add piece of cinnamon and bake for 3 hours.   MISS PORCHER.

RICE PUDDING.

Boil half a pound of rice in milk until it is quite tender, beat it well with a wooden spoon to mash the grains; add three-quarters of a pound of sugar, and the same of melted butter; half a nutmeg, 6 eggs, a gill of wine, some grated lemon peel; put a paste in the dish and

73

bake it. For a change it may be boiled and eaten with butter, sugar and wine.

VIRGINIA HOUSEWIFE.

RICE PUDDING.

Boil 1 cup of rice for half an hour, then pour in a quart of milk and simmer slowly. Put into four teacups, let cold and take out, lay on a dish, on the top of each mould make an opening with a spoon and fill with jelly, then pour in the dish a custard. Let cool and eat with sugar and wine.

MRS. PARKER.

RICE PUDDING.

One tablespoonful of rice boiled soft, 1 quart milk, 8 eggs well beaten, 1 tablespoonful butter, 8 tablespoonfuls sugar, one-half teaspoonful salt, 1 stick cinnamon. Bake in a quick oven and take out before it is quite done, as it hardens more afterwards.

MRS. C. W. KOLLOCK.

RICE PUDDING.

One-quarter pound of rice boiled until soft. While boiling stir frequently to prevent scorching. While warm add to it one-quarter pound of butter. To 6 eggs beaten separately and afterwards mixed, add one-quarter pound of sugar, a wineglass of rosewater, or any flavour preferred Eat with transparent sauce. Put a meringue over this. Bake in dish.

MRS. HILL.

RICE PUDDING.

Boil a teacup of rice in quart of milk, add a
pound of sugar, one-half pound of butter and 6
eggs. Flavor to taste and bake. Eat with
butter sauce.   MRS. PARKER.

RICE PUDDING.

Soak 1 cup of rice for 4 hours, drain, and
put in a pan; add 1 cup of sugar and half
a gallon of milk. Flavour to taste. Bake 4
hours in a slow oven. Sprinkle the top with
sugar and grate nutmeg over. Eat without
sauce.   MRS. PARKER.

RICE PUDDING.

Boil 3 cups of rice in a quart of milk; when
tender add a pint of milk, 2 cups of sugar, a
glass of wine, half a cup of butter one-half
pound of seeded raisins, a pound of currants,
one-half pound of sliced citron, teacupful of
grated cocoanut, one-half pound of blanched
almonds pounded. Beat 10 eggs (leave out the
whites of 6) and mix in. Pour over it a teacup
of brandy. Put into a pan and bake 2 hours.
Make meringue of 6 eggs and a teacup of sugar,
flavor with an extract of nutmeg. Eat without
sauce.   MRS. PARKER.

PINOPOLIS RICE PUDDING.

Four tablespoonfuls of soft-boiled rice, one-
quarter pound of butter, 1 quart of milk, 8 eggs,
scald the milk, add a few sticks of cinnamon,

and, while warm, stir in the rice, butter and eggs, which must be first beaten. Sweeten to taste and bake in a dish.

GERMAN RICE PUDDING.

Boil 3 pints of milk and, as soon as it boils, throw into it one-half pint of rice, nicely picked and washed, and boil half the milk away; then mix in a bowl one-half pint of cream, 1 egg, one-half teaspoonful of salt, a tablespoonful of brown sugar and pour the mixture in the rice and the milk on the fire; boil it for 5 minutes, stirring it all the time. Pour in your dish and sprinkle sugar over it.

CAROLINA HOUSEWIFE.

SNOWBALL PUDDING.

Boil 1 quart of rice and thicken with rice flour. Beat the yolks of 4 eggs with 3 tablespoonfuls of sugar. Mix all together in a pudding dish and bake. Beat the white of the eggs to a froth, add 4 tablespoonfuls of sugar, one-half a teacup of rice well boiled, flavoured with lemon. Drop in little balls over the pudding. Set back in the oven to brown. MRS. PARKER.

SMALL RICE PUDDINGS.

Wash two large tablespoonfuls of rice and simmer it with half a pint of milk until thick, then put in a piece of butter the size of an egg, and nearly half a pint of thick sweet cream, and give it one boil; when cold mix four yolks and

two whites of eggs well beaten, sugar and
nutmeg to taste; add grated lemon and a little
cinnamon. Butter little cups and fill them
three-quarters full, putting at the bottom some
orange or citron. Bake three-quarters of an
hour in a slow oven; serve hot with sweet sauce.
MARYLAND KITCHEN.

RICE PUDDING.

Pick and wash 1 pint of rice, boil soft.
Drain off the water and let rice dry and get
cold. Then mix with it an ounce of butter, 4
ounces of sugar and stir into a quart of milk.
Beat 4 or 5 eggs very light and add them gradually to the mixture; stir in at the last a tablespoonful of mixed nutmeg and cinnamon. Bake
it an hour in a deep dish. MRS. BLAKE.

RICE PUDDING.

Boil one and one-half gills rice rather soft;
while hot mix with it 2 tablespoonfuls of sugar
and 1 of butter, and put into your dish while
hot. Grate in a little nutmeg and put in a few
pieces of cinnamon, put on rice when cold a
few lumps of butter, then mix 4 eggs well beaten
with 1 pint of milk and sugar to taste, pour it
on the rice and set to bake for about half an
hour. MRS. BLAKE.

WOODLAWN RICE PUDDING.

One and one-half pint of fresh milk in a pan
with 1 tablespoonful of raw rice (carefully

washed), 1 teaspoonful of butter; place in the pan in an oven, stirring occasionally. When the milk and rice are boiled to a thick gruel stir in a half pint of milk, some cinnamon and sweeten to taste. Then put it back in the oven for a few minutes. It is as nice cold as hot.

MAUM MARIA.

POOR MAN'S PUDDING.

One tablespoonful rice, 1 quart milk, 1 teaspoonful vanilla, sugar to taste. Boil rice, sugar and milk together for several hours till mixture is thick and smooth; add flavoring. Put in baking dish and brown in a quick oven.

MRS. BURCKMYER.

RICE FLOUR PUDDING.

Mix 3 tablespoonfuls of rice flour into a pint of milk and boil to a pap; then stir in one-half pound of fresh butter. When almost cold add 3 well beaten eggs, sugar to your taste, and a glass of wine, a grated nutmeg and a little salt. Lay crust on shallow plate and bake. Dust some sugar over them. CAROLINA HOUSEWIFE.

WALWORTH BAKED RICE FLOUR PUDDING.

One-quarter pound of rice flour and 1 quart of milk boiled to a pap; when cold add one-quarter pound of sugar and 4 eggs. Bake in dish.

RICE FLOUR PUDDING.

One quart of milk, a quarter of a pound of butter, 4 eggs beaten separately, 5 tablespoonfuls of rice flour, 6 of sugar and the rind of 1 lemon. Beat the yolks very light, add the sugar and lemon peel, boil the milk, mix up the rice flour with a little cold water, pour on it the boiling milk, beat in three yolks and put it back on the fire until it thickens a little, then stir in the butter; pour in the baking dish, add the whites of the 4 eggs beaten very light and bake quickly.   MARYLAND KITCHEN.

RICE FLOUR PUDDING.

One quart of milk, one-half pound of rice flour, 10 ounces of butter and the yolk of 10 eggs. Scald the milk and pour it, boiling, on the flour; then add the butter; beat the eggs and stir them in the mixture, with sugar to taste. Bake in a dish, in a Dutch oven, which must be hotter at the bottom than at the top. Spices may be added if desired.

CAROLINA HOUSEWIFE.

RICE FLOUR PUDDING.

One pint of milk and one-quarter of a pound of butter, 5 teaspoonfuls of rice flour, a glass of wine, a teaspoonful of grated nutmeg, 4 eggs and one-quarter pound of stoned raisins, sugar to taste. Mix the flour with a little cold milk into a thin paste; boil the milk and add flour to it, and stir constantly until it becomes of the consistency of pap. While warm stir in the batter, eggs, which must be first beaten until quite light, the nutmeg, wine and sugar, and lastly the raisins. Bake in rather a quick oven for 15 or 20 minutes.

CAROLINA HOUSEWIFE.

RICE DUMPLINGS.

Pick and wash a pound of rice, boil gently in 2 quarts of water till it becomes dry, keeping the pot well covered and not stirring it. Take off the fire and spread out to cool on bottom of an inverted sieve, loosening the grains lightly with a fork, that all moisture may evaporate. Peel a dozen large, juicy apples, core them and fill cavity with marmalade or lemon and sugar. Cover every apple all over with a thick coating of the boiled rice, tie up each in a separate cloth and put in pot of cold water. They will require one and one-quarter hours after they commence to boil, perhaps longer. Turn out in large dish, be careful not to break the dumplings. Eat with wine sauce or butter, sugar and nutmeg beaten together.

MRS. BLAKE.

RICE CHEESE CAKES.

Boil a quarter of a pound of rice until tender, drain it and add 4 eggs well beaten, half a pound of butter, 1 pint of cream, 6 ounces of

sugar, a grated nutmeg and a glass of ratafia
or brandy. Beat all well together. Lay a light
paste in your patties, fill with the mixture and
bake in a moderate oven.

CAROLINA HOUSEWIFE.

RICE MILK FOR A DESSERT.

Boil half a pint of rice in water till tender,
pour off the water, and add a pint of milk with
2 eggs beaten well stirred into it; boil all together 2 or 3 minutes; serve it up hot and eat
with butter, sugar and nutmeg. It may be
sweetened and cooled in moulds, turned out in
a deep dish and surrounded with rich milk,
with raspberry marmalade stirred into it, and
strained to keep back the seeds—or the milk
may be seasoned with wine and sugar.

VIRGINIA HOUSEWIFE.

RICE PIE.

Turn 1 quart of boiling water on 1 teacup of
rice, boil soft, take from the fire and add a
quart of milk, 5 eggs, a teaspoonful of extract
of lemon and nutmeg, a teacup of sugar and
one-half pound of stoned raisins. Bake in deep
cans lined with puff paste.   MRS. PARKER.

SNOW BALLS.

Wash and pick one-half pound of rice, boil
it, cover with water 10 minutes, drain through
a sieve and spread on a dish to dry. Peel and
core 6 apples, medium size. Divide the rice

into 6 parts; envelop each apple in a portion of rice (the cavities first filled with powdered sugar and cinnamon). Tie separately in cloths loosely. Boil 1 hour. Eat with sauce.

Mrs. Hill.

SNOW ICE CREAM.

Put in a stew pan 4 ounces of rice flour, 2 ounces of sugar, a few drops of essence of almond or any other you chose, with 2 ounces of butter, add a quart of milk, boil from 15 to 20 minutes till it forms a smooth substance, though not too thick, then pour into a mould previously oiled, and serve when cold. It will turn out like jelly. Mrs. Blake.

RICE FLOUR PUFFS.

One pint of rice flour, one and one-half pint of milk, 4 eggs. Boil the milk and while hot stir in gradually in the flour, then add the eggs, which must first be beaten very light, drop in the batter from a spoon into the boiling lard. Eat with sugar and wine.

Carolina Housewife.

RICE CROQUETTES.

Boil 1 pint of rice, mash it fine, season with butter add 1 or 2 eggs well beaten, mix very light. Squeeze in the juice and grate the rind of one orange, make in the form of corks and sprinkle with powdered sugar. · Serve as a second course, vegetables or dessert.

Maryland Kitchen.

RICE BLANC MANGE.

Boil a teacupful of rice in a very small quantity of water till it is near bursting, then add half a pint of milk, boil it to a mush, stirring all the time; season it with sugar, wine, nutmeg; dip the mould in water and fill it; when cold, turn it in a dish and surround it with boiled custard, seasoned, or syllabub; garnish it with marmalade.   MARYLAND KITCHEN.

RICE BLANC MANGE.

One quart of milk, 6 tablespoonfuls of rice and 1 of moss farina; boil, sweeten and flavour with extract of rose.   MRS. PARKER.

RICE FLOUR BLANC MANGE.

Half a pint of rice flour, mixed with a small quantity of cold milk. When smooth, pour on it one quart of boiling milk already sweetened, and stir it constantly before the fire until it thickens. Flavour with rose or peach water pour into molds. It is generally served with cream and sugar.   MARYLAND KITCHEN.

RICE BLANC MANGE No. 1.

Boil the rice very tender and press it through a sieve; sweeten with loaf sugar; blanch some almonds and pound them very fine, adding gradually a little rose or peach water; mix all together and put into the mould while hot. Make a thin custard and pour over the blanc mange.   CAROLINA HOUSEWIFE.

83

RICE BLANC MANGE No. 2.

Boil half a pint of whole rice in as little water as possible till all the grains lose their form and become a solid mass. Next put in a sieve and drain and pass out all the water. Then turn into the saucepan and mix it with half a pint of rich milk and a quarter of a pound of powdered sugar. Boil again till the whole is reduced to a pulp. Remove it from the fire and stir in while hot a wineglass of rose water.

Dip your moulds into cold water, and fill them up with the rice; set then on ice, and when quite cold turn out this blanc mange; serve it on a dish with a sauce tureen of sweetened cream, flavored with nutmeg.

CAROLINA HOUSEWIFE.

RICE FLUMMERY.

Boil 6 ounces of rice flour in a quart of milk, slowly add a little lemon peel, 20 bitter almonds chopped very fine, and about a quarter of a pound of loaf sugar; stir it all the time it is on the fire, and when almost boiled to a consistency pour into a mould and let it stand all night or until it becomes stiff enough to turn out. Serve up with cream and preserves.

CAROLINA HOUSEWIFE.

RICE FLUMMERY.

To 1 large cup of rice flour take 1 quart of new milk. Put on a vanilla bean with the milk to boil. Smooth the rice flour down to a paste with some milk and when the quart of milk boils pour it on the rice flour. Sweeten it and put it on the fire, stirring it all the while. When it is done it will be about the consistency of thick mush. To be eaten with a rich custard. MARYLAND KITCHEN.

SWEET RICE BREAD.

One tablespoonful of hominy, 1 tablespoonful of butter, 2 of sugar (either brown or white), and 2 of wheat flour, a tumbler and a half of rice flour, half a tumbler of warm water, a quarter of an yeast biscuit or a tablespoonful of liquid yeast and 3 eggs. Rub the hominy, butter, sugar and eggs lightly together and add the wheat flour, then the yeast, which must be first dissolved in the water with a little salt; stir in the rice flour and turn the mixture into a well greased pan. When well risen, bake in a moderate oven about half an hour. Some persons allow the mixture to remain all night in the bowl, and next morning stir in a quarter of a teaspoonful of saleratus dissolved in a little water, before putting in a pan. This bread is very nice for either breakfast or tea, and may be made without sugar.

CAROLINA HOUSEWIFE.

RICE CUPS.

Sweeten to your taste 1 pint of milk with loaf sugar and boil it with a stick of cinnamon; stir in rice flour until thick; take it off the fire and add the beaten whites of 3 eggs; stir it again over the fire for a few minutes, then put it into teacups previously dipped in cold water. When cold, turn them out and pour round them a rich custard, made with the yolks of eggs alone. Place upon the rice a little raspberry jam or any other sweetmeat.

CAROLINA HOUSEWIFE.

RICE SPONGE CAKE.

Ten ounces of powdered sugar, half a pound of rice flour, the yolk of 15 eggs and the whites of 7, the grated rind of 2 lemons, and a little orange flour (or peach) water; beat the yolks for half an hour, and then add the sugar and flour and the essences, beat the whites of 7 eggs very light and stir them in. Pour the mixture into a deep pan and bake immediately in a quick oven. CAROLINA HOUSEWIFE.

A RICE CAKE.

Six ounces of wheat flour, 6 ounces of rice flour, three-quarters of a pound of powdered sugar, 9 eggs, 1 tablespoonful of orange and 1 of rose water, and the grated peel of a lemon. Beat these ingredients together and bake an hour.   CAROLINA HOUSEWIFE.

RICE FLOUR CAKE.

Two teacups of rice flour, 1 cupful of sugar, 1 of butter. Season with nutmeg, brandy and almond or rose water. Beat all well together.
                              MARYLAND KITCHEN.

RICE CROQUETTES.

Boil one and one-half cups of rice; when cold add 2 eggs, one-half cup of flour, one-half teaspoonful of salt and 1 tablespoonful of sugar. Mix well and fry same as crullers, making croquettes egg shaped.

RICE CROQUETTES.

Thoroughly wash one-half pound of rice, add one-half cup of sugar, the rind of 1 lemon cut very thin, a piece the size of a walnut, and a pinch of salt, together with 1 pint of milk. Cook in double boiler until soft. When cold enough mould into balls and fry in hot lard. To be served with jelly or hard sauce.

RICE CUSTARD.

Mix a pint of milk, one-half pint of cream, 1 ounce of rice flour, 6 bitter almonds, blanched and pounded, with 2 tablespoonfuls of rose water; sweeten with loaf sugar, and stir it over the fire till it nearly boils; then add the well beaten yolk of 3 eggs; let it simmer for about 1 minute, stirring all the time. Pour it into a dish or cups, with sugar and nutmeg over it.

CAROLINA HOUSEWIFE.

RICE CUSTARD.

Pick and wash 1 tumbler full of rice and boil it in a pint of milk or water. Take it up, mash well, and strain through a colander; add 1 pint of sweet milk and one-half tumbler full of melted butter. Beat 3 eggs well and add to the rice when cool; sweeten and flavor to taste. Bake in puff paste.

This may be baked without a paste and raisins or currants added if liked. If used stir them in when the custard is least half done; if added earlier they will settle at the bottom. Should be eaten with cream sauce. Meringue this.

MRS. HILL.

INVALID DIET.

BEEF OR MUTTON BROTH.

Cut in small pieces 1 pound of either meat, put in 2 quarts of cold water and boil 2 hours, then add half a cup of rice and boil half an hour. Strain and season lightly.

RACAHAUT.

One pound rice flour, one-half pound cocoa or grated chocolate, 2 tablespoonfuls of arrowroot, one-half pound of sugar.

Mix all well together and make with milk as you would chocolate. To 1 quart of milk 4 dessertspoonfuls of the mixture. Mix to like starch in a little water, and pour the boiling milk upon it. Then put on fire and let it boil well. Mrs. Blake.

CHICKEN BROTH FOR AN INVALID.

Cut old fowl into pieces, wash in cold water, put into saucepan with 1 quart of cold water and a little salt; let it boil gently, skim it well; add a little celery and parsley, also onion if desired. Boil the broth for an hour, then strain it. Add 2 tablespoonsful of rice to the broth when first put on, as it makes it more nourishing.

RICE PAP.

Take 2 tablespoonsful rice flour to 1 pint water and a little salt. Stir well and boil till it thickens. Mrs. Blake.

RICE MILK.

Boil a cup of rice in water, pour off when tender, add milk; sweeten and flavor.

RICE GRUEL.

Two tablespoonfuls of rice flour, wet it up with cold water; boil 20 minutes in 1 pint of boiling water; then add 1 tumbler full of fresh sweet milk. Season to taste. Caudle is made by adding the gruel, wine and a little grated cracker.

ST. JOHN'S RICE MILK.

One pint of rice parboiled in water, the water poured off and 1 quart of milk added and boiled very soft and thick. Beat 6 eggs and 1 pound of sugar together. Stir in with a little nutmeg and cinnamon. MISS PORCHER.

GROUND RICE MILK.

Mix in a bowl 2 tablespoonsful of rice flour with sufficient milk to make a thin batter. Then stir into it gradually 1 pint of milk and boil with salt, or lemon peel and sugar, or nutmeg and sugar. MRS. BLAKE.

RICE JELLY.

A quarter of a pound of rice, picked and washed; half a pound of loaf sugar, and enough water to cover it. Boil until it becomes a glutinous mass. Strain and season it with what you fancy and let it get cold.

MARYLAND KITCHEN.

RICE JELLY.

Mix 1 large tablespoonful of rice flour in cold water, put it in a pint of boiling water and sweeten with a lump of sugar. break in while boiling 1 stick of cinnamon. Pour in moulds.

MRS. PARKER.

RICE AND MUTTON MUSH FOR INVALIDS OR CHILDREN.

Take one-half teacupful rice to a piece (two inches long) of lean mutton from the neck. Put the meat on with 1 pint cold water, and when it comes to a boil put in your rice, well washed. Boil to a soft pap and take the meat out before serving. The leg of a fowl or a scrap of beef can be used instead of mutton if preferred. MRS. S. D. STONEY.

PLAIN RICE PUDDING.

One-half cup rice; one and one-half quarts milk; one-half cup sugar; 1 tablespoonful butter; add a little salt and raisins; grate nutmeg over top. Bake slowly until it thickens.

RICE PUDDING.

One small teacup of boiled rice, 3 well beaten eggs, 1 pint of sweet milk, nutmeg and sugar to taste. Bake in a moderate oven until the custard sets. Boiled rice seasoned with orange peel, milk and sugar is a good dish for invalids. Use a little butter if permitted; a little wine is also relished. MRS. HILL.

RICE PUDDING.

One quart of milk, 2 tablespoonsful raw rice, sugar and flavor to taste. Bake 3 hours in a slow oven.   MRS. C. W. KOLLOCK.

SOFT RICE.—A BREAKFAST DISH.

To a half pint rice add 1 and one-half pints cold water; let it boil till the grains are perfectly soft, then add one-half pint milk. Let it boil again, stirring frequently, for 5 minutes, then add salt and serve. Do not put the salt in till ready to serve.   MRS. BARKER.

RICE WAFERS, TO BE BAKED IN A WAFER IRON.

One pint of rice flour, 1 gill of milk and 1 of water, a dessertspoonful of butter and a little salt. Bake a light brown.

CAROLINA HOUSEWIFE.

RICE WAFERS No. 2.

To a pint of warm water put a pint of rice flour and a teaspoonful of salt. This will make 2 dozen wafers.

RICE FLOUR CEMENT.

Mix the flour (as much as is needed) with cold water; pour into boiling water; let it simmer until a transparent paste is formed. When co d use it.   MRS. HILL.

APPENDIX 1

Errata in the Text of the
Carolina Rice Cook Book

I do not note every departure from the text of published works used as sources by Mrs. Stoney, such as running paragraphs together, changing punctuation or spelling, nor even her inimitable way of adding rice where not called for or of omitting mention of alternative grains in specific receipts—that would be tedious—but only errors of some substance or interest.

Note particularly the following section, where I give what would appear to be a more complete and more accurate version of the receipts attributed by Mrs. Stoney to the *Charleston Gazette*, April, 1830, than that which she presents (F 12–14). Ideally, a search should have been made of the files, if they still exist for that period, but that was impracticable and would not necessarily have been productive. (Richard Hooker's search through the files of the *Annual Register* for a similarly attributed receipt for rice bread was fruitless, for example, as I noted earlier.[1]

It was not until I had sent up my work to the publishers and was working on the Bibliography that I realized I had another version, material that I am unable to fully integrate into my text. I stress that I have not been able to verify the version from the *Confederate Receipt Book* either, but at least it does suggest how the receipt "To Make Wafers" came to be so garbled. In addition, the receipts are from South Carolina, and are thus of interest to us.

F 10, line 1 should read: "Wash and gravel one pint of Rice. . ." Omitted receipts for this operation are presented in chapter 2, "To Boil the Rice."

F 13, "To Make Wafers" is hopelessly muddled up with "Rice Puffs," as may be seen in the section immediately following these corrections.

F 20, line 2 should read: ". . . half an hour. Bake in a quick oven. A little . . ."

F 31, last line should read: ". . . 2 teaspoonfuls of baking powder . . . ," NOT tablespoonfuls.

F 44, line 2, last word should be: "picked."

F 45, "Rice Soup," line 5, add: "*A German Receipt.*"

F 51, *"Poulet au Riz"* is repeated on F 64 in more faithful form.

F 54, Mrs. Blake's "Carolina Pilau," line 6 clearly should read: "... Cover the fowl with it [the rice]...." Not verifiable.

F 55, " A French Pilau" is misattributed and has an error: it is properly given and attributed on F 51.

F 62, line 7 should read: "...a teaspoonful of (Dr. Price's) extract of celery..."

F 64, *"Poulet au Riz,"* antepenultimate line should read: "Serve in the same dish...."

F 81, line 4, last sentence should read: "Eat with a rich sauce."

F 82, "Rice Blance Mange" is misattributed to *Maryland Kitchen*; it comes from *The Virginia House-Wife* by Mary Randolph (1831 edition, p. 147; 1984 facsimile edition of 1824 edition, p. 240).

F 82, "Rice Flour Blanc Mange," line 2 should read: "...quantity of cold new milk...."

F 91, "Rice Wafers No. 2," should be attributed to *The Carolina House-wife* by Sarah Rutledge.

Recipes for Making Bread, &c., from Rice Flour, ostensibly from the *Charleston Gazette*, as they appear in the *Confederate Receipt Book* (1863)

Russel County, Ala., September 8th, 1862.

Editors Columbus Sun: I read an article in one of your papers lately in which recipes for making different kinds of bread with rice flour were enquired for, and having a few that I think will be found very good I send them to you. They were printed in Charleston, S.C., several years ago.

Elizabeth B. Lewis.

To make Loaf Rice Bread. Boil a quart of rice soft, add a pint of leaven, then three quarts of rice flour, put it in a tin or earthen vessel, until it has raised sufficiently; divide it into three parts, and bake it as for other bread, and you will have three large loaves, or scald the flour, and when cold mix half wheat flour or corn meal, raised with leaven in the usual way.

Another. One quart of rice flour, make it into a stiff pap, by wetting with warm water, not so hot as to make it lumpy, when well wet add boiling water, as much as two or three quarts, stir in continually until it boils, put in half pint of yeast when it cools, and a little salt, knead in as much wheat flour as will make it a proper dough for bread, put it to rise, and when risen add a little more wheat flour; let it stand in a warm place half an hour, and bake it. This same mixture only made thinner and baked in rings make excellent muffins.

Journey or Jonny Cakes. To three spoonfuls of soft boiled rice add a small tea cup of water or milk, then add six spoonfuls of the rice flour, which will make a large Jonny cake or six waffles.

Rice Cakes. Take a pint of soft boiled rice, a half pint of milk or water, to which add twelve spoonfuls of the rice flour, divide it into small cakes, and bake them in a brick oven. [The same receipt on F 13 calls for a *brisk* oven, it will be noted.]

Rice Cakes Like Buckwheat Cakes. Mix one-fourth wheat flour to three-fourths superfine rice flour, and raise it as buckwheat flour, bake it like buckwheat cakes.

To make Wafers. Take a pint of warm water, a teaspoonful of salt, add a pint of the flour and it will give you two dozen wafers.

To make Rice Puffs. To a pint of the flour add a teaspoonful of salt, a pint of boiling water, beat up four eggs, stir them well together, put from two to three spoonfuls of lard in a pan, make it boiling hot and fry as you do common fritters.

To make a Rice Pudding. Take a quart of milk, add a pint of the flour, boil them to a pap, beat up six eggs, to which add six spoonfuls of Havana sugar and a spoonful of butter, which when well beaten together add to the milk and flour, grease the pan it is to be baked in, grate nutmeg over the mixture and bake it.

Rice Flour Sponge Cake. Made like sponge cake, except that you use three-quarters of a pound of rice flour, thirteen eggs, leaving out four whites, and add a little salt.

Rice Flour Blanc Mange. Boil one quart of milk, season it as to your taste with sugar and rose water, take four table-spoonfuls of the rice flour, mix it very smooth with cold milk, add this to the other milk while it is boiling, stirring it well. Let all boil together about fifteen minutes, stirring occasionally, then pour it into moulds and put it by to cool. This is a very favorite article for invalids.

Rice Griddle Cakes. Boil one cup of whole rice quite soft in milk, and while hot stir in a little wheat flour or rice flour when cold, add two eggs and a little salt, bake in small thin cakes on the griddle.

In every case in making rice flour bread, cake or pudding, a well-boiled pap should be first made of all the milk and water and half the flour, and allowed to get perfectly cold before the other ingredients are added. It forms a support for them and prevents the flour from settling at the bottom, stir the whole a moment before it is set to cook.[1]

[These receipts may be compared with those attributed to the *Charleston Gazette*, April, 1830, F 12–14.]

A Brief Glossary

Gill (pronounced *jill*), a measure of capacity equivalent to four American fluid ounces, or half a cup.

Hominy in South Carolina is cooked grits, and *grits* is coarsely milled dried maize according to John Martin Taylor.

Middlings, small rice, grades of broken rice.

Plate of shrimps, equivalent to one pint according to *Old Receipts from Old St. John's* [1920s].

Yeast powder, effectively baking powder. A receipt from *Old Receipts from Old St. John's* calls for: $1/2$ lb. cream of tartar, $1/4$ lb. baking soda, and $1/4$ lb. flour, all well sifted together. Mrs. Hill of Georgia (1872), says: "An even teaspoonful of cream of tartar, and a quarter of a teaspoonful of soda [as a substitute for] yeast powders." I infer from this and several mentions in the receipts compiled by Mrs. Stoney that "yeast powders" were packaged in premeasured amounts equivalent to one teaspoonful of baking powder in leavening qualities.[1] One such mention is in the receipt "Ashley Rice Bread" of Miss Rutledge (F 14).

Notes

Works that are cited in the text but not included in the Bibliography are supplied with the necessary bibliographical information in these notes, particularly place of publication, which I have deemed unnecessary for those works that are included in the Bibliography. Once a work has been described, either in the text or in a first reference, succeeding notes usually refer only to the author or a shortened title, whichever seems more recognizable. For example, *Two Hundred Years of Charleston Cooking*, the work of four authors, all of whom are duly listed under its title in the Bibliography, is referred to in these notes as *Two Hundred Years...*, naming a contributor or one of the authors when pertinent. *Fifty Years in A Maryland Kitchen* is referred to as *Maryland Kitchen*.

Such abbreviations as are occasionally used in referring to basic references I have listed at the beginning of the Bibliography.

ACKNOWLEDGMENTS AND EXPLANATIONS

1. "To Make a French Pilau," (F 51); culinary manuscript of 1226 translated as *A Baghdad Cookery-Book* by A. J. Arberry; Harvey Levenstein, *Revolution at the Table*. New York (1988), 4.

CHAPTER 1: THE RICE KITCHEN OF THE SOUTH CAROLINA LOW COUNTRY

1. As transcribed in *Recipe Book, Eliza Lucas Pinckney, 1756* (1956), 25; Smart-Grosvenor (1986), 4; Lord Curzon, as cited by Nesta Ramazani, *Persian Cooking* (1974), 105.
2. John Fryer, as cited by Ramazani, 105.
3. *OED*, under *Achar*; Horry, as transcribed in *A Colonial Plantation Cookbook*, ed. Richard J. Hooker (1984), 86; Howard, 279; Glasse (1755, also 1747), 334; *same* (1796), 308; Rutledge (1847), xii, 179, index.
4. Jenkins, *New York Times*, May 3, 1989.
5. Walker, telephone interviews, 1990.
6. Karen Hess, Introduction to *The Virginia House-Wife* by Mary Randolph, facsimile edition (1984), xxix–xxxi, other entries as indexed.
7. Peter H. Wood, *Black Majority* (1974), 224–225.

8. Claude Neuffer and Irene Neuffer, *Correct Mispronunciations of Some South Carolina Names* (1983), under the various names; *Huguenot Society of South Carolina*, 1954.
9. Wood, 167-191; Charles Joyner, *Down By the Riverside* (1984), 2, 196-224; cited by Daniel C. Littlefield, *Rice and Slaves* (1981), 31.
10. Joyner, 43-48, 70-89, 95-96; Littlefield, 5; Julia Floyd Smith, *Slavery and Rice Culture in Low Country Georgia, 1750-1860* (1985), 114-118.
11. J. F. Smith, 34-35; Herbert Ravenel Sass and D. E. Huger Smith, *A Carolina Rice Plantation of the Fifties* (1936), 13.
12. Doar, 8; Littlefield, 96-97; Wood, 10.
13. Doar, 8; Duncan Clinch Heyward, *Seed From Madagascar* (1937), 9-10; also cited by Littlefield, 107.
14. John Gerarde, *The Herball* (1636), 79-80 (also 1597), under *Ryce;* Littlefield, 100, 105.
15. *OED,* Robert, *American Dictionary of the English Language,* all under *Rice*; George Usher, *Dictionary of Plants Used by Man* (1974), under *Oryza,* 427-28; Littlefield, 80-88.
16. Joyner, 171; Wood, 178-79.
17. Wood, 60; Littlefield, 8-9, 103.
18. Littlefield, 113; Wood, 28-32; Joyner, 70-89.
19. Littlefield, 93-98, 108.
20. Wood, 61.
21. Joyner, 14, 34.
22. Doar, 44.
23. Salmon, under *Rice,* 943; Beeton, 677; Favre, under *Riz,* 4:722.
24. Littlefield, 101-102; Doar, 51-52.
25. The Rice Council for Market Development, *Rice is In* (no date, unnumbered, sheet 9), drawn from *U.S. Bureau of Census Historical Statistics of the United States; Colonial Times to 1970* (1975), Part 2, Sec. 481-82, p. 1192 (with thanks to Lisa Pasquale, who had assisted in preparing *Rice is In*).
26. *Thomas Jefferson's Garden Book, 1766-1824,* ed. Edwin Morris Betts, (1944), 26, 123, 124-25, 131, 143.
27. Joyner, 34.

CHAPTER 2: TO BOIL THE RICE

1. Toussaint-Samat, *Afrique Noire,* 79-80; Ramazani, 107-108; Joyner, 92, 96-98; Rundell (1808), 137-38 (also 1807, indexed but inadvertently omitted, 1817); Brown, 71; Eustis, *Cooking in Old Créole Days,* 14; Hill, 245; Rutledge (1847), 93-94.

2. Apicius, *The Roman Cookery Books,* Latin with English translation by Barbara Flower and Elisabeth Rosenbaum (1958), under *Amulatum aliter,* 66–67; Eliza Acton, *Modern Cookery,* Philadelphia (1845), 54; also see "Rice, as Cooked in Japan," in *Creole Cookery,* Christian Woman's Exchange of New Orleans (1885), 72.
3. Littlefield, 79.
4. Smart-Grosvenor, 4; *The South Carolina Cook Book* (1954), 70–71; Ramazani, 129; receipts from Vietnam recorded by Martha Hess, 1989.
5. Joyner, 210.
6. *OED,* under *Rice;* Margaret Wade Labarge, *A Baronial Household of the Thirteenth Century,* London (1965), 99; Robert, under *riz; Traité de Cuisine Écrit vers 1300,* published with *Le Viandier de Taillevent,* ed. Jérôme Pichon and Georges Vicaire, (1892), 222; *Un Manuscrit valaisan du "Viandier" attribué à Taillevent,* ed. Paul Aebischer, in *Vallesia* (1953), 93; *Curye on Inglysch,* ed. Constance B. Hieatt and Sharon Butler, (1985), 64, 75.
7. Favre, 4:1722–23, under *Riz; La Cuisine de Madame Saint-Ange* (1927), under *Riz,* 878; *The Closet of Sir Kenelme Digby Opened* (1669), 171; Glasse (1755, also 1747), 101; Rundell (1808), 137–38; Acton, 54; Mrs. Parker, *see* under "Contributors" in this work.
8. Eliza Leslie, *Directions for Cookery* (1837), 202–203; *Mrs. Hale's New Cook Book* (1873), 281–82; *Mrs. Lincoln's Boston Cook Book* (1883, all editions), 306–307; *Mrs. Rorer's Philadelphia Cook Book* (1886), 356; *Mrs. Rorer's New Cook Book* (1902), 294–95; Rombauer, *The Joy of Cooking,* Indianapolis (1936), 55. I note that it was Anne Mendelson who noticed the Rombauer receipt and sent it to me.
9. Walker, telephone interviews, 1990; Parker (1891), 240; Taylor, telephone interviews, 1990.
10. Mary Stuart Smith, *Virginia Cookery Book* (1885), 136; Randolph (1824), 94, 137–38; Hill, 6.
11. Julie Sahni, *Classic Indian Cooking* (1980), 358.
12. Hill, 245; I do not find specific confirmation of the presence of Carolina Gold in Georgia, but considering the historical ties between the plantation owners in the two states, referred to earlier, and that a certain amount of the Georgia crop was sold out of Charleston, I think that they must have grown Carolina Gold (This last according to J. F. Smith, 23). In certain states there are ordinances prohibiting the sale of rice accompanied by instructions to wash it or to cook it in water that is then discarded.
13. Sahni, in conversation, 1989.

CHAPTER 3: PILAU AND ITS KIND

1. Sir Thomas Herbert, 97, as cited in *OED* under *Pilau*; Fryer, as cited by Ramazani, 105.
2. Neuffer, under *Pilau*; *OED*, under *Pilau*, as well as various relevant cookbooks; Favre, Vol. 4, under *pilaf*, 1583; Madame Saint-Ange, 878; Auguste Escoffier, *Le Riz* (1927), 10.
3. *A Baghdad Cookery-Book*, in *Islamic Culture*, hereafter, simply *Baghdad Cookery*, (January, 1939), 43; *Traité de Cuisine*, 220; *Le Ménagier de Paris*, ed. Jérôme Pichon, (1846), Vol. 2: 214–215.
4. *Baghdad Cookery* (January, 1939), 34–47; various Arab cookbooks, see Bibliography; on "Persian milk:" *Laban* is the name for yoghurt, or forms of it, in much of the Middle East, and a receipt for "*Labaniya*" (*Baghdad Cookery* [January, 1939], 42) calls for "Persian milk." Also see, Claudia Roden, *A Book of Middle Eastern Food* (1972), 79; Ba'albaki, under *jambalaya;* Corominas, under *arroz, pailla*; *OED*, under *Rice*; Robert, under *poêle*.
5. Favre, Vol. 4, under *pilaf*, 1583; Robert, under *pilau*.
6. *Curye on Inglysch*, 89; examples of *blanc manger* made of pounded rice or rice cooked to a mush may be found on the same page and scattered throughout the work.
7. Glasse (1755, also 1747), 101–102, (1796), 130; E. Smith (1742), 28, (1773), 74; Hale (1873), 222. In the Hale work, the receipt is indexed under *T,* as "*Turkish pillau,*" and the page number is given incorrectly. I have also found a few more receipts, each sillier than the last; the Smith receipt had the virtue of demonstrating a relationship with Carolina receipts, however much she had muddled it, and this is why I included it, even at the last minute without being able to incorporate it into the text.
8. Thornton, 139; Leslie, 147, 202–203.
9. *The Travels of William Bartram* [1773–1777], Naturalist's Edition, ed. Francis Harper, (1958), 41, 157; Amelia Simmons, *American Cookery* (1796), 34; Anna Wells Rutledge, *Preliminary Checklist of South Carolina Cookbooks Published Before 1935*, in *The Carolina Housewife*, facsimile edition (1979), 225; for *The Centennial Receipt Book*, see Bibliography; Thornton, facsimile edition (1984), Shirley Abbot, Introduction, 3.
10. Webster (1806), under *bacon*; Brown, 53, 67; Ramazani, 107–57; Martha Logan's calendar, in *Palladium of Knowledge: or, the Carolina and Georgia Almanac 1798* (Early American Imprints, Evans No.

33255); Rutledge (1851), 196; *same* (1847), 219; *Two Hundred Years
. . .,* Hamilton, Foreword, viii, x.

11. *Charleston Receipts,* Foreword, 3. Further support can be found in
Joyner, 80–81; and Fox-Genovese, 158–61.

12. Harris, in manuscript reader's comments; *OED,* under *Gumbo*; Rundell (1808), 42.

13. *Two Hundred Years. . .,* 45; *same,* Hamilton, Foreword, xiii–xvii.

14. *Two Hundred Years. . .,* 54–55.

15. Mistral, under *pelau, tian*; Méry, as given by André Castelot, *L'Historie à Table* (1972), under *Pilau,* 532; *Dictionnaire Languedoçien-
Francais,* under *cassolo.*

16. Durand, 34–35; Morard, 408; Reboul, 87; Armisen and Martin, 54.
(I note that it was Rudolf Grewe who brought the Durand work to
my attention and sent me the receipt.)

17. Stouff, 257, 260, 467–77; *Le Viandier,* 22 entries for *cretonnée* in the
index.

18. Alfred W. Crosby, Jr., *The Columbian Exchange,* Westport, Conn.
(1972), 168–69.

19. Rutledge (1847), 63; C. Chanot-Bullier, *Vieii Receto de Cousino
Prouvençalo* [1972], 130–31; Eugène Blancard, *Mets de Provence,* 5th
ed. (no date; after 1926), 74; Jean-Noel Escudier, *La Véritable Cuisine Provençale et Niçoise* (1964), 191 (Contemporary receipts tend to
be modernized, often omitting the marinade because it is no longer
necessary to assure tenderness, but the flavor is no longer the same. I
have had many conversations concerning this subject in France.); L.
Liger, *Dictionnaire Pratique du Bon Ménager de Campagne et de
Ville* (1715), under *Daube,* Vol. 1:260; Randolph (1824), 97–98, 187–
89; *same* (facsimile edition, 1984), xxx, xxxii, 257–58.

20. Morard, 113–16; Durand, 34; Reboul, 173–75; Méry, see Castelot,
532; also, *Nouveau Larousse Gastronomique* (1967), 221.

21. Chanot-Bullier, 50–51, 128–29, etc.; Escudier, 179; Toussaint-Samat,
Provence, 128–29; Bonnefons, 157 (Concerning the *mouclade,* northern writers often delicately omit the saffron, as Curnonsky did in *Recettes des Provinces de France,* Paris [1962], 126); *Two Hundred Years
. . .,* Hamilton, Foreword, x; Laurel Thatcher Ulrich, *A Midwife's
Tale: The Life of Martha Ballard, Based on Her Diary, 1785–1812*
(1990), 38; Bernard McMahon, *The American Gardener's Calendar*
(1806), 598; *Thomas Jefferson's Garden Book,* 337.

22. Robert, under *bacon*; Mistral, under *bacoun*; Forot, 52; de Croze,
La Psychologie de la Table (1928), 187–90.

23. De Croze, *Les Plats Régioneaux de France* (1928), 361; Vernon, by telephone, 1990; Robert, Durand, under *bouillabaisse*.
24. *Webster* (1961), under *pilau*; Farmer, *The Boston Cooking-School Cook Book,* (1896), 89–90; *The Fannie Farmer Cookbook,* rev. Marion Cunningham with Jeri Laber (1979), 318–19; Rombauer, *The Joy of Cooking,* Indianapolis (1975), 209, 433; Beard, *American Cookery,* Boston (1972), 578–79; Mariani, *The Dictionary of American Food and Drink,* New Haven (1983), 298; Evans, *American Food,* New York (1975), 269–70.
25. Mistral, under *Jambalaia*; Eustis, *Cooking in Old Créole Days,* 13; Begué, 62; *The Creole Cookery Book* (1885), 67.
26. Jouveau, 138; *NLG* (1967), under *Jambalaia,* 608; Hearn, 106; Begué, 62, 63; *Picayune,* 181, 182; *Creole Cookery* (1885), 39; Rutledge (1847), 82–83 (also F 51); Eustis, *Cooking in Old Créole Days,* 15 (I say "makeshift" because *paella* is properly cooked over a wood fire in its huge shallow pan); both *Websters,* under *jambalaya*; *Baghdad Cookery* (January, 1939), 34, 35, 37; Grewe, *Libre de Sent Sovi,* 246; Corominas, under *escabeche*; *Le Ménagier de Paris,* Vol. 2:100, 175; Ada Boni, *Italian Regional Cooking* (1969), 194; Waverley Root, *The Food of Italy,* New York (1977), 373, 522; Glasse (1755), 259; *Baghdad Cookery* (January, 1939), 46.
27. Stouff, 16, 145, 212, 215, 247, 257, 467–77, and *passim*; *OED,* under *Collard*; Franklin, 85; Root, *Food,* New York (1980), 414; *NLG* (1967), under *Riz,* 899. On the subject of cultivation of rice in France, see my discussion of Root's report further on (p. 00). I note that Maguelonne Toussaint-Samat claims that rice was planted for the first time in the Camargue by "a battalion of Indochinese" in 1940 (*Provence,* 128.). I believe that she is in error here, but it may be that it was they who truly made a success of it at last. She is not Provençal, and while her receipts generally reflect current practice, she did no research on rice aside from speaking to "a charming old gentlemen" of her acquaintance, implying that it did not enter the Provençal diet until after it became "naturalized" in the 1940s, ignoring the evidence of nineteenth-and early twentieth-century cookbooks as well as the medieval records unearthed by Stouff. Certainly, the cultivation of rice may have increased its consumption, particularly in the Camargue itself, large tracts of which have historically been something of a wilderness, a land of saline marshes, Gypsies, and steers and half-wild horses tended cowboy-style by *gardianes,* with few settled cities. The Camargue is changing, of course, but it is still a land apart.

28. Harrison, trans., *The Song of Roland,* 51.
29. Duconquéré, 33–34, 61; Harrison, 9.
30. *Little Book of Jewish Cookery,* 67, 90–91; Machlin, 116; Johnston, 226.
31. *Encyclopedia Judaica* (1972), under *Provence* (as well as individual cities, as *Arles, Avignon,* etc.), *Persia, Barcelona, Food, Rice*; Machlin, 116; Bacon (1986), 67–69.
32. Glasse (1796), 293–94, 295; *same* (1755, also 1747), 259; Platt (1623, reprint by Violet and Hal W. Trovillion, 1942), 69 (I have seen the receipt in editions as early as 1603 and believe it to be in all editions under *Cookery and Huswiferie,* No. 17); Hess, *Martha Washington's Booke of Cookery,* 177–78; *OED,* under *Caveach*; E[liza] Smith, 33; Pinckney (1756), 15; Horry, 58; Rutledge (1847), 52; also *see* receipt for *Escobeche* in *The Jewish Manual,* 39.
33. Mistral, under *Ris.* Obviously, Purim has nothing to do with carnival, the pre-Lenten feast of Christendom, but they are both early spring festivals.
34. Stouff, 261–62, 332 (There are other entries concerning saffron in rice, such as *"Pro croco in risu posito,"* 1397, also from Avignon; *Croco,* as in *Crocus sativus,* is elsewhere identified in records as *alias safra.* The meaning is roughly the same as the translation given in text), 330, 332; *The Jewish Manual* (1846), 126–27; Durand, (1837); Thornton (1845); McDougal, by telephone, 1990; Root, *Food,* 414–15. (I make a point of not having verified Root's report more than I did; he was a journalist and a raconteur, not a historian, and much of his information on the history of rice is quite unreliable, in particular where it concerns South Carolina. I have, however, seen mention of the decree of 1603 elsewhere).

CHAPTER 4: THE RICE CASSEROLES
OF SOUTH CAROLINA

1. Horry, 62; *Dictionnaire Portatif de Cuisine,* under *Castrole,* 135; Glasse (1755, also 1747), 53–54 (also 1796, 79); Rundell (1817), 207.
2. L. Liger, *Dictionnaire Pratique du Bon Ménager* (1715), Vol. 1, under *Casserolle,* 139; Antonin Carême, *Le Patissier Royal* (1815), Vol. 1:138 (also 1854): also in *NLG* (1967) in a somewhat shortened form, with no plates, *"Casserole au Riz à l'ancienne,"* 291–92; Rutledge (1847), Preface, v; A Boston Housekeeper [Mrs. N. K. M. Lee], *The Cook's Own Book* (1832), "Rice Casserole," 174. Mrs. Lee went through cookbooks like a vacuum cleaner, simply alphabetizing the receipts.
3. Ramazani, 122–23, 129–31; Rundell (1817), 237, 241, 243; Mistral, under *cassola* (with myriad forms), and *tian*; Coromias, under

cazo; *Baghdad Cookery* (January, 1939), 46 (the translation is "Garnish with poached eggs," but this is disputed by some, saying it should be "hard-cooked eggs" or even "yolks of hard-cooked eggs." In any event, it is hard-cooked eggs in modern Eastern receipts). South Carolina is too hot for mussels, and I suggest that shrimps replaced them for this reason.

4. *Old Receipts from Old St. John's,* no paging, sheet 8; *South Carolina Cook Book,* "Mum Rosie's Rice Pie," 177.

CHAPTER 5: HOPPIN' JOHN AND OTHER BEAN PILAUS OF THE AFRICAN DIASPORA

1. *Baghdad Cookery* (January, 1939), 44; Ayensu, *West African Cooking,* 109, 110–11; Brown, 91; Eustis, *Cooking in Old Créole Days,* 10, 16; *South Carolina Cook Book,* 234; Vernon, correspondence, 1990.
2. Ramazani, 108–57, *passim*; Littlefield, 83; Harrison, trans., *The Song of Roland,* 100–101, 100–11, 150.
3. *Baghdad Cookery* (January, 1939), 47; C. J. Hylander and O. B. Stanley, cited by William Ed Grimé, *Ethno-Botany of the Black Americans,* 20; names of rice-and-bean dishes largely from *The Complete Book of Caribbean Cooking,* by Elizabeth Lambert Ortiz (1973), but any serious work on the cooking of that region, or that of the African Diaspora, such as *Iron Pots and Wooden Spoons* by Jessica B. Harris (1989), which came out after I had done the bulk of my research on this section, will bear out most of the names if one simply consults the index under *Rice,* or *Peas,* or *Beans,* always keeping in mind that names are changeable from one district to another, often maddeningly so. But that is part of the charm and, more important, part of the history of the Diaspora.
4. Tussac, Lunan, Catesby, and P. Brown all cited by Grimé, 20–21, 159, 191; Dooley, *Puerto Rican Cookbook,* 78.
5. Usher, under *Vicia faba, Vigna,* 600; Grimé, 27, 191; *Jefferson's Garden Book,* 252.
6. *WNNCD,* under *hopping John*; Grewe, in conversation, 1990; Wehr, 77; *Sturtevant's Edible Plants of the World* (1972); actually it dates from the late nineteenth century), under *Vicia sativa,* 596; names all drawn from various sources already cited; photograph of black–eye-peas-and-rice dish in Saigon taken by Martha Hess, 1990.
7. *Baghdad Cookery* (January 1939), 46; Veeraswamy, 21; Indra Majupuria, 74; *OED,* under *Asparagus, Sparrow-grass, Kickshaws*; Wehr, under *Petra.*
8. Ortiz, *Caribbean Cookery,* 293, 296–97 (I emphasize that she does not characterize "*Moros y Cristianos*" as a pilau, nor any other rice-

and-bean dish that is cooked similarly, reserving the term *pilau* for dishes of Indian origin, and this accords with the practice of other writers); Jenkins, *New York Times,* February 28, 1990; Harris, by telephone, 1990; Harris, *Iron Pots,* 103–104; *WNNCD,* under *hopping John,* presumably based on *Recollections of A Southern Matron,* Caroline Gilman (1838), 124, where it is described by her fictional heroine.

9. William Woys Weaver, in *America Eats* (New York, 1989), 28–29, 71, goes so far as to specifically exclude those works, as well as those of Lettice Bryan, *The Kentucky Housewife* (1839) and Mrs. B. C. Howard, *Fifty Years in A Maryland Kitchen* (1873), from his bibliography in a work purportedly surveying "traditional" regional cookery; Rutledge (1847), 44, 45, 46, 83, etc.; *Two Hundred Years...,* 58.

10. Brown, *Domestic Cookery,* 91; Hill, 196; Eustis, *Cooking in Old Créole Days,* 14, 16; *Picayune,* 114, 182; Ortiz, *Caribbean Cookery,* 286; Sturtevant, 124–25; Phillips, *American Negro Slavery,* 255, as graciously supplied to me by Amelia Wallace Vernon; *Jefferson's Garden Book,* 143, 380, 381; Rice Council, by telephone, 1990; Nowick, by way of Vernon, 1990; Vernon, from excerpts from her forthcoming work on subsistence rice farming in South Carolina, and correspondence, 1990.

11. Rice Council, *Rice Is In,* sheets 9–10; [Mme. Utrecht-Friedel], *La Petite Cuisinière Habile* (1840); Lafcadio Hearn, *La Cuisine Creole* (1885), 10, 80: *Creole Cookery* (1885), 39, 70, 72, etc.

12. Thomas Hill and Nell Hill, in conversation, 1990; Walker, by telephone, 1990; Harris, *Iron Pots,* 106; Rutledge, F 60–61; Vernon, in correspondence, 1990; Taylor, *New York Times,* December 28, 1988.

CHAPTER 6: RICE SOUPS

1. Rundell (1817), 211, also 117–18, virtually the same.

2. *OED,* under *Gumbo, Pepper-pot, Mulligatawny;* Usher, under *Hibiscus esculentus,* 303; Harris, manuscript reader's comments, 1990; Grimé, under *Abelmoschus esculentus,* 19; Rutledge (1851), 36; Randolph (1824), 96.

CHAPTER 7: THE RICE BREADS OF SOUTH CAROLINA

1. Horry, 120–21; Rundell (1817), 243 (also 1814); Rutledge (1847), 12; Thornton, 111–12; *Centennial Receipt Book,* 64; Porter, 171.

2. Elizabeth David, *English Bread and Yeast Cookery* (1980 and 1982), 71; Calvel, 349–51.

3. David, 71, 292; Rutledge (1847), Preface, v.

4. Rutledge (1847), 31–32; *same* (1851), 20–21; Thornton, 139, where he suggests the use of "pearl Barley as a Substitute for Rice," claiming that it cost "one-third the price [of ground rice]"; this is in inland Camden.

5. *OED,* under *Lady*; David, 155–90; *same,* Hess, Introduction to the American Edition, xii–xix; Hess, "The American Loaf: A Historical View," *Journal of Gastronomy,* Vol. 3, no. 4 (Winter 1987/1988): 2–23, 11–16.

6. Taylor, reader's comments, 1990; Brown, 98–99, 104, 110; Thornton, 107–108; *Creole Cookery,* Christian Woman's Exchange of New Orleans (1885), 92; Horry, Introduction by Richard J. Hooker, 10–11; "Boston Housekeeper" [Mrs. N.K.M. Lee], *The Cook's Own Book,* under *Bread, Rice,* 26; I am not about to document the poor receipts for rice bread from the counterculture, leaving that to the reader; David, 290–92.

7. Romans, as cited in *OED* under *Johnny-cake*; Horry, 135; Simmons, 34; Thornton, 116; Rutledge (1847), 27; *Centennial Receipt Book,* 64–65.

8. Hess, "*The Jonny-Cake Papers, and Other Tales,*" in *A Conference on Current Research in Culinary History,* Schlesinger Library of Radcliffe College and the Culinary Historians of Boston (June 1985, 46–55), 48, from which work I have heavily borrowed in this section, but with certain important emendations; Taylor, in correspondence, 1990.

9. Hess, "*Jonny-Cake Papers,*" 46–55; *OED,* under *Johnny, Johnny-cake.*

10. *DAE,* under *Jonikin*; *OED,* under *Jannock, Bannock*; Halliwell, under *Jannocks*; *Webster* (1806), under *Bannoc*; *WNNCD,* under *Bannock.*

11. Horry, 64, 135; Hill, 236–37; Bryan, *Kentucky Housewife,* 315; *Picayune,* 404; *Maryland Kitchen,* 236; *Charleston Receipts,* 180.

12. Rundell (1817), 237.

13. Simmons, 35, 36; John Beale Bordley, *Essays and Notes on Husbandry and Rural Affairs,* 2d ed. Philadelphia (1801), 411–12.

14. Eustis, *La Cuisine Créole,* 108; *Creole Cookery* (1885), 130.

15. *OED,* under *Fritter*; Brillat-Savarin, *Physiologie du Goût* (1826), in reprint edition, Pierre Waleff (1967), under "*Théorie de la Friture,*" 103; *Picayune,* 184; Harris, *Iron Pots,* 27–31; Ortiz, *Caribbean Cooking,* 32–35, 422; Dr. André Nègre, *Les Antilles À Travers Leur Cuisine* [1967], 18–19, listing eleven receipts for *acras*; *Baghdad Cookery* (April, 1939), 213; Ayensu, 114–15; Alex D. Hawkes, *The Flavors of the Caribbean* (1978), 34; Robert, under *beignet.*

16. Bertrand Guégan, *Les Dix Livres de Cuisine D'Apicius* [1933], 208, Note 300; *Baghdad Cookery* (April, 1939), 213; Yianilos, *The Complete Greek Cookbook,* New York (1970), 167–68, where the name is *loukoumathes,* but the more usual transcription is *loukoumades;* *Ménagier de Paris,* Vol. 2:224, 225, 229; *Viandier,* 124–25; *Curye on Inglysch,* 53, 67, 132, etc., variously called *fritur, cryspys,* etc.; Jacques Médecin, *La Cuisine du Comté de Nice* (1972), 76–77; Randolph (1824), 160; Bryan, 298.

17. *Le Pastissier François,* Troyes 1690(?), as reprinted with and under the title of *Le Cuisinier François,* ed. Jean-Louis Flandrin, Philip Hyman, and Mary Hyman (1983), 410; *Le Pastissier François* (1653), chapter 20, no. 2.

18. Daniel Roche, Introduction, *"Les Livrets Bleus"* (in *Le Cuisinier François,* ed. Flandrin, Hyman, and Hyman), 3–5; *La Cuisinière Bourgeoise* (1753), 334–37; La Varenne, *Le Cuisinier François* (1654), 110; Antonin Carême, *Le Cuisinier Parisien* (1828), 388; Menon, *Les Soupers de la Cour* (1755), Vol. 2:15–16, among 24 receipts for *baignets; Dictionnaire Portatif de Cuisine* (1772), 75. In regard to use of French cookbooks in Carolina, it is to be noted that Sarah Rutledge acknowledges that "a few [receipts were] translated from the French," presumably those attributed to Madame de Genlis, in *La Maison Rustique,* a work I do not know; Rutledge (1847), v, 49, 72, etc., ten receipts in all. And there is Mrs. Stoney's citation from Bouillet's *Dictionnaire Universel* (1854), F 11. That is, there seems to have been a certain flow of works from France to Carolina.

19. Maestro Martino, *Libro de Arte Coquinaria,* as reprinted in *Arte della Cucina...dal XIV al XIX Secolo,* Vol. 1:175, 177; Platina, *De Honesta Voluptate* (1475), *Liber Nonus...Frictellas...,* unpaged 141, 142, beginning after the table of contents; Francisco Martinez Motiño, *Arte de Cozina* (1611), folio 140 *verso,* 141 *recto,* 143 *verso; Fettiplace,* ed. Hilary Spurling, 84.

20. Nègre, 18–19, as well as other Caribbean references already given; Rice Council, *Rice Is In,* sheets 9–10; *Creole Cookery* (1885), 39, 70, 72; Eustis, *La Cuisine Créole,* 94.

21. Mary Stuart Smith, 14; Mrs. Parker's Complete Housekeeper *(1891),* 35.

CHAPTER 8: SWEET RICE DISHES OF
SOUTH CAROLINA

1. De Croze, 82, 116; Rutledge (1847), 126.

2. *Two Hundred Years...* (1976), Foreword, x; *same,* 54–55, 247; Rutledge (1855), 118.

3. Hess, *Martha Washington's Booke of Cookery*, 125–26, 131; *Nouveau Larousse Gastronomique* (1967), 851; Madame Saint-Ange, 925–26 (Don't ask me why it is *gâteau de riz* but *pouding au riz*, but this is the way it is); Longone, *American Cookbooks and Wine Books: 1797–1950*, 37; Jean Seguin, *vieux mangers, vieux parlers bas-normands*, 2d ed. [1938], 138–39; Curnonsky and Austin de Croze, *Le Trésor Gastronomique de France* (1933), 71; Roger Lallemand, *La Vraie Cuisine de la Normandie* [1972], 171–72; also, Simone Morand, in *Gastronomie Bretonne* (1965), 389, 390, gives two receipts in this regard: *"Riz Chaud Quimperois"* and *"Riz 'Dans les Mottes' ou Taouac'h,"* the latter a slightly elaborated version; Digbie, 161–62.
4. *Lucayos Cook Book*, 28, no. 137; Glasse (1796), 341; *same* Alexandria (1805), 291.
5. Rundell (1808), 152–53; *same*, (1817), 191; *Picayune*, 186, 276, 277; Curnonsky and de Croze, 70; Lallemand, 152–53; Beeton, 621, 622–23, 627; Hill, 269–70.

CHAPTER 9: RICE IN INVALID COOKERY

1. Salmon, under *Rice*, 943; Favre, Vol. 4, under *Racahout*, 1691–1692; Lincoln, 427. (I note that it was Anne Mendelson who brought this last to my attention.)
2. *NLG* (1967), *Grand Larousse* (1977), Bloch, all under *Racahout*; John Peachie, *Some Observations Made Upon the Root Called Serapias, or Salep. Imported from Turkey, Showing Its Admirable Virtues in Preventing Womens Miscarriages* (1694), 3–6; Dufour, *De L'Usage du Caphé, du Thé, et du Chocolate* (1671), 75–188, *passim*; Dufour, *Traitéz Nouveaux et Curieux du Café, du Thé, et du Chocolate* (1688), 310; Diana Kennedy, *The Cuisines of Mexico* (1972), 349, 350; Brillat-Savarin, 100.
3. *Maryland Kitchen*, 349; *Wise Encyclopedia*, under *Rachahout*.

CHAPTER 10: A FEW WORDS ON THE *CAROLINA RICE COOK BOOK* AND ITS CONTRIBUTORS

1. Mrs. Stoney's full name has been communicated by John Bennett, a kinsman of the Stoney's referred to earlier, and forwarded by John Taylor, 1991; Taylor, *Omnibus*, Charleston (May 1991), 7; Mc-Dougal, by telephone, 1990; Anna Wells Rutledge, Introduction to facsimile edition of *The Carolina Housewife* (1979), vii; *same, A Preliminary Checklist...*, 231; Parker, F 46; *Charleston Receipts...*, 107, Bennet also explained (by telephone, 1991) that "Mrs. Albert Simons (Harriet Stoney)" was a daughter of our Mrs. Stoney, that is, an aunt of Harriet McDougal.

APPENDIX 1: ERRATA IN THE TEXT OF
THE CAROLINA RICE COOK BOOK

1. Horry, 120.

APPENDIX 2: RECIPES FOR MAKING BREAD, &C.,
FROM RICE FLOUR

1. *Confederate Receipt Book* (1863), as an appendix, 25–27.

APPENDIX 3: A BRIEF GLOSSARY

1. *Old Receipts...*, unnumbered, sheets 9, 16; Hill, 245.

Bibliography

BASIC REFERENCES, INCLUDING
ABBREVIATIONS WHERE USED

I list works by their most recognizable name, whether it be title, author, or editor. This results in considerable inconsistency in style, a fault which I feel is justified by greater ease in use by the reader. Also, among the established reference works I do not always include names of editors, often very numerous, for which I apologize. In certain cases, none is given on title page.

American Heritage Dictionary of the English Language. Boston, 1969.

Ba'albaki, Munir. *Al-Mawrid, A Modern English-Arabic Dictionary.* Beirut, 1969.

Bitting, Katherine Golden. *Gastronomic Bibliography.* San Francisco, 1939.

Bloch, Oscar. *Dictionnaire Étymologique de la Langue Française.* Paris, 1964.

Brown, Eleanor, and Bob Brown. *Culinary Americana...from 1860 through 1960.* New York, 1960.

Cambridge History of Islam (Vol. 2 A, 'The Indian Sub-Continent, South-East Asia, Africa, and the Muslim West'). Cambridge, England, 1970.

Colomer, Jordi. *Diccionari Anglès-català—Català-anglès.* Barcelona, 1979.

Corominas, Joan. *Breve Diccionario Etimológico de la Lengua Castellana.* Madrid, 1980.

Dictionary of American English. Sir William A. Craigie and James R. Hulbert, eds. Chicago, 1938. (*DAE*)

Encyclopedia of Islam. Leiden, Holland, 1960.

Encyclopedia Judaica. Jerusalem, 1972.

Godefroy, Frédéric. *Dictionnaire de l'Ancienne Langue Française et de tous ses Dialects du IX au XV Siècle.* Paris, 1881–1902.

Grimé, William Ed. *Ethno-Botany of the Black Americans.* Algonac, Mich., 1979.

Halliwell, James Orchard. *Dictionary of Archaic and Provincial Words.* London, 1889.

d'Hombres, Maximin, and Gratien Charvet. *Dictionnaire Languedocien-Français.* Alais, France, 1884.

Larousse de la Langue Française, Grand. Paris, 1976.

Larousse Gastronomique, Nouveau. Paris, 1967. (NLG)

Larousse, Nouveau Petit. Paris, 1930.

Littré, Émile. *Dictionnaire de la Langue Française.* Paris, 1863–1877, 1957.

Longone, Janice B., and Daniel T. Longone. *American Cookbooks and Wine Books, 1797–1950.* Ann Arbor, Mich., 1984 "The Clements Library & The Wine and Food Library."

Lowenstein, Eleanor. *Bibliography of American Cookbooks, 1742–1860.* Worcester, Mass. and New York, N.Y., 1972.

McMahon, Bernard. *The American Gardener's Calendar.* Philadelphia, 1806.

Mistral, Frédéric [1830–1914]. Lou Tresor Dóu Felibrige. *Dictionnaire Provençal-Français* [1878–86]; 3d ed., Barcelona, 1968.

Neuffer, Claude, and Irene Neuffer. *Correct Mispronunciations of Some South Carolina Names.* Columbia, S.C., 1983.

Neuman-Holzchuh, Ingrid, ed. *Textes anciens en créole louisianais.* Hamburg, Germany, 1987.

Nouveau Larousse Gastronomique; see Larousse.

Nouveau Petit Larousse; see Larousse.

Oxford, Arnold Whitaker. *English Cookery Books to the Year 1850.* London, 1913.

Oxford English Dictionary. London, 1971. (OED).

Read, William A. *Louisiana-French.* Rev. ed. Baton Rouge, La., 1963.

Robert, Paul, *Dictionnaire de la Langue Française.* Paris, 1985.

——— *Dictionnaire Alphabétique & Analogique de la Langue Française.* Paris, 1967. Unless otherwise indicated, it is this latter edition, sometimes called *Petit Robert,* to which I refer.

Rutledge, Anna Wells. *A Preliminary Checklist of South Carolina Cookbooks Published Before 1935.* (In facsimile edition of The Carolina Housewife; *see* Rutledge, Sarah.

Sturtevant, Edward Lewis [1842–1898]. *Sturtevant's Notes on Edible Plants.* Edited by U. P. Hedrick. Albany, N.Y., 1919. In facsimile as *Sturtevant's Edible Plants of the World.* New York, 1972.

Usher, George. *Dictionary of Plants Used by Man.* New York, 1974.

Vicaire, Georges. *Bibliographie Gastronomique. . . . depuis le XVe siècle jusqu'à nos jours.* Paris, 1890. In facsimile, with Introduction by André L. Simon. London, 1954.

Webster, Noah, Esq. *A Compendious Dictionary of the English Language.* New Haven, 1806. In facsimile, New York, 1970.

Webster's New International Dictionary of the English Language. 2d ed., unabridged. Springfield, Mass., 1961.

Webster's Ninth New Collegiate Dictionary. Springfield, Mass., 1983. (*WNNCD*)

Wehr, Hans. *A Dictionary of Modern Written Arabic.* Edited by J. Milton Cowan. Wiesbaden, Germany, 1979.

READING LIST

This is a personal reading list. I have not thought it necessary to include titles to which I have referred either in passing or in a critical way; they are duly attrributed in my notes, and there is no need to discuss them further, although I was sorely tempted in instances where American regional cookery is involved.

There are no works listed here on technical aspects of rice culture. Those seeking such information shall have to look elsewhere. Good sources for works on related subjects are the bibliographies of some of the works here listed. Nor does my list include all the works I consulted, which would have increased its length hundredfold. Even so, I may have missed works of great importance. Surely I have.

I include historical works that have strong sections on rice cookery or were so important for popular American cookery that they could hardly be omitted. I include works from lands where pilau is traditional, particularly those from Provence because of the historical association betwen the pilaus of Provence and those of Carolina. (I also include works from other lands of the *langue d'oc* so that readers might get some feeling for the separate culinary traditions of the French Midi, in particular the role of *petit salé*, or cured pork, one that also came to Carolina, particularly in rice cookery.) I do not include works from the Maghreb; the historical associations seem tenuous, and rice cookery took a somewhat different path there. Even with Spain and Italy, I confine myself to works cited in the text for their historical associations. In any event, the list would be endless if I included contemporary works from those lands.

I include a sampling of works from the African Diaspora, the Caribbean and New Orleans, in particular, because of their primordial association with the rice kitchen of Carolina. As in all categories, these lists are incomplete; perforce one works with sources that fall to hand, those in nearby libraries or my own extensive collection. And I have my favorites.

I think it useful to note reprint or facsimile editions where known to me. Courtesy requires listing the name of the editor or writer of the introductions, which are in many cases perfectly unspeakable from any point of view, historical or culinary. I am so grateful to have the facsimile text that I try to close my eyes to the awfulness of these introductions, but I resent having to place them on an apparently equal footing with the delightful one of Anna Wells Rutledge, for example. (I exclude one facsimile edition because I would have to note and explain that it was actually falsified so as to make the original edition appear to be several years earlier that it is—this in addition to a spiteful introduction and the usual wretched "modernized" receipts that certain reprint houses feel constrained to inflict upon us.) I should note that I do occasionally make use of minor biographical details concerning the original writer, attributing them when I do so.

Bracketed material refers to information obtained from various sources, often from one of the standard bibliographies listed above. The date, where none is given on the title page of the work, may refer to the date of printing, which is often given in French works. In cases where a work was published long after the author's death, I include biographical dates, also in brackets. These dates are often of importance in evaluating the work. In the same manner, I include the date of old manuscripts when not part of the title or description. Other pertinent information, such as the date of William Bartram's travels, is treated likewise. I do not think it necessary to attribute each of these instances unless it is significant.

French names with a *particule*, that is, beginning with a lowercase *de* or *du*, are alphabetized under the name proper, for example, Austin de Croze is listed under *C.* American practice is spotty in this regard, but Katherine Bitting follows French practice, and it is just as well to get used to it.

Acton, Eliza. *Modern Cookery in All its Branches.* London, 1845. The Whole Revised and Prepared for American Housekeepers by Mrs. S[arah] J. Hale. Philadelphia, 1845. The extent of her revision is clearly stated, consisting of the inclusion of a number of American receipts, all of which are enclosed within brackets, although this is not always understood by writers. The work went through nine American editions by 1860 and so had considerable influence.

Aebischer, Paul, ed. *Un manuscrit valaisan du "Viandier"* [about 1300] *attribué à Taillevent.* In *Vallesia,* 1953, 73–100. A most important document for understanding the development of French medieval cuisine.

Apicius; see Guégan, Bertrand; also, Flower, Barbara; and Elisabeth Rosenbaum. [Apicius died about 30 A.D.,] but his work as it survives probably dates from the fourth century A.D., with the earliest extant manuscripts dating from the ninth century.

Arberry, A. J., ed. *A Baghdad Cookery-Book,* translated from a manuscript by Muhammad ibn al-Hasan ibn Muhammad ibn al-Karīm al-Kātib al-Baghdādī, 1226. In *Islamic Culture, Hyderabad Quarterly Review,* January, 1939, 21–47, and April, 1939, 189–214.

Armisen, Raymond, and André Martin. *Les Recettes de la Table Niçoise.* Strasbourg, 1972.

Atwood, Mary S. *Adventures in Indian Cooking.* Bombay, 1969, 1972. This work was recommended to me by my Indian supplier of basmati rice.

Audot, L[ouis]-E[ustache]. *La Cuisinière de la Campagne et de la Ville.* 3d ed. Paris, 1823. An enormously influential work.

Austin, Thomas, ed. *Two Fifteenth-Century Cookery-Books.* London, 1888, 1964.

Ayensu, Dinah Ameley. *The Art of West African Cooking.* New York, 1972.

Bacon, Josephine Levy. *Jewish Cooking From Around the World.* Woodbury, N.Y., 1986.

Baghdad Cookery-Book, A.; see Arberry, A. J.

Barberousse, Michel. *Cuisine Provençale.* Seguret, Vaucluse, [no date]. Often cited by writers of the past several decades.

Bartram, William, The Travels of [1773–1777]. Naturalist's ed. Francis Harper. New Haven, 1958.

Beecher, [Catherine Esther]. *Miss Beecher's Domestic Receipt-Book.* New York, 1846, 1855.

Beeton, Mrs. Isabella. *The Book of Household Management.* London, 1861; in facsimile, London, 1968.

Begué, [Elizabeth Kettenring Dutrey]. *Mme. Begué and her Recipes: Old Creole Cookery.* Copyright in Houston, 1900. In French, with English translations. Also including a section of receipts by Monsieur Victor. In facsimile, Introduction by Shirley Abbot. Birmingham, Ala., 1984; *same,* 5th ed., under the title *Mme. Bégué's Recipes of Old New Orleans Creole Cookery.* New Orleans, 1937. (I should note that editions vary in the placement of accents in her name; I do not know which is correct, although some sources make a point of saying that the name is pronounced thus: *Bay-GAY,* which would require the spelling of *Bégué.* I have not been entirely consistent.

Les Belles Recettes des Provinces Francaises. (Les Sans-Filistes Gastronomes). Paris, 1929. A lovely receipt *"Pilau de Langouste De La Ciotat."*

Blancard, Eugène. *Mets de Provence.* 5th ed. Grenoble, France, [1926].

Blot, Pierre, *Hand-Book of Practical Cookery.* New York, 1868. 1869 edition in facsimile, with Introduction by Louis Szathmary. New York, 1973. Blot was a French chef who founded The New York Cooking Academy.

Boissard, Pierre. *Cuisine Malgache, Cuisine Créole.* Madagascar, 1983. Bilingual text, Malagasy and French. (By the good graces of John Taylor.)

Boni, Ada. *Italian Regional Cooking.* Trans. Maria Langdale and Ursula Whyte. New York; 1969.

Bonnaure, André. *La Cuisine Rustique: Languedoc.* Forcalquier, Haute-Provence, 1971.

[Bonnefons, Nicolas de]. *Les Delices de la Campagne...Dedié aux Dames Mesnageres.* 3d ed. Paris, 1662.

Boston Housekeeper; *see* Lee, Mrs. N. K. M.

Brillat-Savarin [Jean Anthelme]. *Physiologie du Goût.* Paris, 1826. Reprint, Paris, 1967.

Bringer, Rudolphe. *Les Bon Vieux Plats du Tricastin.* Pierrelatte, Drôme [no date].

Brissenden, Rosemary. *South East Asian Food: Indonesia, Malaysia, and Thailand.* Harmondsworth, England, 1970.

Brown, Theresa. *Theresa C. Brown's Modern Domestic Cookery.* Charleston, 1871. In facsimile, with Foreword by Harriet R. Holman, Pendleton, S.C., 1985.

Bryan, Mrs. Lettice. *The Kentucky Housewife.* Cincinnati, [no date] (copyright 1839). In facsimile, Paducah, Ky., [no date]; *same,* with Introduction by Bill Neal. Columbia; S.C., 1991.

Buc'hoz, [variously J.-P., Pierre Joseph, or simply M. for Monsieur]. *Dissertations sur l'utilité et les bons et mauvais effets du tabac, du café, et du thé.* 2d ed. Paris, 1788.

———. *Traité usuel du chocolat,...de la canelle, de la vanille, du salep de Perse, de l'ambre gris, du sucre.* Paris, 1812.

Buckeye Cookery. Minneapolis, 1880. In facsimile, with Introduction by Virginia M. Westbrook. St. Paul, Minn., 1988.

Carême, Antonin. *L'Art de la Cuisine Française au Dix-Neuvieme Siècle.* 3 vols. Paris, 1833–1835, 1847. In facsimile, including vols. 4 and 5 completed by Plumery, Paris, 1981.

———. *Le Cuisinier Parisien.* Paris, 1828; in facsimile, Luzarches, 1975.

———. *Le Patissier Royal Parisien.* Paris, 1815.

Castelot, André. *L'Histoire à Table.* Paris, 1972. For Méry's receipt for pilau.

Centennial Receipt Book, Written in 1876 By A Southern Lady ["Miss Mary Joseph Waring, 1851–1947," according to a hand-written note on title page, with the ex libris of Dorothy T. Waring on facing page]. Charleston [?], according to Anna Wells Rutledge, who does not give an author. This work is all but unknown. (Sent to me by John Taylor.)

Chang, K. C., ed. *Food in Chinese Culture: Anthropological and Historical Perspectives.* New Haven; 1977. Invaluable.

Chanot-Bullier, C. *Vieii Receto de Cousino Prouvençalo.* 3d ed. Marseilles, no date.

Charleston Receipts. Collected by The Junior League of Charleston. Charleston, 1950. Reprinted many times.

Charleston Receipts Repeats. Recipes compiled by the Junior League of Charleston. Charleston, 1986.

Childs, Arney R., ed. *Rice Planter and Sportsman: The Recollections of J. Motte Alston.* Columbia, S.C., 1953.

Clinton, Catherine. *The Plantation Mistress.* New York; 1982. It is difficult to get past the title of chapter 2, "Slave of Slaves," an unforgivable lapse. That said, there is valuable primary material presented in the work.

Confederate Receipt Book. A Compilation of Over One Hundred Receipts Adapted to the Times. Richmond, 1863. Reprint, with Introduction by E. Merton Coulter. Athens; Ga., 1960 (this a gift of Jan Longone). In facsimile, with Introduction by Shirley Abbot. Birmingham, 1985.

Copage, Eric V. *Kwanzaa: An African-American Celebration of Culture and Cooking.* New York, 1991.

Creole Cookery Book, The. Christian Woman's Exchange of New Orleans, La. New Orleans, 1885. This is the earliest of the extant Creole cookbooks. The Exchange was a Protestant organization, this in Catholic New Orleans. Judging by the names of the people on the Board of Managers and of the contributors, there was a striking absence of a French influence. There is a "Mammy" figure facing the title page. The work of Lafcadio Hearn followed in the same year; it was not until the turn of the century that Creole works written by French Creoles began to appear, insofar as I can ascertain. (It was Mary Lou O'Keefe who helped me obtain a copy of this work.)

de Croze, Austin. *Les Plats Régioneaux de France.* Paris, [1928]; in facsimile, Luzarches, Seine-et-Oise, 1977.

———. *La Psychologie de la Table.* Paris, 1928.

Le Cuisinier Durand; *see* Durand.

La Cuisinière Bourgeoise; *see* Menon.

Curnonsky and Austin de Croze. *Le Trésor Gastronomique de France.* Paris, 1933.

Curye On Inglysch; *see* Hiett, Constance B., and Sharon Butler.

David, Elizabeth. *A Book of Mediterranean Food.* Harmondsworth; England, 1950, 1955.

———. *English Bread and Yeast Cookery.* American ed. with Intro. by Karen Hess. New York, 1980, 1982. First published in London, 1977.

———. *A Book of Mediterranean Food.* Harmondsworth, England, 1955. First published in 1950. For many of us, this was our introduction to the incomparable Elizabeth David.

———. *French Country Cooking.* London; 1958. First published in 1951.

———. *French Provincial Cooking.* New York, 1962.

———. *Italian Food.* London, 1965. First published in 1954.

———. *Spices, Salt and Aromatics in the English Kitchen.* Harmondsworth, England, 1970. There is a receipt for rice bread in the book on bread, and strong rice sections in the other works.

Davidson, Alan. *Mediterranean Seafood.* Harmondsworth, England, 1976.

DeWitt, Antoinette, and Anita Borghese. *The Complete Book of Indonesian Cooking.* Indianapolis, Ind., 1973.

Dictionnaire Portatif de Cuisine. Paris, 1772.

Digbie (variously Digby, etc.). *The Closet of the Eminently Learned Sir Kenelme Digbie K'. Opened.* London, 1669.

Doar, David. *Rice and Rice Planting in the South Carolina Low Country.* Edited by E. Milby Burton. Charleston, 1936. Also including other authors listed under their respective names.

Dooley, Eliza B. K. *Puerto Rican Cookbook.* Richmond, Va., 1948, 1950.

Duconquéré, Paulona. *Cosina Occitana del País d'Agde.* Picpol, Lot-et-Garonne, 1987.

Dufour, Philippe Sylvestre. *De l'Usage du Caphé, du Thé, et du Chocolate.* Lyons, 1671.

———. *Traitez Nouveaux et Curieux du Café, du Thé, et du Chocolate.* Paris, 1688.

Durand. *Le Cuisinier Durand.* Nîmes, 1837. This is considered to be the earliest Provençal cookbook.

Easterby, Harold J., ed. *The South Carolina Rice Plantation.* Chicago, 1945.

Egerton, John. *Southern Food.* New York, 1987.

Escoffier, A[uguste]. *Le Guide Culinaire.* 4th ed. Paris, 1921.

———. *Ma Cuisine.* Paris, 1934.

———. *Le Riz. Aliment Le Meilleur, Le Plus Nutratif. 130 recettes pour l'accomoder.* Paris, 1927. (This sent to me by Philip and Mary Hyman.)

Escudier, Jean-Noel. *La Véritable Cuisine Provençale et Niçoise.* Toulon, 1964.

Eustis, Célestine. *Cooking in Old Créole Days, La Cuisine Créole à l'Usage des Petits Ménages.* New York, 1904. These are actually two separate works in a single volume, with separate indexes, not simply a bilingual edition. Many receipts are in one that do not appear in the other. In facsimile, with Introduction by Louis Szathmary. New York, 1973. The French work has been excised from the modern edition without so much as a mention of the fact, so that it is a mangled edition.

Farah, Madelain. *Lebanese Cuisine.* Portland, Oreg., 1975.

Favre, Joseph. *Dictionnaire de Cuisine et d'Hygiène Alimentaire.* 4 vols. Paris, 1883–1891.

Fettiplace; *see* Spurling, Hilary.

Flandrin, Jean-Louis, Philip Hyman, and Mary Hyman. *Le Cuisinier François.* Introduction by Daniel Roche. Paris, 1983. This work gives the texts of *Le Cuisinier François, Le Pastissier François, Le Confiturier François,* and *Almanach pour l'An de Grace, Mil Six cens Quatre-vingts trois,* as well as a learned discussion of their historical importance.

Flower, Barbara, and Elisabeth Rosenbaum, trans. *Apicius: The Roman Cookery Book.* New York, 1958. (Bilingual ed., with Latin and English on facing pages.)

Forot, Charles. *Odeurs de Forêt et Fumets de Table.* Saint-Félician, Ardeche, 1964.

Fox-Genovese, Elizabeth. *Within The Plantation Household: Black and White Women of the Old South.* Chapel Hill, N.C., 1988. A valuable source book.

Franklin, Alfred. *La Vie Privée d'Autrefois: La Cuisine.* Paris, 1888.

Genovese, Eugene D. *Roll, Jordan Roll: The World the Slaves Made.* New York, 1974.

Gerarde, John. *The Herball or General Historie of Plantes.* London, 1597, 1636.

[Glasse, Hannah]. *The Art of Cookery, Made Plain and Easy...By A Lady.* London, 1747, 1755. *same,* by Mrs. Glasse, 1796 (and innumerable interim editions). 1796 edition in facsimile, Hamden, Conn., 1971. *same,* Alexandria, Va., 1805, which includes some interesting American receipts but little in the way of rice, not even what appeared in the English editions. (I believe that there is also a facsimile of the 1747 edition.)

de Goustine, Françoise, and Luc de Goustine. *Lo Topin de la Marieta.* Tulle, Correze, 1979.

Grewe, Rudolf. *Libre de Sent Sovi.* Barcelona, 1979. Transcription of a fourteenth-century Catalan manuscript, with commentary, all in Catalan. Catalan medieval cuisine was perhaps the most highly regarded in Europe, and this admiration was reflected in Platina's *De Honesta Voluptate,* 1474.

Grubb, Alan. *House and Home in the Victorian South: The Cookbook as Guide.* In *In Joy and in Sorrow,* edited by Carol Bleser, New York, 1991.

Guégan, Bertrand. *Les Dix Livres de Cuisine d'Apicius.* Paris, [1933]. Translated, with voluminous and scholarly commentaries.

Hale, Sarah Josepha. *Mrs. Hale's New Cook Book.* Philadelphia [1873, as dated in Preface]; also *see* Acton, Eliza.

Harland, Marion. *Common Sense in the Household.* New York, 1871, 1881. The 1871 edition, in facsimile, with Introduction by Shirley Abbot, Birmingham, Ala., 1985. While Marion Harland wrote for a general readership, and very successfully, she was a Virginian and her work shows it, including a receipt for rice bread, for example, and expressing utter contempt for *yellow* corn-meal of the North, which "Southerners regard as only fit for chicken and cattle-feed."

Harleian Manuscripts; *see* Austin, Thomas.

Harris, Jessica B. *Iron Pots and Wooden Spoons.* New York, 1989. The cooking of the African Diaspora in the New World.

Harrison, Robert, trans. *The Song of Roland.* New York, 1970.

Hawkes, Alex B. *The Flavors of the Caribbean & Latin America.* New York, 1978.

[Hearn, Lafcadio]. *La Cuisine Creole.* New Orleans, copyright 1885. In facsimile as *Lafcadio Hearn's Creole Cook Book,* with Foreword by Hodding Carter. Gretna, La., 1990. (Also includes other related writings.) *Same,* 2d ed., copyright 1885. In facsimile, Louisville, Ky., 1966. Hearn was an American writer,

born on the Greek island of Levkas of Greek and Irish parentage, who spent
but ten years in New Orleans before ending up in Japan—this according to
John Thorne (*Mange Tout,* Steuben, Me., Spring/Summer 1990)—so that it
is not surprising that his work is highly idiosyncratic.

Hearn, Lafcadio. *"Gombo Zhèbes," Little Dictionary of Creole Proverbs.* New
York, 1885. Excerpts of this work are included in the *Lafcadio Hearn's Creole Cook Book* noted above. The African-American French language of the
New World is referred to *Gombo,* or *Gumbo;* the word also refers to any of a
number of soupy stews (originally based on okra from Africa), as well as
having a figurative meaning of *olio,* so that the title is a pun.

Hess, John L., and Karen Hess. *The Taste of America.* New York; 1977; 3d ed.,
Columbia, S.C., 1989.

Hess, Karen. *Martha Washington's Booke of Cookery.* Transcription of an early
seventeenth-century family manuscript having been in the keeping of Martha
Washington, 1749–1799, with historical commentary. New York; 1981.

———. *The Virginia House-Wife,* by Mary Randolph. A facsimile of the first edition, 1824, along with additional material from the editions of 1825 and
1828, thus presenting a complete text. Historical Notes and Commentaries.
Columbia, S.C., 1984.

———. *"The Jonny-Cake Papers, and Other Tales: Problems in American Culinary Research." Proceedings of a conference on Current Research in Culinary History: Sources, Topics, and Methods.* Boston, 1985; 46–55.

———. *"The American Loaf: A Historical View."* In *The Journal of Gastronomy,* Vol. 3, no. 4 (Winter 1987/1988): 2–23. Also *see* David, Elizabeth, *English Bread and Yeast Cookery.*

Heyward, Duncan Clinch. *Seed From Madagascar.* Chapel Hill, 1937.

Hiett, Constance B., and Sharon Butler, eds. *Curye on Inglysch.* English Culinary
Manuscripts of the Fourteenth Century. (Including *The Forme of Cury*).
London, 1985.

Hill, Mrs. A. P., Widow of Hon. Edward Y. Hill, of Georgia. *Mrs. Hill's New
Cook Book.* New York, 1872. In facsimile, with Introduction by Shirley Abbot, Birmingham, Ala., 1985.

Hooker, Richard J., ed. *A Colonial Plantation Cookbook: The Receipt Book of
Harriott Pinckney Horry, 1770.* Columbia, S.C., 1984.

———. *Food and Drink in America: A History.* Indianapolis; Ind., 1981.

Horry, Harriott Pinckney; *see* Hooker, Richard J.

Howard, Mrs. B. C. *Fifty Years in Maryland Kitchen.* Baltimore, 1873. Beware of
the 1944 "revised" edition, mangled beyond recognition.

Hyman, Philip and Mary; *see* Flandrin, Jean-Louis.

Indra Majupuria. *Joys of Nepalese Cooking.* Kathmandu, Nepal, 1983–84.
(Name as given, Indra being the family name.)

Jaffrey, Madhur. *An Invitation to Indian Cooking.* New York; 1973.

———. *A Taste of India.* New York, 1986.

Thomas Jefferson's Garden Book, 1766–1824. Edited by Edwin Morris Betts.
Philadelphia, 1944.

Jewish Cookery, The Little Book of; see *The Little Book of Jewish Cookery.*

The Jewish Manual. Edited by A Lady. London, 1846. In facsimile, with Introduction by Chaim Raphael, New York, 1983. This may be the earliest Jewish cookbook in English. It contains several receipts for rice, the most interesting historically being "Almond Rice," effectively the *ris a l'amelo,* mentioned by Mistral as being associated with the celebration of Purim in Provence, that is, one possible version.

Johnston, Mireille. *The Cuisine of the Sun: Classic Recipes from Nice and Provence.* New York, 1976.

Jouveau, René. *La Cuisine Provençale de Tradition Populaire.* Berne, [no date].

Joyner, Charles. *Down by the Riverside: A South Carolina Slave Community.* Urbana, Ill.; 1984.

Kennedy, Diana. *The Cuisines of Mexico.* New York, 1972.

Khawam, René R. *La Cuisine Arabe.* Paris, 1970.

La Varenne. *Le Cuisinier François.* Paris, 1651, 1654; Amsterdam, [1700?]. This last edition in facsimile, Luzarches, Seine-et-Oise, 1976; also *see* Flandrin, Jean-Louis.

[Lee, Mrs. N. K. M.] *The Cook's Own Book.* By A Boston Housekeeper. Boston, 1832. In facsimile, New York, 1973.

Leslie, Miss [Eliza]. *Directions for Cookery in its Various Branches.* Philadelphia, 1837, 1848. 1848 edition in facsimile, with Introduction by Louis Szathmary. New York, 1973.

Liger, L. *Dictionnaire Pratique du Bon Ménager de Campagne et de Ville.* Paris, 1715.

Lincoln, Mrs. D. A. [Mary Johnson]. *Mrs. Lincoln's Boston Cook Book.* Boston, 1883, 1893. Innumerable editions, not changing materially until well into the twentieth century.

The Little Book of Jewish Cookery. London, no date [about 1912]. In facsimile, with Introduction by Elaine D. Frumer. New York, 1986.

Littlefield, Daniel C. *Rice and Slaves: Ethnicity and the Slave Trade in Colonial South Carolina.* Baton Rouge, La., 1981. A most important work.

The Lucayos Cook Book. (The Bahamas, so named by Columbus.) Being an Original Manuscript, 300 years old, never published. Found in the Bahamas. Kept for 30 years to Test-Refine from AD 1660 to 1690 by a Noble family of Elizabethan England. Long lost to Epicureans and the World. . . . Reproduced faithfully from the penned Manuscript to safeguard Continuity of Quaint Old Kitchen Phrases and Customs. . . . Nassau, Bahamas; 1959.

Machlin, Edda Servi. *The Classic Cuisine of the Italian Jews.* New York, 1981. (Now published by Giro Press, Croton-on-Husdon, N.Y.)

Majapuria, *see* Indra.

Martino, Maestro. *Libro de Arte Coquinaria.* In *Arte della Cucina. . . dal XIV al XIX Secolo.* Vol. 1. Edited by Emilio Faccioli. Milano, 1966. The manuscript of the *Libro,* from the last half of the fifteenth century, is transcribed. (A gift from Elizabeth David.)

McCulloch-Williams, Martha. *Dishes and Beverages of the Old South.* New York, 1913. In facsimile, with Introduction by John Egerton. Knoxville, Tenn., 1988.

McKellar, Doris. *Afghan Cookery.* Kabul, Afghanistan, 1967. A charming and, I believe, authentic work, including some lovely receipts for *pálów* and *chálów,* in other words, a strong Persian presence. (A gift from Rudolf Grewe.)

Médecin, Jacques. *La Cuisine du Comté de Nice.* Paris, 1972.

Mendes, Helen. *The African Heritage Cookbook.* New York, 1971.

Le Ménagier de Paris; see Pichon, Jérôme.

[Menon]. *La Cuisinière Bourgeoise.* Paris, 1746, 1753; Amsterdam, 1774. This last edition in facsimile, with Postface by Alice Peeters. Paris, 1981.

———. *Les Soupers de la Cour.* 4 vols. Paris, 1755. In facsimile, Paris, 1978.

Merlin A., and A. Y. Beaujour. *Les Mangeurs de Rouergue.* Paris, 1978.

Meynier, Yvonne and Job de Roincé. *La Cuisine Rustique: Bretagne, Maine, Anjou.* Forcalquier, Haute Provence, 1970.

Montagné, Prosper. *Le Festin Occitan.* I know the work only in fascimile, in which neither date nor city of the original is given [1930s?]. In facsimile, Terre d'Aude, 1980. (A gift from Philip and Mary Hyman.)

Morand, Simone. *Gastronomie Bretonne d'Hier et d'Aujourd'hui.* Paris, 1965. She gives two versions of the Norman/Breton rice pudding that came to be known variously as *poor buckra pudding,* etc., in Carolina: *"Riz Chaud Quimperois"* and *"Riz 'Dans les Mottes' ou Taouac'h."*

Morard, Marius. *Manuel Complet de la Cuisinière Provençale.* Marseilles, 1886. In facsimile, Marseilles, 1984.

Motiño, Francisco Martinez. *Arte de Cozina, Pasteleria, Vizcocheria, y Conserueria.* Madrid, 1611. (By the good graces of Rudolf Grewe.)

Nègre, Dr. André. *Les Antilles à Travers Leur Cuisine.* 2d ed. No city (printed in Caen), [1967].

Old Receipts from Old St. John's. Village of Pinopolis: Civic League, no date [1920s?]. A typewritten collection, with pasted-in photographs of a number of plantations. (A gift from John Taylor.)

Ortiz, Elizabeth Lambert. *The Book of Latin American Cooking.* New York, 1980.

———. *The Complete Book of Caribbean Cookery.* New York, 1973.

Paige, Howard. *Aspects of Afro-American Cookery.* Southfield, Mich., 1987.

Parker, Mrs. [Eliza R.]. *Mrs. Parker's Complete Housekeeper...* By A Veteran Housekeeper. New York, 1891. This edition is in none of my bibliographies, but the title page is pristine. The name Eliza is taken from Bitting for an 1888 edition. (Jan Longone sent me photocopies of relevant pages.)

Le Pastissier François. Paris, 1653. Also see Flandrin, Jean-Louis.

La Petite Cuisinière Habile; see Utrecht-Friedel.

Philippon, Henri. *La Cuisine Provençale.* Paris, [1966].

Phillips, Ulrich B. *American Negro Slavery.* Baton Rouge, La., 1966.

Picayune's Creole Cook Book. 2d ed. New Orleans, 1901. In facsimile with Introduction by Shirley Abbot. Birmingham, Ala., 1984. In facsimile, New York; 1971.

Pichon, Le Baron Jérôme, and Georges Vicaire, eds. *Le Viandier de Guillaume Tirel Dit Taillevent.* Paris, 1892. Manuscript from about 1375, also including *Traité de Cuisine Écrit vers 1300.* Facsimile, with new material, notably facsimile of *Le Manuscrit de Sion,* the subject of Paul Aebischer's works, which *see.*

Pinckney, Eliza Lucas, *Recipe Book of.* Belmont, S.C., [no date]. The Committee on Historic Activities of the South Carolina Dames of America. (A gift of Edward R. Pinckney, M.D., and Cathey Pickney.)

Platina (i.e. Bartolomeo de Sacchi dei Piadena). *De Honesta Voluptate.* Venice, 1475. In facsimile, Vol. 5. Mallinckrodt Collection of Food Classics. A bilingual Latin/English translation. (By the good graces of Philip and Mary Hyman.)

de Pomiane, Édouard. *Le Code de la Bonne Chère.* Paris, [1925].

Porter, Mrs. M. E., Prince George Court-House, Virginia. *Mrs. Porter's New Southern Cook Book.* Philadelphia, [1871]. Facsimile, with Introduction by Louis Szathmary. New York, 1973.

Pringle, Mrs. Elizabeth Watris. *A Woman Rice Planter.* New York, 1913.

Ramazani, Nesta. *Persian Cooking.* New York, 1974. (Now Charlottesville, Va.)

Randolph, Mary. *The Virginia House-Wife.* Washington [D.C.], 1824; 2d ed., 1825; 3d ed., 1828. For facsimile, *see* Hess, Karen.

Ransinangue, Danielle, and Denis Peaucelle. *La Grande Lande Dans Son Assiette.* La Grande Lande, 1984.

Ravenel, Rose Pringle [1850–1943]. *Charleston Recollections and Receipts: Rose P. Ravenel's Cookbook.* Edited by Elizabeth Ravenel Harrigan. Columbia, S.C., 1983. There is much delightful material including Rose Ravenel's Charleston drawings, here, but what a pity that we could not have *all* of her receipts as she wrote them down, rather than a few "modernized" ones.

Ravenel, Theodore. *The Last Days of Rice Planting.* Read at the meeting of the Carolina Plantation Society, March 2, 1935; *see* Doar, David.

Rawlings, Marjorie Kinnan. *Cross Creek Cookery.* New York, 1942. This interesting work contains six receipts for pilau, which she effectively claims for Florida, saying that "William Bartram found it here on his travels and spelled it 'pillo.' We pronounce the word 'pur-loo.' " As noted in chapter 3, "Pilau," it was Bartram's bearers from South Carolina who cooked the *pillo,* and it occurred in a then wilderness area of Florida long before rice was cultivated in the state. That is, rice and pilau came from Carolina, along with the pronunciation. Early Florida cookery is very poorly documented.

Rayess, George N. *Rayess' Art of Lebanese Cooking.* Translated from Arabic by Najla Showker. Beirut, Lebanon, 1966.

Reboul, J.-B. *La Cuisinière Provençale.* Marseilles, no date [first published in 1895].

Roden, Claudia. *A Book of Middle Eastern Food.* New York; 1972.

Rodinson, Maxime. *"Recherches sur les Documents Arabes Relatif à la Cuisine." Revue des Études Islamiques.* Paris, 1949–1950.

———. *"Ma'mūniyya* East and West." Trans. by Barbara Inskip. *Petits Propos Culinaires 33.* London, 1989.

Rorer, Sarah Tyson. *Mrs. Rorer's New Cook Book.* Philadelphia, [1902].
———. *Mrs. Rorer's Philadelphia Cook Book.* Philadelphia, [1886].
Rosengarten, Dale. *Row upon Row: Sea Grass Baskets of the South Carolina Lowcountry.* Columbia, S.C., 1986.
Royer, Bernard. *La Fricassée: Histoire et tradition de l'élevage porcin.* Poitiers, 1981.
[Rundell, Mrs. Maria Eliza]. *A New System of Domestic Cookery...* By A Lady. Boston, 1807; Exeter, 1808; New York, 1814, 1817.
[Rutledge, Sarah]. *The Carolina Housewife, or House and Home:* By A Lady of Charleston. Charleston, 1847. In facsimile, with Introduction by Anna Wells Rutledge. Columbia, S.C., 1979. 2d ed., 1851; 3d ed., 1855; an undated 4th ed.
Sahni, Julie. *Classic Indian Cooking.* New York, 1980.
Saint-Ange, Madame E. *La Cuisine de Madame Saint-Ange.* Paris, [1927], 1958.
Salley, A.S. *The True Story of How the Madagascar Gold Seed Rice Was Introduced into South Carolina; see* Doar, David,
Sass, Herbert Ravenel, and D. E. Huger Smith. *A Carolina Rice Plantation of The Fifties.* New York, 1936.
Seguin, Jean. *vieux mangers, vieux parlers bas-normands.* 2d ed. Avranches, Manche, [1938].
Simmons, Amelia. *American Cookery.* Hartford, 1796. In facsimile, with Introduction by Mary Tolford Wilson. New York, 1958. Facsimile edition reissued as *The First American Cookbook,* New York, 1984. Mrs. Wilson's introduction is a model for such works and an early one.
Singh, Dharmjit. *Indian Cookery.* Harmondsworth, England, 1970.
Smart-Grosvenor, Vertamae. *Vibration Cooking, or The Travel Notes of a Geechee Girl.* New York, 1986. 1st ed., 1970.
Smith, E[liza?]. *The Compleat Housewife.* Williamsburg, Va., 1742. This is the earliest extant printed cookbook in what came to be the United States, actually a reprint of a London work from earlier in the century, beginning 1727.
Smith, Julia Floyd. *Slavery and Rice Culture in Low Country Georgia 1750-1860.* Knoxville, Tenn., 1985.
Smith, Mary Stuart. *Virginia Cookery-Book.* New York, 1885.
South Carolina Cook Book. Rev. ed. Columbia, S.C., 1954. Collected and edited by the South Carolina Extension Homemakers Council and the Clemson Extension Home Economics Staff.
South Carolina, Indian and Freedmen Occupation at the Fish Haul Site, Beaufort Country. Research Series 7, edited by Michael Trinkley. Columbia, S.C., 1986. (Chicora Foundation, Inc.)
Spurling, Hilary. *Elinor Fettiplace's Receipt Book: Elizabethan Country House Cooking.* New York; 1986.
Stephan, Lily, *Lebanese Dishes.* Beirut, Lebanon, [no date].
Stoney, Samuel Gaillard. *Plantations of the Carolina Low Country.* New York and Charleston, 1989. First published in 1938.
Stouff, Louis. *Ravitaillement et Alimentation en Provence Aux XIVᵉ et XVᵉ Siècles.* Paris, 1970. A tome of invaluable primary material.

Taillevent, *see* Pichon, Jérôme and Georges Vicaire; also *see* Aebischer, Paul.

Taylor, John Martin. *"Carolina Gold Returns!" Carologue* (Winter 1988).

――. *"Carolina Gold: A Rare Harvest." New York Times,* December 28, 1988.

――. *"Food and History in the Carolina Low Country," The Journal of Gastronomy,* 4, no. 3 (Autumn, 1988): 2–19.

――. *Hoppin' John's Lowcountry Cooking.* New York, 1992.

Thorne, John. *Rice and Beans. The Itinerary of A Recipe.* Boston, 1981. (First published by Speculum Press, now Jackdaw Press, Castine, Maine.)

Thornton, P[hineas], of Camden, South Carolina. *The Southern Gardener and Receipt Book.* 2d ed. Newark, N.J., 1845 (copyright 1839). In facsimile, with Introduction by Shirley Abbot. Birmingham, Ala., 1984. 3d ed. rev. and enl. by Mrs. Mary L. Edgeworth, Philadelphia, 1859 (Mrs. Edgeworth neglects to note the name of Thornton, so that this edition is always mistakenly credited to Mrs. Edgeworth; *see* Lowenstein, 120).

Toussaint-Samat, Maguelonne. *La Cuisine Rustique: Afrique Noire [et] Madagascar.* Forcalquier, Haute Provence, 1970.

――. *La Cuisine Rustique: Provence.* Forcalquier, Haute Provence, 1971.

Traité de Cuisine Écrit Vers 1300; *see* Pichon, Jérôme and Georges Vicaire, *Le Viandier. . .*

The Travels of William Bartram; *see* Bartram, William.

The Tuesday Soul Food Cookbook. New York, 1969. Hoppin' John and collards, as expected, but lots more.

Two Hundred Years of Charleston Cooking. Receipts gathered by Blanche S. Rhett, edited by Lettie Gay, with Introduction by Helen Woodward and a new Foreword by Elizabeth Hamilton. Columbia, S.C., 1976. First published in 1930 and later revised, but the present edition is based on the first.

[Utrecht-Friedel, Mme.] *La Petite Cuisinière Habile. . .écrit sous la dictée de Mlle. Jeannette, par un gastronome de ses amis. Nouvelle-Orléans,* 1840. According to Vicaire, this work first appeared in Paris in 1814 as *Le Petit Cuisinier. . .par Mme. Fr.,* in 1821 as *La Petite Cuisinière,* and in later editions dropping *Mme. Fr.* in favor of a *Mlle. Jeannette.* At first glance it appears to be a perfectly typical early nineteenth-century work intended for home kitchens, but it contains a receipt *"Bouillabaisse,"* most unusual, as well as *"Ayoli"* (the garlic mayonnaise of Provence); I do not know how far back those receipts started appearing in that work, but it is an early appearance in any event. (This work may explain the presence of *bouillabaisse* in New Orleans cuisine.) There are a few other Provençal traces in this otherwise solidly French work. Mme. Utrecht-Friedel was German, by the way, the widow of a famous confectioner from Berlin; Mlle. Jeannette may well have been her cook. (I thank Mary Lou O'Keefe for her help in obtaining a copy of this all-but-unfindable work.)

Valldejuli, Carmen Aboy. *The Art of Caribbean Cookery.* Garden City, N.Y., 1957.

Veeraswamy, E. P. *Indian Cookery.* Bombay, 1956.

Vernon, Amelia Wallace. *African-Americans at Mars Bluff, South Carolina.* In press.

Le Viandier; *see* Pichon, Jérôme, and Georges Vicaire; *also* Aebischer, Paul.

Waring, Miss Mary Joseph; *see Centennial Receipt Book.*

Martha Washington's Booke of Cookery; *see* Hess, Karen.

Williams, Cindy. *Bahamian Cookery: Cindy's Treasures.* (Printed at) Boynton Beach, Fla., 1976, 1984. Lots of rice receipts, including pigeon peas and rice, but I was taken with one for "Hop and John," calling for black-eye peas and *Guinea corn,* which normally refers to durra, or sorghum, native to Africa. (John Taylor sent me this work.).

Wheaton, Barbara Ketcham. *Savoring the Past: The French Kitchen and Table from 1300 to 1789.* Philadelphia; 1983. Rice is barely mentioned, which reflects fairly accurately its status in the establishment cuisine of northern France, particularly in the postmedieval period.

Wilson, C. Anne. *Food and Drink in Britain: From the Stone Age to Recent Times.* Harmondsworth, England, 1973. As in the Wheaton work, rice is hardly mentioned, and for the same reasons.

Wilson, Mrs. Henry Lumpkin. *Tested Recipe Cook Book.* Atlanta, 1895. In facsimile, *The Atlanta Exposition Cookbook,* with Introduction by Darlene R. Roth. Athens, Ga., 1984. The receipts are all contributed, some of them pretentious and poorly understood—*"Fillet of Flounder a la Joinville,"* or *"Turbot a la Creme,"* for example—but there are a number of more interesting ones with roots in the land, "Rice Bread," for example. A number of contributors are from South Carolina.

Wood, Peter H. *Black Majority: Negroes in Colonial South Carolina from 1670 through the Stono Rebellion.* New York, 1975. A pioneering work in this field, ranking with that of Daniel Littlefield, indeed often cited by him.

A Note on the Indexes

In the Receipt Index, all entries are for actual receipts save two, where a detailed description seemed to warrant inclusion. (Other receipts discussed in the text may be found in the General Index, within quotation marks.) Contributors, when named, are given in parentheses, following Mrs. Stoney to the letter where receipts from her work are concerned. All contributors, with page references, are listed in the General Index. As in the text, F numbers refer to the facsimile of Mrs. Stoney's work. In an effort to avoid confusion, they are grouped together following all other page numbers. In all cases, numbers in boldface refer to the receipt.

Since rice is the principal ingredient in these receipts, I have not followed standard cookbook procedure in the Receipt Index, preferring to simply group them according to their construction, the more since many of them are fancifully entitled, even misleadingly so. Cross-references were not deemed necessary. Many receipts defied given categories and are to be found under Miscellaneous Receipts.

General Index

Pinckney, Eliza Lucas, **1**, 25, 80, 188
Pinckney, Harriott, 44
Pinckney, Mrs. Charles Cotesworth, **51–52**, 58
pirjokes, 100
pita, 73
plantains, F 43
plantation, rice, 8, 9–11
  self-sufficiency of, 14
  task system, 8
  working on, 8, 14–15
  also see African-Americans; Carolina; pounding
plate of shrimps, 163; F 68
Platina, 136, 188
Platine en françoys, 136
Platt, Sir Hugh, 80, 170
pois de pigeon, 98, 100
"*Pois et Riz Colles,*" 96
pollo, 26, 36, 42, 46, 79, 94. *Also see* pilau
"Poloe, To make a," 42–43
pone, 44
poor buckra, 187, F 72. *Also see* Receipt Index
Porcher, Miss, 155; **F 20, 72, 89**
Porcher, Miss M. E. [same?], 155; **F 18, 18–19**
pork, 45, 46, 62, 72, 74, 101
  pickled, 61
  proscriptions. *See* dietary laws
  salt, 94, 59, 61, 62
  smoked, 45, 46
  also see bacon; ham; hog; hog jowl; jambon; petit salé
Porter, Mrs. M. E., **115**, 188
"*Pouding au riz,*" 143, 175
poule au riz, 41
"*Poule au riz au Safran,*" 60
pounding of rice, 14, 106, 107
  women's work, 14, 107
"Pourprion au Riz," 60
Practical Notes on
  Boiling long-grain rice, 32–35
  Bread, 138–40
  Journey or Johnny Cakes, 140
  Rice Casseroles, 90–91
presoaking rice, 32, 33, 34. *Also see* soaking
Pringle, Elizabeth Allston, 15
pronunciation, 6, 58, 165

Protestant. *See* Huguenots
Provence, Provençal, 37, 46, 52–83 passim
  cuisine, foods
    disdain of French for, 63–64, 65–66
  dishes
    lou pelau, 52. *Also see jambalaia;* pilau, Provence
    also see bouillabaisse; daube; rizotte; soupe courte
  historical foods. *See* Stouff, Louis
  receipts, 52–55
    in Carolina, xiii, 47. *Also see* "French Pilau," receipts for
  rice
    cultivation of, 11, 71, 82–83, 169, 170
    importation of, 71
    preference for long-grain, 71
    with almond milk, 81
  saffron, 52, 53, 59, 60, 82, 170
  spices, 60, 81
  suppression of by France, 55. *Also see langue d'oc*
  wars against, 55, 73–74
  word forms in Carolina, 57, 84, 89
  also see Arabs, in French Midi; Arles, Avignon; Camargue; Crusades; Jews of; Marseilles; Mistral, Frédéric
pudding rice, 31. *Also see* short-grain rice
puddings, 142. *Also see* Receipt Index
Puerto Rico, 96, 183
pullau, 36, 42, 52
  a Muslim dish, 39
"Pullow," **36**, 41
pulse, in pilau, 54–62. *Also see* hoppin' John
Purim, 81
purlow, 3, 43

qasa, 88

racahout, 147–51 passim. *Also see* Receipt Index
raccoon, 44, 50
Ramazani, Nesta, **22–23**, 79, 86, 87, 188
Randolph, Mary *(Virginia Housewife, The, which also see),* 30, 121, 185, 188
Ravenel, Theodore D., 15, 152, 188
Reboul, J.-B., **53–54**, 59, 188

Receipt Index

Boiling, Preparing the Rice

Breads

Cakes Baked on a Griddle or Various Irons

Journey or Johnny Cakes

Miscellaneous Receipts

Pilaus and Related Dishes